The Truth of Islam and Christianity

The Deep End of Islam and Christianity

B.T.

WESTBOW°
PRESS
A DIVISION OF THOMAS NELSON
& ZONDERVAN

Scripture taken from the King James Version of the Bible.

WestBow Press books may be ordered through booksellers or by contacting:

WestBow Press
A Division of Thomas Nelson & Zondervan
1663 Liberty Drive
Bloomington, IN 47403
www.westbowpress.com
1 (866) 928-1240

Because of the dynamic nature of the Internet, any web addresses or links contained in this book may have changed since publication and may no longer be valid. The views expressed in this work are solely those of the author and do not necessarily reflect the views of the publisher, and the publisher hereby disclaims any responsibility for them.

Any people depicted in stock imagery provided by Thinkstock are models, and such images are being used for illustrative purposes only. Certain stock imagery © Thinkstock.

ISBN: 978-1-4908-4681-1 (sc)
ISBN: 978-1-4908-4683-5 (hc)
ISBN: 978-1-4908-4682-8 (e)

Library of Congress Control Number: 2014913927

Printed in the United States of America.

WestBow Press rev. date: 10/16/2014

Special thanks to my husband for his insight and wisdom, and to my three precious daughters who always an encouragement to me.

Dear earnest reader! I presented this masterpiece to understand the truth of Islam and Christianity. These two great religions have drawn my attention to search the truth because both religions started with same God and end up with Jesus coming in the end days with a goal of reaching heaven or hell but both have a great gulf in between them. Both religions have great number of followers. Are these followers climbing up with understanding or not? In any religion most of the people blindly cling to a belief simply because their parents or culture is closely tied to it. The traditions and beliefs are being passed on from generation to generation without any knowledge in their religion. Some people believe that religion takes them to eternity. They embrace religion because of a fear of death. On the other hand there are a few people who really assess their core beliefs based on truth and reason. Some people are still in research of truth. These both religions started at one point and are going in two different directions with their divergent understanding and are trying to reach the same destination. It is very impressive to see that both religions are eagerly looking forward for Jesus and rewards from Him. For all these reasons I tried my best to bring attention of those people to the detail of two religions in which I laid out various topics and great deal of discussion so that it is easy to discern which way is the best to reach the destination. My aim is that people should understand the truth in it where there is a straight way. The amazing thing about this book is while you are reading this book; you could compare, contrast and reason it to make your wise decision which leads you to the destination where you will be in peace and safety forever with joy and happiness.

Contents

The Prologue

Islam and Christianity are two great religions in the world. The Islam originated in Arabia in the early 7th century. The beliefs in the Islam were founded by Prophet Muhammad in 622 CE, its adherents world wide today are an estimate of 1.3 billion. There are two main sects in the Islam: Sunni and Shi'ite. The Sunni concept of predestination is called divine decree, while the Shi'a version is called divine justice. The main theme of the Islam is "Live for Allah and die for Allah." However, the main concept of the Islam centers on a faith in Allah. The Christianity was founded in early 1st century CE. The Christianity focuses on the teaching, miracles, crucifixion and resurrection of Jesus Christ. Today it is the largest religion in the world, with around 2 billion followers.

The Bible teaches that the Christianity was built on the foundation of the apostles and the prophets, with Christ Jesus Himself as the chief cornerstone. God, as Jesus Christ, came and died for all the people in the world. Only by the grace of God the mankind could be saved from the eternal destruction to get back to the eternal life not with their self efforts. The Christianity has a wide variety of forms, beliefs and practices, but it all centers around the faith in Jesus Christ.

These two religions share the same origin, theme, and expectation. They share the belief in their expectation of Jesus Christ's second return during the end times. Islamic eschatology is concerned with the Qiyamah (end of the world) and the final judgment of humanity.

The Qur'an says Jesus will come as a just ruler; he will defeat Dajjal, and pay wages to everybody according to their works.

The Christians also have the same view; however, this shared expectation has caused division between both beliefs. These differences occur in between both the religions view in their hope to enter into paradise, the second coming of Jesus Christ, and His Title as Son of God.

The Muslims consider that Muhammad and Jesus both were prophets, but the latest prophet was Muhammad, who professed to proclaim a revelation from God. So the Muslims believe the Islam is the final teaching of God.

On the other hand, the Christians believe that Jesus is the Son of God and is the only way to reach the eternity. They say that everyone has to follow Jesus Christ the Messiah, because in Him there is an assurance of the paradise and the eternal life. Jesus Christ said that He is the only way to enter into the kingdom of God.

God sent many prophets but it was in vain. Because of that reason God Himself came and made the way to sinners to enter into the heaven. Jesus Christ came to fulfill the prophecies of the previous prophets and accomplished the task of salvation and promised them the eternal life. He promised the believers that He will come back to the earth to take them with Him. In their opinion no other prophet is needed after Jesus Christ.

However, the Muslims say that we have to follow Muhammad, because he said that if anybody testifies that Muhammad as a prophet of Allah, then he or she will be granted the paradise. So here is where the conflict arises, and who do we follow Jesus or Muhammad? – Which is the right path?

There is much dispute in this matter throughout the world between these two religions. If Allah was not pleased with the teachings of Jesus, why did Allah gave Messiah such an authority in the end days? Why did God plan to send Jesus in the end days as a just ruler? Why should we be judged by Jesus? Whose teachings do we follow, Muhammad's or Jesus'? Please read and find out the answer.

The Islam and the Christianity have a unifying beginning. They both originated from Judaism. They both have the common origin of creationism, prophets such as Adam – creation of God, Noah, Abraham, Joseph, Moses, David, Solomon and other Biblical figures. The Qur'an recognizes reality of previous divine revelations from God, the Torah, the Scriptures, and the Gospel. This makes it clear that God of Muhammad and God of Israel is the selfsame God – however, the both religions do not have a unifying end.

One common theme in the both religions is that they do not believe in reincarnation. Both religions believe the human race was created by one God. Whoever born they die, and are resurrected, because there is life after death. They believe in heaven and hell, and their ultimate hope in waiting for Jesus Christ's second return is the same. However, the Islam and the Christianity differ in the understanding of how a person reaches the heaven. I tried my best went deep down into the two religions to present the truth to find out the right way.

To investigate the truth, I needed the base of the Islam and the Christianity. They both stand firmly on the word of God. The Muslims believe that Quran was sent by Allah through angel Gabriel and the Prophet Muhammad had revelations from Allah. When he was telling those revelations, his companions wrote them and also added the explanation and interpretations of those revelations in Hadiths. From the Muslim perspective, the Hadiths are as important as the Noble Qur'an. I took references from the Qur'an, Hadiths such as Sahih Bukhari, Tirmidhi, Sahih – Muslim, and Abu Da'ud. A few references were taken from Muwatta of Ibn Malik and Musnad of Ahmad Ibn Hanbal.

From the Christian perspective, I took references of the Holy Bible. (King James Version) The Bible is in two parts, the Old Testament and the New Testament. The Torah and the Scripture comes under the Old Testament. The four Gospel, the Acts, the Epistles and the last book Revelation belong to the New Testament. The Christians believe the Bible is holy and it is the word of God and was written by many prophets in different time periods. The Bible composed of sixty six books. But it is one continuous book revealing the past, the present and the future things of the human history right from the beginning of the world and it ends with the new earth and the new heaven.

I hope from this research we all can find out the true way in reaching the eternal life. Just to note in my writing I substituted "Allah" for "God", since Allah is quite literally the Arabic word which means God.

Important note: The Muslim beliefs differ in between sects and individual believers. The Christians also differ in their practices and there are many denominations. This book presents the truth in both the religions and was explored in greater depth.

God Speaks if we Listen

Every one has their own ideas and assumptions about this topic. It is a unique and awesome experience if any one hears God's voice. There are some people who could witness about the voice of God. His voice is always there. But most of the people don't perceive it. He speaks with the Prophets, and also with the simple people. In fact He speaks with every one in every turn. But everybody is very busy to hear His voice. No one pays any attention because He is invisible.God speaks, and He speaks only if we listen and believe. But who is the true God that will speak? Unless we hear the voice of God, we will never know who is the true God? Have you ever wondered who the true, living, and speaking God is? Have you ever heard God's voice and experienced walking with Him? Or do you think that God is very distant and can not be reached?

Despite of our efforts in keeping up with the traditions in religion if we do not hear God's voice and experience Him in our life time, our efforts are useless. If we are willing to walk with God then we have to humble ourselves. The Most Holy, the Most Merciful, and the Most Compassionate God want to walk with us, talk with us, answer our prayers, and He never abandons us.

What is the name of this God? Some say Jehovah God, Yahweh, or some say Allah, and some have so many names for God. But, what is His actual name?We have evidence in the Old Testament. In the Torah, Exodus 3:13 &14, Moses asked God what His name was?

1

The verse states His name is as follows: '¹³And Moses said unto God, "Behold, when I come unto the children of Israel, and shall say unto them, The God of your fathers hath sent me unto you; and they shall say to me, what is His name? What shall I say unto them?" '¹⁴And God said unto Moses, **"I Am That I Am":** and He said, Thus shalt thou say unto the children of Israel **I Am** hath sent me unto you.'

God's name "I AM" indicates that He is a God of the present. God is past, present and future. His presence is always there. God's deity reveals the fullness of His nature.

There is nobody that can be compared with God. He is the supreme. His wisdom is infinite, and He never makes mistakes. He never changes His word.

God is a speaking God. He spoke with the Prophets, even with the Egyptian maid servant of Sarah. The Old Testament of the Bible recorded this truth, and He comforted Hagar the mother of Ishmael – proving that He speaks. It verifies the fact that God does not belong to any nationality; He is not a partial God.

Hagar was an Egyptian. She was given as a maid to Abraham's wife, Sarah. Later on she fled from Sarah. But God did not ignore Hagar. God spoke and comforted her. She called the name of the Lord that spoke unto her, **'Thou God seest me'** for she said, have I also here looked after him that seeth me? This passage can be read in the book of Genesis 16:13 from the Bible.

Even in the present times, God speaks to the people who incline their ears to Him. All the human beings get tempted and go through critical situations and problems, that is why, God gave us these encouraging and guiding words in Isaiah 30:21. As per this verse, everyone can hear His voice in everyday life saying, "This is the way walk in it." We hear it in every turn, either good way or bad way. Even in the simple things in life, His still small voice comes to us saying: "Don't do this or don't go that way. There is danger in that, or there will be bad consequence by doing that" etc. Several times people don't incline to that voice and do whatever they wish to do.

That is how we ignore His soft voice and go in our own way and face many consequences for rejecting God's voice.

We can not hear His voice with the worldly wisdom. In order to hear His voice we have to have a peace of mind and be obedient to His soft and sweet voice. We have to make a firm decision to hear His voice and to yield.

My experiences about God have clarification to the existence and almost "tangible" realness of God. I was obedient to Him, I heard His voice, and I submitted to Him; by doing this, I have walked with Him and experienced His direction, guidance, faithfulness and love throughout my life. For this reason I have peace and do not fear death or the dangers to come in the end days. If you want to have the same experience with God and desire to walk with Him then stop, be obedient, and read carefully about the Truth and hear His voice.

I am sure that God will speak with you while we discuss the comparisons and differences between the Islam and the Christianity and the truth about them. I pray that this book gives you a clear understanding to discern and choose the correct path. The truth that God reveals to you should not be rejected.

The Danger of death and the End days according to the Noble Qur'an

Every person has to face the death. Muslims believe in "the punishment of the grave" which takes place between the death and the resurrection. According to the Noble Qur'an there is the death and the punishment of the grave. Sahih Bukhari, book 9 and volume 88 (This Hadith wrote about the end days.) In volume 2, book 23, number 454: Bukhari, the prophet talks about how; there is torment and the punishment in the grave.

"Narrated Masruq: Aisha said that a Jewess came to her and mentioned the punishment in the grave, saying to her, "May Allah protect you from the punishment of the grave." Aisha then asked Allah's Apostle about the punishment of the grave. He said, "Yes, there is punishment in the grave." Aisha added, "After that I never saw Allah's Apostle but seeking refuge with Allah from the punishment in the grave in every prayer he prayed." The prophet feared. In other words he feared danger of death."

The torment in the grave is clearly taught in the Islam and in the traditions of the Prophet. In Bukhari, volume 2, book 23, number 456 we read the following: "Narrated Anas bin Malik: Allah's Apostle said, "When (Allah's -) slave is put in his grave and his companions return and he even hears their footsteps, two angels come to him and make him sit and ask, 'what you used to say about this person (i.e. Prophet Muhammad -by showing his picture)?" 'The faithful Believer will say, "I testify that he is Allah's' Abd' and His Apostle. Then they will say to him, "look at your place in the Hell Fire; Allah has given you a place in Paradise instead of it.' So he will see both his places."

Qatada said, "We were informed that his grave would be made spacious." Then Qatada went back to the narration of Anas who said; "Whereas a hypocrite or a non-believer will be asked, "what did you use to say about this man?" He will reply, "I do not know; but I used to say what the people used to say." So they will say to him, "neither did you know nor did you take the guidance." Then he will be hit with iron hammers once, that he will send such a cry as everything near to him will hear, except Jinns and human beings. [Bukhari -volume 2, book 23, number 456]

In the above narration, we read that the paradise was sanctioned to a slave not based on his good deeds or his bad deeds but only by testifying that Muhammad is the Prophet of Allah. If that is the standard to enter into the paradise, why does Muhammad have no authority to enter into the paradise? Why should he fear the punishment of the grave? Why should he seek refuge from the punishment of the grave and affliction of Messiah and Ad-Dajjal?

"Narrated by Aisha (R.A): (Aisha was wife of the Prophet Muhammad) The Prophet (P.B.U.H) used to invoke Allah in the prayer saying, "O Allah, I seek refuge with you from the punishment of the grave and from the affliction of Messiah, Ad –Dajjal and from the affliction of life and death. O Allah, I seek refuge with you from the sins and from being in debt."

Aisha, 'the Prophet Muhammad's favorite wife, relates Muhammad's comments about the punishment in the grave.' She stated how Muhammad feared punishment in the grave and prayed that he would be kept from it. Moreover Muhammad (peace be upon him) said, "In order to escape the hell fire we must take God's guidance and follow it." The afflictions in the end days are also explained by the Prophet in Hadith no. 63, volume 8. Part of our faith is based in our belief in the Day of Judgment. The signs about "this coming day" are mentioned in the Fitna.

The great tribulation i.e, Fitna of Dajjal is yet to come and it is stated that even the Prophet used to seek refuge. In the Islam the end days are explained by the Prophet. 'Narrated Abu Huraira, the prophet said, "The time will pass rapidly, good deeds will decrease, and miserliness will be thrown in the hearts of the people, afflictions will appear and there will appear much. 'Al-Harj?" He said, "Killing! Killing!" This Hadith is clearly states, that when Christ peace be upon him, returns he will govern the people. Hudhaifa b. Usaid Ghifari reported: "Allah's Messenger (May peace is upon him) came to us all of a sudden as we were busy in a discussion. He said: What do you discuss about?

They (the Companions) said, we are discussing about the Last Hour. Thereupon he said: "It will not come until you see ten signs before and (in this connection) he made mention of the smoke, Dajjal, the beast, the rising of the sun from the west, the descent of Jesus son of Mary (Allah be pleased with him), the Gog and Magog, and land-sliding in three places, one in the east, one in the west and one in Arabia at the end of which fire would burn forth from the Yemen, and would drive people to the place of their assemble."

"Jesus shall be a Sign (for the coming of) the Hour (of Judgment): therefore have no doubt about the (Hour), but follow ye me: this is a Straight Way. (Quran, Az-Zukhuruf, 43:61) Allah will send Maseeh ibne Maryam (Messiah son of Mary). Thus he will descend near the White Eastern Minaret of Damascus, clad in two yellow sheets, leaning on the shoulders of two angels."(Sahih Muslim, vol. 8, p. 192-193) The son of Mary will kill the Anti-Christ (Dajjal) at the door of Ludda. (Tirmidhi and Ahmad) By Him in Whose Hand is my life, Ibn Maryam (Jesus Christ) would certainly pronounce Talbiyah for Hajj or for Umrah or for both (simultaneously as a Qarin) in the valley of Rawha." [Sahih Muslim book 7, number 2877]

Sahih Bukhari, volume 3, book 34, number 425: 'Narrated Abu Huraira: "Allah's Apostle said, "By Him in Whose Hands my soul is, son of Mary (Jesus) will shortly descend amongst you people (Muslims), as a just ruler and will break the Cross and kill the pig and abolish the Jizya (a tax taken from the non-Muslims, who are in the protection, of the Muslim government). Then there will be abundance of money and no-body will accept charitable gifts." In addition to the Qur'an, the Hadith (or traditions) focuses on the end-times and refers to it as the Last hour. The Hadith Sahih Muslim also deals with the topic of the Last Hour; furthermore, Muslims view events leading to the return of Jesus, Son of Mary. Sahih Muslim lists ten signs leading up to the return of Jesus.

Sahih Muslim book 041, number 6932 says: "By Him in whose hand is my life, the son of Mary, peace is upon him, will soon descend among you as a just judge. He will break crosses, kill the swine and abolish the poll-tax (Jizya), and wealth will pour forth to such an extent that no one will accept it."

In Sahih Muslim, book 1, number 287, it is very clear that when Christ, peace be upon him, returns he will govern the people according to the teachings of Islam. The Prophet, peace is upon him, also said: By Him in whose hand is my soul, the son of Mary will approach the al-Rawhâ pass (between Mecca and Medina), to perform Hajj, Umrah, or both. The above two references from the Hadith Sahih Muslim are clear proof that the Prophet Muhammad life and the soul are in the hands of Jesus (Son of Maryam) and he feared the punishment of the grave.

The Prophet Muhammad completely relied on Jesus Christ for rescue from the coming danger in the end days. Now we have to ask ourselves the question: If Muhammad relied on Jesus to rescue him from the coming danger, whom do we have to seek refuge? from Jesus or Muhammad?

The Death and the End Days according to the Holy Bible

According to the Holy Bible, there is no torment or state of punishment in which the soul suffers for a time in order to be cleansed before going to the paradise. Roman Catholics believe that there is a punishment and money must be paid for Masses to the relief of the soul. This is completely against to the scriptures.

Paul stated in 2 Corinthians 5:6–8, '⁶Therefore we are always confident, knowing that, whilst we are at home in the body, we are absent from the Lord: ⁷For we walk by faith, not by sight. ⁸We are confident, I say, and willing rather to be absent from the body, and to be present with the Lord.' According to the Holy Bible, it is very clear that once we are absent from this body, we will be present with the Lord. There is no explanation or mention of purgatory in the Bible. The physical death is inevitable – we live only for a limited amount of the time.

In the Holy Bible, the life of a person is compared to grass, flower, shadow and a vapor.

Here below are some references from the Holy Bible:

'⁶The voice said, "Cry." And he said, "What shall I cry? All flesh is grass and all the goodliness thereof is as the flower of the field." (Isaiah 40:6–7)

'Is there not an appointed time to man upon earth? Are not his days also like the days of a hireling?' (Job7:1)

'11My days are like a shadow that declineth; and I am withered like grass.' (Psalms102:11).

'9For we are but of yesterday, and know nothing, because our days upon earth are a shadow.'(Job8:9)

'Whereas ye know not what shall be on the morrow. For what is your life? It is even a vapor that appeareth for a little time, and then vanisheth away.' (James 4:14).

'5Behold, thou hast made my days as a handbreadth; and mine age is as nothing before thee: verily every man at his best state is altogether vanity. Selah. 6Surely every man walketh in a vain shew: surely they are disquieted in vain: he heapeth up riches, and knoweth not who shall gather them.' (Psalms 39:5-6)

We all knew 'the life on the earth' is temporary. When Jesus Christ was on the earth, He told a parable about the mystery of the life on the earth to the innumerable multitude of people who gathered to hear His words and for the miracles.

The parable is written in Luke Gospel 12:16–21. 'And Jesus spoke a parable unto them, saying, "the ground of a certain rich man brought forth plentifully: 17And he thought within himself, saying, what shall I do, because I have no room where to bestow my fruits? 18And he said, this will I do: I will pull down my barns, and build greater; and there will I bestow all my fruits and my goods. And I will say to my soul, Soul, thou hast much goods laid up for many years; take thine ease, eat, drink, and be merry. 20But God said unto him, Thou fool, this night thy soul shall be required of thee: then whose shall those things be, which thou hast provided? [21]So is he that layeth up treasure for himself, and is not rich toward God."

The parable explains that no one knows at what time the death occurs or our soul is required by God. We have to leave this world, whenever God calls us. It is true. We see many unexpected deaths around the world in our daily life.

When Jesus was on the earth, Jesus' disciples asked Him about the end days. He explained them very clearly. Authors of the three Gospels Mathew, Mark and Luke had written about it in detail. I had taken some of the verses from Mathew 24th chapter and Luke 21.

'[3]And as He sat upon the Mount of Olives, the disciples came unto Him privately, saying; "tell us, when these things shall be? And what shall be the sign of thy coming, and of the end of the world?" [4]And Jesus answered and said unto them, "Take heed that no man deceive you. [5]For many shall come in my name, saying, I am Christ; and shall deceive many. [6]And ye shall hear of wars and rumors of wars: see that ye be not troubled: for all these things must come to pass, but the end is not yet. [7]For nation shall rise against nation, and kingdom against kingdom: and there shall be famines, and pestilences, and earthquakes, in divers' places.' (Mathew Gospel 24:3-7)

'[8]All these are the beginning of sorrows. [9]Then shall they deliver you up to be afflicted, and shall kill you: and ye shall be hated of all nations for my name's sake. [10]And then shall many be offended, and shall betray one another, and shall hate one another.[11]And many false prophets shall rise, and shall deceive many.[12]And because iniquity shall abound, the love of many shall wax cold. [13]But he that shall endure unto the end, the same shall be saved. [14]And this gospel of the kingdom shall be preached in the entire world for a witness unto all nations; and then shall the end come.' (Mathew Gospel 24: 8-14)

'[32]Now learn a parable of the fig tree; When his branch is yet tender, and putteth forth leaves, ye know that summer is nigh: [33]So likewise ye, when ye shall see all these things, know that it is near, even at the doors. [34]Verily I say unto you, this generation shall not pass, till all these things be fulfilled. [35] Heaven and earth shall pass away, but my words shall not pass away. [36]But of that day and hour knoweth no man, no, not the angels of heaven, but my Father only. [37]But as the days of Noah were, so shall also the coming of the Son of man be. [38]For as in the days that were before the flood they were eating and drinking, marrying and giving in marriage, until the day that Noah entered into the ark, [39]And knew not until the flood came, and took them all away; so shall also the coming of the Son of man be." (Mathew 24:32–39)

There are some more signs about His coming that Jesus talked about. We read them in Luke Gospel. In Luke Gospel 21:25–28, "[25]And there shall be signs in the sun, and in the moon, and in the stars; and upon the earth distress of nations, with perplexity; the sea and the waves roaring; [26]Men's hearts failing them for fear, and for looking after those things which are coming on the earth: for the powers of heaven shall be shaken. [27]And then shall they see the Son of man coming in a cloud with power and great glory. [28]And when these things begin to come to pass, then look up, and lift up your heads; for your redemption draweth nigh." We see many of these signs are happening in our life time.

Whatever man faces – the death or the end days – everyone must be prepared to face the reality of life. Jesus promised that He will return and will take them whoever believes in Him. Those who do not accept Jesus Christ as their Savior will be left on the earth for the tribulation period, in which God is going to pour down His wrath. These prophecies are all written in the Holy Bible.

How can we know that there is surety of the paradise to those who believe in Jesus Christ? We could read the evidence from the Holy Bible in Luke Gospel 23:38–43. '[38]Then were there two thieves crucified with him, one on the right hand, and another on the left. [39]And one of the malefactors which were hanged railed on him,' saying, "if thou be Christ, save thyself and us."

"40But the other answering rebuked him, saying, dost not thou fear God, seeing thou art in the same condemnation? 41And we indeed justly; for we receive the due reward of our deeds: but this man hath done nothing amiss." 42And he said unto Jesus, "Lord; remember me when thou comest into thy kingdom." 43And Jesus said unto him, "Verily I say unto thee, today shalt thou be with me in paradise." The murderer became saint to enter into paradise. What a grace! What a power in Jesus words.

This above context gives us such a clear understanding that Jesus had authority over the paradise. Those who believe in Jesus will enter into the paradise when they die. That is why it is written, 'Blessed are the dead, which die in the Lord.' (Revelation 14:13)

One day the disciples of Jesus Christ were wondering, what benefit they will receive if they follow Him? In Mark Gospel 10:28-30, "28Then Peter began to say unto him, lo, we have left all, and have followed thee." 29And Jesus answered and said, "Verily I say unto you, there is no man that hath left house, or brethren, or sisters, or father, or mother, or wife, or children, or lands, for my sake, and the gospel's, 30But he shall receive a hundredfold now in this time, houses, and brethren, and sisters, and mothers, and children, and lands, with persecutions; and in the world to come eternal life."

According to the holy Bible, the name sake Christians have no guarantee to enter into the kingdom of God. Those who repented of their sins and come under His Lordship, them only inherit the kingdom of God. In 2 Timothy 2:11-12, "11It is a faithful saying: For if we be dead with him, we shall also live with him: 12If we suffer, we shall also reign with him: if we deny him, he also will deny us:

The Christians anticipate that the Biblical prophecy about the end days will be literally fulfilled. The Christians see the current world events, regional wars, and natural disasters as the beginning of the birth pains of the end times. The Christian believers have no fear of death, and no anxiety for the end days, because they have full assurance of their life from standing on Jesus promises. The Christian believers anticipate the future, because they know one day they will meet Jesus face to face with no shame but inexpressible joy. This is a believer's ultimate hope.

Who is Jesus Christ exactly, and why do we wait for in with such hope? This is a great question to be answered to a great many people who follow the Islam and the Christianity. The ultimate goal for both the religions is looking forward for Jesus return in the end days.

The Titles of Jesus in the Noble Qur'an

Jesus is a Noble Messenger of Allah, the Word of God, Allah's Spirit, and a Bright Light, A Prophet, Speech of Truth and Messiah.

We read in Hadith Anas Bin Malik – Mutiara Hadith, page 353, and also in Qur'an, Surah – Al Nisa section 4, 24:171, as ----- Jesus is the Noble Messenger of Allah and His Word. 171. "O people given the book! Do not exaggerate in your religion nor say anything concerning Allah, but the truth; the Messiah, (ISA) the son of Mary am, is purely a Noble Messenger of Allah; and His Word; which He sent towards Mary am, and He is a Spirit from Him."

In Dr. Hasbullah Bakry's book "Nabi Isa dalam Al-Qur'an enz" he states, "Jesus is the Prophet." In the Qur'an, Page 109: 'The Prophet Jesus is called "Kalimatu Allah" which means 'The WORD of GOD' because He is incarnation of the WORD of GOD which was designated to Mary to bear the Prophet Jesus. It means that "the word of God" itself was made flesh (human). Jesus was not made when God sent a word. God's word itself became Jesus Christ. His name itself is "the word of God". There is much difference in understanding this concept because of the different views of people.

Therefore to make it clear let us discuss further for clarification. Surah 4:171 states that Jesus Christ is "HIS WORD" meaning, the Title itself is the expression of Jesus Christ. There is no reason to be mistaken with Adam. When God created Adam, He did not called him to be as "HIS WORD." Later on, it was never even mentioned in the Qur'an that Adam was the word of God.

Jesus Christ did miracles, revived even the dead persons. This is the reason why Jesus alone was called the "word of God?" when both Adam and Jesus were created in the same way as we read in Surah 3:59. Jesus Christ in His life time proved that He is the "Word of God". The title reflected in every action of His entire life. Jesus words were very authoritative, powerful, and at the same time very merciful and gracious. Moreover, He was pure and holy. What ever Jesus said it was truth from Allah. All God's will was fulfilled in Him. The statement in Surah - 4:171, it is clear about Jesus' title "The word of God."

The Title of Jesus Christ as a "Spirit from God" as mentioned in the Qur'an, Surah 4:171, is a bit difficult to explain from the Islam perspective. But the express title for Jesus in the Islam is "Ruhullah" which means 'the Spirit of God.' The Spirit of God Himself came as Jesus according to this word "Ruhullah."

The Holy Spirit which is mentioned several times in the Qur'an was interpreted as the angel Gabriel. We read in the Qur'an, Surah 16 (An-Nahl) ayat that the angel Gabriel (Jibreel) sent by Allah to assist His chosen servants in their divinely ordained missions. Gabriel was only a messenger.

In any way in the Noble Qur'an, there is lot of confusion about this title that 'Jesus is Spirit from God or Spirit of God.' If Jesus came as a Spirit of God according to the verse Surah 4:171, no one should object it. If any one opposes it, they are answerable to Allah's words since they believe that the "Qur'an" is Allah's own words. "The Messiah, (ISA) the son of Maryam, is purely a Noble Messenger of Allah; and His Word; which He sent towards Maryam, and He is a Spirit from Him." It is true because Jesus is a Spirit from God, because Allah said, 'I receive you to "Myself." And Allah received Jesus to be in His abode. No one else in the world was received by Allah directly to the heaven, except Jesus.

Now, if we accept the fact that God is a Spirit, then we assume Jesus is God's son in a spiritual sense. It is very wrong to understand that God had sexual contact to get a son. It is strictly opposed to this opinion because God is holy and He is the Holy Spirit. Since Jesus had no physical father, He was born with the Holy Spirit of God. In other words the Holy Spirit is God Himself. There is none holy except God. The word 'Holy' implies only to God. But it is a bit confusing in the Qur'an that the angel Gabriel was regarded as the Holy Spirit. It is giving the scope to the people to understand the angel Gabriel himself is God as He was considered as a Holy Spirit in the Qur'an.

But the Muslims don't accept that Jesus Christ is the "son of God" They assume the angel Gabriel brought the Holy Spirit. If we think deeply about this fact, how angel could bring the Holy Spirit of God? The angel Gabriel was only a messenger. Only with the power of God's Holy Spirit it is possible to Mary to conceive Jesus. God sent His Spirit to become a human. The word "Ruhullah (The Spirit of God) explained it with a correct sense that Jesus is the Spirit of God.

Jesus was not born like all other human who transmitted God's breath from Adam. Here we could understand the truth that, 'the impossible things are possible to God.' God had been sending the prophets to the world since from the beginning of the creation but it did not work out the purpose of God to redeem the human from their sins and weaknesses. Man is always susceptible to the sin.

God wanted every one to be holy to enter into His kingdom. As per the Qur'an, only the prophets are supported by the Holy Spirit. But every human needs the support to live holy. God does not have favoritism and partiality. Everybody is equal and precious to God. God always regards those whoever pays attention to Him. Even the prophets went astray and committed wrong things. So when the time was fulfilled, God had accomplished His purpose by coming Himself to the world. He made Himself of no reputation but humbled Himself to be one of us. Therefore His Holy Spirit came into Mary as a Son of God and became a son of woman. Thus Jesus came as a human and was called as "the Son of man."

"Walad" in the Qur'an means the son born by a sexual act between God and Mary. We all reject this type of an idea about the Holy God.

By using the WORD "Ibn," by this term Jesus is not called a biologically begotten Son. Jesus stated these terms in order to explain the relationship between the Father and the Son. He is an exact replica of the Father in Heaven but left all His glory to dwell among the mankind on the earth.

In the Qur'an, Surah Al-Nisa 4 section 24: 172-174, Jesus is very significant. He came to the world with full authority. '172 verse says, "The MESSIAH" ---- whoever hates worshipping HIM and is conceited --- so very soon He will gather them all towards Him.' The verse 173 says, "Then to those who believed and did good deeds, He will pay their wages in full and by His munificence, give them more, and those who hated (worshipping Him) and were proud, He will inflict a painful punishment; and they will not find for themselves other than ALLAH, any supporter or any aide."

The Surah 4:173 is such a powerful statement that all the people should fear to. Here Jesus had all the authority to give their wages and those who are disobedient, to inflict a painful punishment and there will be none to support except Allah. It is a very terrible statement.

In the verse 174 in the Qur'an, Allah sent Jesus to the world as a bright light. 174. 'O mankind! Indeed the clear proof from your Lord has come to you, and we have sent down to you a bright light.'

Before we go on any further discussion, let's pause and ask ourselves this question: Who is the Bright Light and the Holy Prophet sent down by Allah as Allah's word? According to the verses above from the Noble Qur'an, it is crystal clear that the Noble messenger of Allah is Isa (Jesus). And He is a bright light. Isa (peace be upon Him) brought the Gospel from Allah as Allah stated it. Whoever rejects this Gospel message is rejecting Allah's message. Whoever hates worshipping Isa (as it was stated in the verse 173) will be inflicted with painful punishment. These specifications about Jesus are very clear in the Qur'an.

Surah Al-Mā'idah 5: 46, 47 in the Noble Quran and Sahih International says:

46) "And We sent, following in their footsteps, ISA, the son of Mary, confirming that which came before him in the Torah; and We gave him the Gospel, in which was guidance and light and confirming that which preceded it of the Torah as guidance and instruction for the righteous."

47) "And let the People of the Gospel judge by what Allah has revealed therein. And whoever does not judge by what Allah has revealed – then it is those who are the defiantly disobedient."

According to the above verses we should not be disobedient to Allah and His Word (Jesus). If we reject the Gospel sent by Allah we will be punished by Jesus when He comes to judge the people.

The Muslims believe in the prophets. They believe that prophets don't commit any big sins. But they do small sins. They all asked for forgiveness of their sins. But every one will accept the truth that the only prophet in the Qur'an who did not commit any sin, is Jesus Christ. Since it is impossible to human beings to be sinless, Jesus Christ must be more than a prophet according to the writings of the Qur'an.

The Qur'an explains that Isa (Messiah) came as a Noble Messenger, the Word of God, Spirit from Allah, Bright Light, and the Prophet sent by Allah. These are all the honorary titles of Jesus that we read from the Surah 4:169-171. He is the Speech of Truth [Surah19:34:35] Jesus was as a sign unto men and Mercy from God. [Surah 19:21]

In the Qur'an, Jonah 10:95, it says, 'And be not thou of those who deny the revelations of Allah, for then wert thou of the losers.

The Titles of Jesus Christ
in the Holy Bible

Every book of the Old Testament and the New Testament in the Bible give complete understanding of Jesus Christ. and He is the central theme of the holy Bible.

Immanuel: Around 700 B.C, Isaiah the Prophet foretold in the Book of Isaiah 7:14, it was written, 'a virgin will give birth to a son and He will be called Immanuel' (meaning "God with us.") Thus the name itself confirmed the Deity of Jesus Christ.

Savior and Christ the Lord (Anointed): About 700 years later, Isaiah's prophecy was fulfilled. Gabriel the Angel appeared and announced to Mary, Joseph (foster Father of Jesus) and also to shepherds. '10And the angel said unto them, "Fear not: for, behold, I bring you good tidings of great joy, which shall be to all people.11For unto you is born this day in the city of David a Savior, which is Christ the Lord. 12And this shall be a sign unto you; ye shall find the babe wrapped in swaddling clothes, lying in a manger. 13And suddenly there was with the angel a multitude of the heavenly host praising God, and saying, 14Glory to God in the highest, and on earth peace, good will toward men. (Luke Gospel 2:10-14)

At the time of His birth, heavenly powers revealed the name of Messiah as Jesus (Savior), Immanuel (God is with us) and Christ (Anointed). The foretold prophecies in the Old Testament about His birth were fulfilled.

Son of God: In Mark Gospel 1: 9-11: "Johnthe Baptist was giving baptism to Jesus in Jordan; he saw the heavens opened, and a Spirit like dove was descending upon Him. "And there came a voice from heaven, saying, "Thou art my beloved son, in whom I am well pleased." In this verse, it confirms Jesus as the Spirit of God and was sent down from heaven as God's Spiritual son. This is witnessed by John the Baptist and the people around Him. They were amazed and could not deny the truth. Jesus Himself said these words. "For God so loved the world that He gave His only begotten Son, that whosoever believeth in Him should not perish, but have everlasting life." John Gospel 3:16. Many people believed it, since His name is SPEECH OF TRUTH.

Arm of God & His righteousness: The event of Jesus coming to the world was prophesied by Isaiah the Prophet 700 years before Jesus was born. He specified in Isaiah 59:16, that Jesus is a God's Spiritual son or a part of God. It was written, 'He saw there was no man, and wondered that there was no intercessor: therefore "His arm" brought salvation unto him: and His righteousness, it sustained him.' This verse explains how Jesus is a part of God. There is a clear explanation that 'The arm of God' that would bring salvation to the people is Jesus.

And it was confirmed by the angel Gabriel at His birth. Angel Gabriel mentioned that His name will be Jesus which means the Savior. Jesus Christ is the Savior who came to the world to save the people from their sins and 'the salvation' given is unto eternity. That is how, He is considered as a part of God or the son of God. We see the linkage of the Old Testament and the New Testament. The foretold prophesies about Jesus were written in the Old Testament and were fulfilled in the New Testament. How beautiful are theses prophesies. They explained the truth. Even the simple can understand the truth.

Spirit of God: To explain, how Jesus is the Spirit of God, we can view God as the original fire and Jesus Christ as a flame. From the original fire a flame came into this world to lighten mankind so that the spirit of man may also burn for God or to have zeal for God. Even though "the flame" left the fire, "the original fire God" is still there. Since I was born in a country, I saw how the fire spreads. If one object ignites, the fire from that object goes and catches fire to an object afar. The first object still burning and it ignites the other one.

'God' is personified as fire to understand this simple truth. There are several incidents and examples in the Torah which contained many references. Awesome God who is beyond human expectation, revealed Himself with these references from the word of God.

God spoke with Moses in the burning bush, yet the bush was not burnt. When the Israelites sinned against God, God's wrath kindled against them and a fire came from the heaven and burnt them. "For our God is a consuming fire." (Hebrews 12:29)

'A part of the original spirit (fire)' is regarded as a Son. In that sense a voice from the heaven confirmed that Jesus Christ is a 'Spiritual Part or Son of God.' But, do not mistake Jesus as a physical son born to God because God is Spirit. The same Spirit came as Jesus. He is the Spirit of God. Since God is omnipotent, God can stay at one place and still be in all places; that is the uniqueness of God. To deny God's uniqueness of being present everywhere we are undermining the greatness of God's wonderful power. God is the original Spiritual fire.

His personality is wide, varied and complex. His Spirit came as a man (Jesus) in the human form because Father God form is unreachable, unapproachable as He was an intense fire. It is written in the scriptures. '16Who only hath immortality, dwelling in the light which no man can approach unto; whom no man hath seen, nor can see: to whom be honor and power everlasting. Amen.' (1Thimothy 6:16) God said "Thou canst not see my face: for there shall no man see me, and live." Do not mistake all the fire on the earth to be God. God is the Spiritual fire. God showed many examples in the Scriptures to make people to understand the concept.

A glimpse of God's extreme greatness can be seen in the Torah. In Exodus 19:18 "And Mount Sinai was altogether on a smoke, because the LORD descended upon it in fire: and the smoke thereof ascended as the smoke of a furnace, and the whole mount quaked greatly." God told Moses to set a boundary round about the people, because whoever would touch the mount would die. Here we are able to see God as an intense fire and greatest power. In Exodus 9:15, Moses turned and came down from the mount, and the mount appears as it was burning with fire. But still the mount was as it was. How can a man imagine God? He is beyond our imagination.

His holiness and power were so great, that humans were unable to approach Him, even though they were sanctified. That is why He made a way for the humans to reach Him. The Spirit of God became man to approach the man kind. If God comes as a snake, animal or in the other form, or with His full glory, we can not communicate or approach and we will die. Our merciful God, who intended to have relationship with the human which was lost in the Garden of Eden, restored it by revealing Himself as a human in the flesh, appeared on the earth as Jesus Christ.

Word of God; Full of grace and truth: In the Gospel of John 1:1 and 14 it is written, "In the beginning was the Word, and the Word was with God, and the Word was God. 14And 'the Word' was made flesh, and dwelt among us, and we beheld his glory, the glory as of the only begotten of the Father full of grace and truth."

His word manifested in the flesh as Jesus Christ. God's word has power. With the same word God created all creation. The same power we can see in Jesus Christ's words. He brought back life and did so many miracles. The Eternal word incarnate in the son of God. In the scriptures the "word of God" was explained in several references. Here below are as follows:

'⁶The words of the LORD.are pure words: as silver tried in a furnace of earth, purified seven times.'(Psalms12:6)

'²⁰He sent his word, and healed them, and delivered them from their destructions.' (Psalms107:20)

Psalms 119 full chapter was written about "His word." Here are some references from the same chapter.

'¹¹Thy word have I hid in mine heart, that I might not sin against thee.'

'⁵⁰This is my comfort in my affliction: for thy word hath quickened me.'

'⁸¹My soul fainteth for thy salvation: but I hope in thy word.'

'⁸²Mine eyes fail for thy word, saying, When wilt thou comfort me?'

'¹⁰³How sweet are thy words unto my taste! Yea, sweeter than honey to my mouth!'

'¹⁰⁴Through thy precepts I understand: therefore I hate every false way.'

'¹⁰⁵Thy word is a lamp unto my feet, and a light unto my path.'

'130The entrance of thy words giveth light; it giveth understanding unto the simple.'

Then in Psalms 138:2, God magnified His word above all His name.

'2 I will worship toward thy holy temple, and praise thy name for thy loving kindness and for thy truth: for thou hast magnified thy word above thy entire name.' (Psalms138:2)

All the above references specified on the "word of God," are the foretold prophecies to indicate Jesus Christ.

The Spiritual meaning of the expression "Son of God" was revealed as His Word had became man in the birth of Jesus Christ which means the "word of God" itself took the form of Jesus. God's word has the life in it. Therefore Jesus Christ is called the LIVING WORD as stated in 1 John 1:1. And He is also called as the living bread.

And the title the "Word of God" is Jesus Christ. It was testified by His disciple John. He verified it by seeing it with His own eyes. He witnessed that he saw Jesus in His glory. John in Patmos Island when the heavens were opened saw visions of God in the heaven. He witnessed it in Revelation19:10-16. This vision was shown to John in about 90A.D.

You could read the whole 19th chapter to understand the meaning of 'the word of God' which implies Jesus fully.

John wrote as it was, '10And I fell at his feet to worship him. And he said unto me, See thou do it not: I am thy fellow servant, and of thy brethren that have the testimony of Jesus: worship God: for the testimony of Jesus is the spirit of prophecy. 11And I saw heaven opened, and behold a white horse; and he that sat upon him was called Faithful and true, and in righteousness he doth judge and make war. 12 His eyes were as a flame of fire, and on his head were many crowns; and he had a name written, that no man knew, but He himself. [13]And he was clothed with vesture dipped in blood: and his name is called The Word of God. [14]And the armies which were in heaven followed him upon white horses, clothed in fine linen, white and clean. [15]And out of his mouth goeth a sharp sword, that with it he should smite the nations: and he shall rule them with a rod of iron: and he treadeth the winepress of the fierceness and wrath of Almighty God. [16]And he hath on his vesture and on his thigh a name written, King of Kings, And Lord of Lords.'

What else we need for clarification that Jesus Christ is the "word of God" and is superior above every one. In the above passage it is clear that angels are under him and are inferior to Him. He is King of kings and Lord of Lords.

"His word" was made as a human on this earth and He is the Lord. Now He is the head of the church. (Group of the believers) The church is His body.

Let us keep on continue about 'His titles',

The Holy one of God: Jesus had the authority to drive out the unclean spirits/demons, and that even the unclean spirits/demons recognized Him as the Holy One of God, as stated in Mark 1:24: "What have you to do with us, Jesus of Nazareth? Have you come to destroy us? I know who you are —The Holy One of God." But some people are not recognizing this truth.

Jesus is the way, the truth & the life: In John Gospel 14:6-7, "[6]Jesus saith unto him, "I am the way, and the truth, and the life: no one cometh unto the Father, but by me. [7]If ye had known me, ye would have known my Father also: from henceforth ye know him, and have seen him." He is exact replica of Father God.

Jesus Christ came to fulfill the scriptures. Here is the evidence. Jesus in His ministry He pointed out to the Old Testament for an understanding of Him and His ways, because the Old Testament always was pointed Him. (Luke24:25-27)

In John Gospel 5:39-46. Jesus said, "³⁹Search the scriptures; for in them ye think ye have eternal life: and they are they which testify of me. ⁴⁰And ye will not come to me that ye might have life. ⁴³I am come in my Father's name, and ye receive me not: if another shall come in his own name, him ye will receive."

He is the bread of life:

In John Gospel 6:35, Jesus had declared that He is the bread of life. '³⁵Jesus said unto them, "I am the bread of life: he that cometh to me shall not hunger, and he that believeth on me shall never thirst."

Almighty controller of the universe:
Lord and Messiah:

Jesus is Lord, in the sense that He has the authority. Jesus stated that He and Father are one and Father gave him authority in heaven and in the universe.

"The Father is in me and I in him." (John 10:28)

"I and my Father are one." (John 10:30)

"He who has seen me has seen the Father." (John 14:9)

"He that honored not the Son honored not the
Father which had sent him." (John 5:23)

Jesus said in Matthew 28:15: "All authority has been given
to me in heaven and on earth." This verse explains that Jesus
is the Almighty controller of everything in the universe.

Even though Jesus is the Almighty controller of everything
in the universe, Jesus our Lord is a humble, sacrificial, and
loving king. He behaved differently in his kingship than what
we have expected- Jesus humbled Himself unto death to save
mankind, rather than taking a prideful position of dominance.
He became as a humble servant of God even though He
had a command over life and the creation." Therefore let
all Israel be assured of this: God has made this Jesus, whom
you crucified, both 'Lord and Messiah'." (Acts 2:3)

Jesus Himself clarified He is the Lord. "These words spoke Jesus,
and lifted up his eyes to heaven, and said, Father, the hour is come;
glorify thy Son, that thy Son also may glorify thee: As thou hast given
him power over all flesh, that he should give eternal life to as many as
thou hast given him. And this is life eternal, that they might know thee
the only true God, and Jesus Christ, whom thou hast sent." John 17: 1-3.

If anyone, whoever inclines their ears to the above statement of
Jesus Christ, they would have never mistaken His Divine entity.

The light of the world: In John Gospel 8:12 "Then spoke
JESUS again unto them, saying, I am the light of the world. He that
follows me shall not walk in darkness, but shall have light of life." In
John Gospel 12:44-46&50, "44Jesus cried and said, "He that believeth
on me, believeth not on me, but on him that sent me. 45And he that
seeth me seeth him that sent me. 46I am come a light into the world,
that whosoever believeth on me should not abide in darkness. 47And if
any men hear my words, and believe not, I judge him not: for I came
not to judge the world, but to save the world." Jesus Christ emphasized
himself as He is light of the world." His own words had confirmed it.

For more clarity to back up these assertions about Jesus let's look at what the Torah says since Torah, the Old Testament prophesied about Jesus. There are one hundred and nine prophecies about Jesus' birth, life, and death. This clarifies, why we consider the Old Testament and the New Testament as a complete book.

More than a Prophet: Moses prophesized about a prophet in Torah, Deuteronomy 18:15. He would be like him, everybody should listen to Him. It states, "The Lord thy God will raise up unto thee a prophet from midst of thee, of thy brethren, like unto me, unto him, ye shall hearken."

Who is the Prophet that everybody has to listen? Let us analyze and come to the conclusion: According to the Moses' prophecy, the Prophet that will arise and whom we must hearken to should be like Moses; carrying traits similar to him. There is much dispute about this matter in between the Islam and the Christianity.

Who is the Prophet that resembles Moses? Jesus Christ or Muhammad? Here below is the comparison and analysis among our three prophets and whoever reads this could discern who the Torah was referring to and who had more similarities of Moses?

Moses	Muhammad	Jesus Christ
During Moses' birth Pharaoh ordered to kill all males under age two.	There no such thing occurred when Muhammad was born.	During the birth of Jesus, Herod ordered to kill all children under age two.
When he was an infant, Moses was protected by the daughter of Pharaoh (foster mother)	When he was a toddler, his mother died and was under the care of his paternal grandfather.	When he was an infant, Jesus was protected by Joseph the foster father. (Guided by angel). He had no father.

During Moses' childhood he lived in Egypt.

During Muhammad's childhood he lived in Mecca in Saudi Arabia

During Jesus' childhood he was taken by Mary and Joseph to Egypt. Guided by angel and was there for some time.

As an adult Moses received power from God. He performed miracles when God told him to do, and served as a messenger of God.

Muhammad had claimed as a messenger of Allah. No evidence of doing any miracles.

Jesus Christ is a Spirit from God in His authority came as the "LIVING WORD," of God. His word has power. He performed many miracles and raised the dead from the grave.

Moses was in the direct presence of God. "Behold, skin of Moses face shone (glowed) from being in direct presence of God's glory. And all Israelites were afraid to come nigh to him." Exodus 34:30 (Torah).

There was no transfiguration witnessed by his companions or no such change found in him.

According to the Gospel of Matthew 17: 1-6, Mark 9:2-8 and Luke 9:28-36: It was written that JESUS CHRIST took His 3 disciples Peter, James and John to a mountain transfigured before them. His face shone and His clothes were whiter than snow, they were afraid to see His face. A cloud overshadowed them; and a voice came out of the cloud, saying, "this is my beloved son: hear him." This is the voice from Heaven, who can deny it?

Moses fasted 40 days and 40 nights.	Muhammad fasted 30 days every year. 9 Ramadan.	Jesus fasted 40 days and 40 nights.
Moses died naturally, as a human being at his old age 120 years.	Muhammad died at the age of 63 by suffering with illness.	There is no record of Jesus Christ's illness. Jesus Christ was crucified at 33. He rose again on third day and appeared to people and ascended to heaven. Two Angels told disciples that He will come back the earth, again second time.

Many similarities existed in between Moses and Jesus Christ, thereby we see the proof that Jesus is the Prophet that was mentioned in the Torah. Thereby everybody has to listen to Jesus as it was written by Moses in Deuteronomy 18:15.

Jesus Christ is a part of God (son of God), who came as a human (son of man) to the world. Jesus Christ is the word of God and the arm of God, thus considered as 'Son of God.' But he came as a human. He experienced life on the earth. He was thirst, hungered, and he was tempted and went through all kinds of situations. He had pity upon people, healed their sicknesses, provided food for them, and raised dead. He showed His compassion and love. God humbled himself and came down in order to be reachable to every person and nations in the world. The blind received their sight, and the lame walked, the lepers were cleansed, and the deaf were heard, the dead were raised up, and the poor heard the Gospel and it was preached to them. (Isaiah 9 and 42 chapters were fulfilled). It demonstrated His unspeakable love towards the mankind whom He created in His likeness.

Even now many miracles are happening in the name of Jesus. In this book we confirmed the titles of Jesus Christ as Immanuel (God is with us) Savior, The arm of God and His righteousness, Son of God, The Holy one of God, the Spirit of God, and the Way, the Truth, the Life, Word of God, Lord, Bright Light & Light of the world, more than a Prophet and Anointed, but altogether in the Old Testament and the New Testament, He had more than 200 names.

Jesus is the light of the world as per the Holy Bible & Jesus is the Bright light as per the Noble Qur'an

---

Dear earnest reader! The Islam and the Christianity, both the religions agree with the fact that Jesus is "the Light to the world."

In the Holy Bible Jesus applied this title to Himself. He declared that He is the light of the world. (John 9:5) In John Gospel 8:12, "12Then spake Jesus again unto them, saying, "I am the light of the world: he that followeth me shall not walk in darkness, but shall have the light of life."

In John 1:9, John the Baptist witnessed that Jesus Christ is the true light.

Whereas in the Noble Qur'an Allah declared that "Jesus is the Bright light," that was sent to the world to all the mankind. In Al Nisa 4:174, we read, 174. "O mankind! Indeed the clear proof from your Lord has come to you, and we have sent down to you a bright light." And in Al- Maidah 5:46.[46] "And We sent, following in their footsteps, ISA, the son of Mary, confirming that which came before him in the Torah; and We gave him the Gospel, in which was guidance and light and confirming that which preceded it of the Torah as guidance and instruction for the righteous." Jesus is the straight path and is a bright light. There is wisdom and light for guidance in His teachings as it was specified in the above statements from the Qur'an.

Here Allah is witnessing that Jesus Christ is the Bright light not an ordinary light. If Allah says some thing there is a deeper meaning in it. Allah sent Him as the bright light so that people could see their filthiness, uncleanness (dirt) and know their sins to repent. Allah mentioned the word the "bright light" only to refer Jesus. In the Noble Qur'an, Allah is addressing to the whole world. Please notice the word "O mankind!" It is not only to the Israel nation. Some people are misunderstanding this important concept and are neglecting Jesus. They are assuming that Jesus is only for the Israel nation. Allah mentioned Jesus as the Bright light to all the mankind.

There is a great deal of significance in this title of Jesus Christ which we need to know it in detail. It is essential to know the truth why Jesus was sent as bright light and why Jesus declared that He is the light of the world?

In the creation, God created the physical light first. (Genesis 1:3) There will be darkness everywhere without the light. If there is light there is inspiration and insight. Otherwise it is void and darkness. The spiritual light works with the same principle. A physically blind person can not see any thing. He needs assistance. In the same way, a spiritually blind person needs spiritual assistance to find a way. Because of this reason, the spiritual light is important as well as the physical light.

God is a Spirit being and is the Spiritual intense light that nobody could approach Him. God is the 'Father of lights' as it is written in the word of God. In 1 Timothy 6:15-16, it is written, "¹⁵Which in his times he shall shew, who is the blessed and only Potentate, the King of kings, and Lord of lords; ¹⁶Who only hath immortality, dwelling in the light which no man can approach unto; whom no man hath seen, nor can see: to whom be honor and power everlasting. Amen. "¹⁷Every --- and cometh down from the Father of lights, with whom is no variableness, neither shadow of turning." (James1:17)

God as an unapproachable light could not come into the midst of the people as He is since no one could stand. Therefore God sent Jesus Christ as the bright light in His appropriate time. That is why, Paul wrote to Galatians' church, "But when the fullness of the time was come, God sent forth his Son, made of a woman, made under the law, ⁵To redeem them that were under the law, that we might receive the adoption of sons." (Galatians 4:4–5)

The importance of having the light and seeing the light are two concepts in this theorem. Otherwise there is no beauty in having the light. God's idea of sending Jesus the Bright light into the world has a vast amount of meaning in both ways physical and spiritual. What a beautiful emphasis about Lord Jesus Christ in the Qur'an and in the Bible! When God says a word, there is a very important meaning embedded in it and it is so powerful because of His infinite wisdom.

We all knew the importance of the light in our daily life. We see beautiful creation only because of the light. We achieve many things in our daily life. The light drives away the darkness where there is fear. There is no appearance of the darkness in the light. The light gives guidance. Whereas in the darkness there is fear and there is no guidance. We can not go forward in the darkness. We can not find out anything. We will stumble and fall.

Besides all these uses, there is one more essential use of the light. It is exclusive resource of energy. Plants use the light for the photosynthesis and provide the food for the living things on the earth. Without the light there is no life and there is no energy. Everything will die and becomes dead world.

As we read in the previous chapters, Jesus Christ is "the word of God" and He is the spiritual food. The word of God gives the energy. Jesus said, "²⁷Work not for the food which perisheth, but for the food which abideth unto eternal life, which the Son of man shall give unto you:" '³⁵ Jesus said unto them, "I am the bread of life: he that cometh to me shall not hunger, and he that believeth on me shall never thirst. ⁵⁸This is the bread which came down out of heaven:

not as the fathers ate, and died; he that eateth this bread shall live for ever." (John 6:27, 35&58) Those days when Jesus said these things, Jews could not understand because they rejected Him. Hence they were left spiritually blind. Their ears were heavy as per the prophecy.

Those who can not see the light are blind that is why whoever does not come to Jesus Christ are blind. They are in their spiritual darkness and are spiritually in lack of food and thereby lack of energy. They stumble and fall in their spiritual life because they are in the darkness. Eventually they are dead. No one on the earth have their own spiritual energy to live righteous life. Every one has to depend upon the light resource. It is written in Romans 8:10, "[10]And if Christ be in you, the body is dead because of sin; but the Spirit is life because of righteousness. In the same way, without Jesus Christ to the world, there is no spiritual energy, thus no spiritual life.

The importance of the light in everyday life metaphorically speaks of Jesus Christ in the spiritual life.

The light we see in our everyday life appears as white and bright but it is very complex in its nature. The light refers to the breadth of electromagnetic spectrum, which includes visible light, yet also includes light with wavelengths that we can not see, such as radio waves, microwaves, infrared, ultraviolet, X-Rays and gamma rays. These different types of light are used in everyday life; however, for example, airport scanners use X-Rays to inspect the contents of suitcases. In medical field X-rays reveal inside disease of the body. In the previous chapters of this book, we had been gone through the situations where we read in the holy Bible that Jesus knew all men. "[24]But Jesus did not commit himself unto them, because he knew all men, [25]And needed not that any should testify of man: for he knew what was in man." (John Gospel 2:24-25)

As we knew that the physical light is with both visible and invisible spectrum, the spectrum of light contains seven distinct colors along with thousands of shade. The color spectrum of the light can be seen in the rainbow.

In the Holy Bible it was recorded the rainbow as a symbol of God's covenant with His people. The rainbow is so beautiful and magnificent. It is symbolic to Lord Jesus Christ with His divine characteristics.

Lord God our creator made rainbow as a token of a covenant so that whenever He sees it He will forgive living creatures of all the flesh. That is how the sins of all the human beings were forgiven in Jesus Christ. To make this concept clear Jesus came as a human and bore everybody's sins, died and buried the sins of all the people and He was arose and ascended into the heaven.

God made it clear in the time of Noah that He will forgive the people when He sees the rainbow. God made this universal covenant at the time of Noah. To understand the concept let us look into a reference in Genesis 9:13-17, "[16]And the bow shall be in the cloud; and I will look upon it, that I may remember the everlasting covenant between God and every living creature of all flesh that is upon the earth." [17]And God said unto Noah, "This is the token of the covenant, which I have established between me and all flesh that is upon the earth." This is God's fore plan. That is why God sent Jesus Christ as the bright light. It shows very clearly that only through Jesus Christ all the people were forgiven. God forgives the people only when He sees Jesus Christ in between Him and the people.

In the Old Testament, God made covenant with all the people and also with the individuals. These covenants were very significant and make us to understand the fore coming things of God and also His fore plans. God revealed His fore plans ahead to the prophets in the Scriptures. Those fore plans are the prophecies. The Holy Bible is written in a sequence that all the Old Testament was a fore plan of God which was accomplished in the New Testament. This proves the word of God is of great infinite wisdom.

As we see seven distinct colors in the rainbow, we see seven covenants in Jesus Christ that God made. We understand how Jesus is the bright light to the world. Only through Him we are able to understand God's will and His plan. Through this we are able to understand the plan of God in sending Jesus as the bright light.

Let us go through the Scriptures how the covenants of God were fulfilled through Jesus Christ. All the seven covenants indicate seven rainbow colors.

The first covenant made by God is in Genesis 3:15. "15And I will put enmity between thee and the woman, and between thy seed and her seed; it shall bruise thy head, and thou shalt bruise his heel." This covenant was made by God in the beginning of the creation when Adam and Eve were deceived by Satan.

This was fulfilled when Lord Jesus Christ came to the world. Jesus did not defeat Satan by His miracles or with His sermons. He defeated Satan on the cross by saying, "It is finished" He fulfilled God's plan and He finished it. Some people may amaze how was Jesus fulfilled it! Jesus Christ was born of the woman means He came to the world without physical father, Genesis 3:15 was fulfilled at the time of his birth. It was fore planed by God. The Satan deceived Adam who was created in the image of God. But God knew how to defeat the Satan by His image (in the form of man.) It did not happen by chance. It happened according to the Scriptures.

According to the history Pontius Pilate was reluctant to condemn Jesus, but was eventually forced to give up when the crowd became unruly. The Jews shouted to crucify Him. That's how the Devil sought to bruise the heel of Lord Jesus Christ but Lord Jesus Christ crushed it's head on the cross. He died according to the Scriptures, He defeated 'the Death' and He rose again according to the Scriptures.

The same promise was given to us in Romans16:20. "20And the God of peace shall bruise Satan under your feet shortly. The grace of our Lord Jesus Christ be with you. Amen." He conquered the Death and rose again. He sent His Holy Spirit into the heart of a believer so that through Him (the Holy Spirit), a believer could conquer the world and be victorious over the Satan.

The second covenant, we read in Genesis 9:15. "¹⁵And I will remember my covenant, which is between me and you and every living creature of all flesh; and the waters shall no more become a flood to destroy all flesh. ¹⁶And the bow shall be in the cloud; and I will look upon it, that I may remember the everlasting covenant between God and every living creature of all flesh that is upon the earth." God is not destroying the whole world with flood like at the time of Noah, even though the world is far more sinful than before.

God keeps on striving for the human race and if we humble ourselves and confess our sins, He will make us His children and come and live in us. God is waiting patiently at the sinner to get back to Him. He will forgive the human because of the covenant that He made with every living creature of all the flesh. Only through Jesus we all will be forgiven.

God made **the third covenant** with Abraham. (Genesis 12:2-3) "²And I will make of thee a great nation, and I will bless thee, and make thy name great; and thou shalt be a blessing: ³And I will bless them that bless thee, and curse him that curseth thee: and in thee shall all families of the earth be blessed. ⁷And I will establish my covenant between me and thee and thy seed after thee in their generations for an everlasting covenant, to be a God unto thee, and to thy seed after thee." Even though Abraham was hundred years old and Sarah was ninety years old, God kept His promise and made them to bear a son named Isaac as a promised son. God kept His covenant.

From the generations of Abraham, Lord Jesus Christ was born. Abraham was strong in faith to experience the impossible thing to happen. Both of their old bodies were revived by the power of resurrection from God. Lord Jesus Christ proved that He had the power of Resurrection. By faith a believer can claim same power for all his or her temptations, trials and sufferings, and achieve the impossible things.

The fourth covenant we read in Deuteronomy 18:5. This covenant was made with Moses. "¹⁵The LORD thy God will raise up unto thee a Prophet from the midst of thee, of thy brethren, like unto me; unto him ye shall hearken;' We already discussed this verse in previous chapters of this book. We were convinced that Lord Jesus Christ is the person who was like Moses but He is greater than Moses and is an ever lasting Prophet. He instructs us and guides us in our daily life. We have to listen to Him.

The fifth covenant was made by God with David in 2 Samuel 7:12-13, "¹²And when thy days be fulfilled, and thou shalt sleep with thy fathers, I will set up thy seed after thee, which shall proceed out of thy bowels, and I will establish his kingdom. ¹³He shall build a house for my name, and I will stablish the throne of his kingdom for ever. ¹⁹All this, said David, "the LORD made me understand in writing by his hand upon me, even all the works of this pattern." God gave David the pattern for the temple of God to be built by his son Solomon. The same way we have received the heavenly pattern of the Heavenly church through Lord Jesus Christ. God is building His bride or house hold of God through Christ by the believers of all over the world. (Revelation 1:10-20)

The sixth covenant was the Lord Jesus Christ Himself, Psalms 2:7-9, '⁷I will declare the decree: the LORD hath said unto me, "Thou art my Son; this day have I begotten thee. ⁸Ask of me, and I shall give thee the heathen for thine inheritance, and the uttermost parts of the earth for thy possession. ⁹Thou shalt break them with a rod of iron; thou shalt dash them in pieces like a potter's vessel." This covenant was fulfilled by the coming of Jesus Christ to the world as a part of God or the Son of God. God gave Him the authority and the power as we had seen in so many illustrations in this book. Through Him, believers also have the same privilege. A believer can win the souls for God with the love of the Son of God.

The seventh and the last covenant God made in Hebrews 10:16-17. "¹⁶This is the covenant that I will make with them after those days, saith the Lord, I will put my laws into their hearts, and in their minds will I write them; ¹⁷And their sins and iniquities will I remember no more."

This covenant was revealed to the Prophet Jeremiah in the Old Testament who lived around 655 BC. He lived in the days of Josiah and Jehoiakim. For many years Jeremiah warned the Jews that God would send the Babylonian armies to punish Jerusalem's ungodliness.

God's word again came to Jeremiah, where we read it in Jeremiah11:10-11. '¹⁰They are turned back to the iniquities of their forefathers, which refused to hear my words; and they went after other gods to serve them: the house of Israel and the house of Judah have broken my covenant which I made with their fathers. ¹¹Therefore thus saith the LORD, Behold, I will bring evil upon them, which they shall not be able to escape; and though they shall cry unto me, I will not hearken unto them. And He continued in Jeremiah 23:10-11. ¹⁰For the land is full of adulterers; for because of swearing the land mourneth; the pleasant places of the wilderness are dried up, and their course is evil and their force is not right. ¹¹For both prophet and priest are profane; yea, in my house have I found their wickedness, saith the Lord.'

God is very compassionate. His mercy endureth forever. He never leaves His children. He is a forgiver. He had forgiven them and made a new covenant.

Later, in chapter 31, God's word came to Jeremiah. We read it in the book of Jeremiah31:31-35, '³¹the days are surely coming, says the LORD, when I will make a new covenant with the house of Israel and the house of Judah. ³²It will not be like the covenant that I made with their ancestors when I took them by the hand to bring them out of the land of Egypt—a covenant that they broke, though I was their husband (master), says the LORD.'

'³³But this is the covenant that I will make with the house of Israel after those days, says the LORD: I will put my law within them, and I will write it on their hearts; and I will be their God, and they shall be my people.' (Jeremiah 31:33) These words of God were fulfilled when Jesus Christ came as the Savior to the world.

The meaning of the name Jesus is the Savior. Before Jesus left from the world, on the Passover day, He told His disciples, '²⁰And he did the same with the cup after supper, saying, "This cup that is poured out for you is the new covenant in my blood. (Luke 22:20) '8There is therefore now no condemnation for those who are in Christ Jesus. ²For the law of the Spirit of life in Christ Jesus has set you free from the law of sin and of death. ³For God has done what the law, weakened by the flesh, could not do: by sending his own Son in the likeness of sinful flesh, and to deal with sin, he condemned sin in the flesh, ⁴so that the just requirement of the law might be fulfilled in us, who walk not according to the flesh but according to the Spirit. (Romans 8:1-4)

'¹⁵For this reason he is the mediator of a new covenant, so that those who are called may receive the promised eternal inheritance, because a death has occurred that redeems them from the transgressions under the first covenant.' (Hebrews 9:15)

Jesus Christ is the bright light to redeem us from the darkness and gives us the spiritual energy to live righteously unto eternity. His Spirit dwells in us. Those who receive Him will become light to the world. We can have direct communication with God only through Jesus. Without the Bright light Jesus, we are in the darkness and stumble in our way to reach God. In John Gospel 3:19-21, it is written that Jesus Christ is the true light. "¹⁹And this is the condemnation, that light is come into the world, and men loved darkness rather than light, because their deeds were evil. ²⁰For every one that doeth evil hateth the light, neither cometh to the light, lest his deeds should be reproved. ²¹But he that doeth truth cometh to the light, that his deeds may be made manifest, that they are wrought in God.'

The invisible spectrum in the light has many amazing properties as we previously discussed, and the human eye cannot fully understand its significance. In a similar way the personhood of Jesus Christ is distinguished in majesty, power and the glory that humans cannot understand or see with their human eyes. On this planet, we only saw His miracles and also came to know that He knew all men. He brought back the dead people to life. We can not hide anything from Him. The most unique thing about Him is He never leaves us nor forsakes us. His Spirit is continuously working in us to be like Him. His greatness is beyond our knowledge. Man is only able to see and understand the greatness of Jesus Christ when he enters into the eternity. Therefore God is quite right to emphasize Jesus as a bright light to all the mankind.

Here is a main inference of Jesus message to all the people in the world. There is no other message to be needed. John Gospel 8:23-24. "²³And Jesus said unto them, ye are from beneath; I am from above: ye are of this world; I am not of this world. ²⁴I said therefore unto you, that ye shall die in your sins: for if ye believe not that I am he, ye shall die in your sins. In Luke Gospel 9:26. ²⁶For whosoever shall be ashamed of me and of my words, of him shall the Son of man be ashamed, when he shall come in his own glory, and in his Father's, and of the holy angels."

Jesus words are very clear in saying that every one in this world should believe in Him otherwise they can not meet Him when He comes at the second time to the world. In fact they will die in their own sins.

The Only One True God in the Islam

God as referenced in the Qur'an is the only God and is said to be the same God worshipped by other Abraham religions such as Judaism and the Christianity. In the Qur'an, it was explained that God is above all comprehension, "No vision can grasp Him, but His grasp is over all vision. He is most courteous well acquainted with all things." (Qur'an 6:103)

The definition of Allah in the Qur'an 6:103 claims that no vision can grasp Him and Allah cannot be represented by any visible image and yet, astonishingly, there are narrations which say that Allah created Adam in his image, and specified even height and length and in His complete image.

Abu Hurairah (Arabic) lived in between 603-681. He was a companion of Islamic Prophet Muhammad. He narrated 5375 ahadith. The meaning of ahadith is a report of deeds and sayings of the Prophet Muhammad. They all were composed in Sahih Muslim book. The following are one of those ahadith.

Abu Hurairah narrated: 'The Prophet said, "Allah created Adam in HIS IMAGE, sixty cubits (about 30 meters) in height. When He created him, He said (to him), 'Go and greet that group of angels sitting there, and listen what they will say in reply to you, for that will be your greeting and the greeting of your offspring.' Adam (went and) said, '(Peace be upon you).' They replied, '(Peace and Allah's Mercy be on you).' So they increased 'wa Rahmatullah' The

Prophet added, 'so whoever will enter Paradise, will be of the shape and picture of Adam." Abu Huraira reported Allah's Messenger (May peace be upon him) as saying: "Allah, the Exalted and Glorious, created Adam in His own image with His length of sixty cubits. So he who would get into Paradise would get in the form of Adam, his length being sixty cubits, then the people who followed him continued to diminish in size up to this day." (Sahih Muslim book 040, number 6809)

This Hadith has been transmitted on the authority of Abu Huraira and in the Hadith transmitted on the authority of Ibn Hatim, a companion of the Prophet Muhammad, Allah's Apostle (may peace be upon him) is reported to have said: "When any one of you fights with his brother, he should avoid his face for Allah created Adam in His own image." (Sahih Muslim, book 032, number 6325) It gives us the understanding that God has the same face like the human in the Islam.

Narrated Abu Huraira: The Prophet said, "Allah created Adam in His complete shape and form (directly), sixty cubits (about 30 meters) in height...(Sahih al-Bukhari, volume 8, book 74, number 246) These Hadiths have caused trouble to explain since they find it difficult to reconcile these statements with their belief that creatures do not resemble Allah. They interpret these reports in the Islam to mean that Allah created Adam in Adam's image, i.e. in the shape and form that Allah had ordained for Adam! It is very difficult to understand the diverse statements about the description of God.

In the Islam we have two diversified ideas about God. One idea is that no vision can grasp God. It means there isn't anything and anyone similar to God. And the other idea is 'man' is in complete image of God. Even height was specified in the Hadiths. When no vision can grasp God, how the height and the face were seen by some one?

Abdur Rahman ibn, one of the Hadith writers narrated about Aisha's statement: Aisha was the wife of the Prophet Muhammad.

Allah's Messenger (peace be upon him) said: "I saw my Lord, the Exalted and Glorious in the most beautiful form. He said: What do the Angels in the presence of Allah contend about? I said: Thou art the most aware of it. He then placed his palm between my shoulders and I felt its coldness in my chest and I came to know what was in the Heavens and the Earth." He recited: 'Thus did we show Ibrahim the kingdom of the Heavens and the Earth and it was so that he might have certainty.'(Tirmidhi, 237)

Masruq Ibn Ajada transmitter of prophetic traditions or Hadith narrated his personal conversation with the wife of the Prophet Muhammad: 'I said to Aisha, "O Mother! Did Prophet Muhammad see his Lord?" Aisha said, "What you have said makes my hair stand on end! Know that if somebody tells you one of the following three things, he is a liar: Whoever tells you that Muhammad saw his Lord, is a liar." Then Aisha recited the Verse: 'No vision can grasp Him, but His grasp is over all vision. He is the most courteous well acquainted with all things' Quran 6:103. It is not fitting for a human being that Allah should speak to Him except by inspiration or from behind a veil.' Quran 42:51

'Aisha further said, "And whoever tells you that the Prophet knows what is going to happen tomorrow, is a liar." She then recited: 'No soul can know what it will earn tomorrow.' (Quran 31.34) She added: "And whoever tells you that he concealed (some of Allah's orders) is a liar." Then she recited: "O Apostle! Proclaim (the Message) which has been sent down to you from your Lord..." (5.67) 'Aisha added. "But the Prophet saw Gibril (Gabriel) in his true form twice." (Sahih al- Bukhari, volume 6, book 60, number 378)

Narrated Masruq: 'Aisha said, "If anyone tells you that Muhammad has seen his Lord, He is a liar, for Allah says: 'No vision can grasp Him.' (6.103) and if anyone tells you that Muhammad has seen the Unseen, he is a liar, for Allah says: 'None has the knowledge of the Unseen but Allah." (Sahih al-Bukhari, volume 9, book 93, number 477)

Aisha recites Surahs 6:103 and 42:51 to prove that Muhammad could not have seen his Lord. When Aboo Tharr asked the Prophet, if he saw Lord, the Prophet replied, there was only light, how could I see Him? (Sahih Muslim1, p 113, number 341)

It is narrated on the authority of Ibn 'Abbas, paternal cousin of the Prophet Muhammad, 'that he (the Prophet) saw (Allah) with his heart.' (Sahih Muslim Book 001, number 0334) It is narrated on the authority of Ibn Abbas that the words: "The heart belied not what he saw" (al-Qur'an, Iiii. 11) and "Certainly he saw Him in another descent" (al-Qur'an, Iiii. 13) imply that he saw him twice with his heart. (Sahih Muslim book 001, number 0335)

The explanation of God in the Islam is varied. Different ideas were exhibited. There is no exact explanation of God's appearance and existence in the Islam. It was not explained how God created man in His likeness.

But in the teaching of the Islam, the Oneness of God is explained in Surah-Al-Ikhlas 112, Surah Al- Nisa 4:171 say, "Do not say that God is three."

Muslim doctrine is very strict about Monotheism (Taw hid), but there are some verses in the Qur'an in which plurality was mentioned, stating "We" the name of Allah in plural. Please see the statement below in Nisa 4:174.

"O mankind! Indeed the clear proof from your Lord has come to you, and 'We' have sent down to you a bright light." (Please refer --- The Holy Prophet is clear proof from ALLAH.)

Even though central theme of the Islam is Monotheism (Taw hid), yet some of the statements of Allah in the Qur'an were specified as plural. Here in the above quotation, we see the word "WE" mentioned many times which is not consistent with Taw hid. It could not explain how the divine plurals can be interpreted to harmonize monotheism. But the Islam is very strict about the Monotheism. They explain that the plurals "WE" is the respectable word to higher authority. "God is one. He is Allah: the Self sufficient, the Eternal

God; He begets not, nor was He begotten; there is none equal to Him." (The Holy Quran, Surah 112:1-4) But there is no explanation in the Islam about "God created man in His own image or in His likeness.

The Only one True God
in the Christianity

———————⬦———————

Now let us see in the Christianity for the evidence of only one God.

In the Holy Bible, Monotheism is persistent. The holy Bible explained in a beautiful and applicable way.

Deuteronomy 6:4-5: "Hear, O Israel, the Lord our God, the Lord is one!"

Exodus 20:3-5: '³Thou shall have no other Gods before me. ⁴Thou shall not make unto thee any graven image, or any likeness of any thing that is in heaven above, or that is in the earth beneath, or that is in the water under the earth. ⁵Thou shall not bow down thyself to them, nor serve them: for I the LORD thy God am a jealous God, visiting the iniquity of the fathers upon the children unto the third and fourth generation of them that hate me.'

There is only one God the Creator of the universe. In the Torah His name was specified as "I am that I am" to Moses. He is a Sovereign and Powerful God whom none can see and live. He is ever existing God.

The book of Hebrews in the Holy Bible explained the sovereignty of God. It is written in the first chapter, 10-12. '¹⁰And, Thou, Lord, in the beginning hast laid the foundation of the earth; and the heavens are the works of thine hands: ¹¹They shall perish; but thou remainest; and they all shall wax old as doth a garment; ¹²And as a vesture shalt thou fold them up, and they shall be changed: but thou art the same, and thy years shall not fail.'

There are some descriptions about God in the Old Testament of the Bible. Some of the descriptions are a bit longer. As we are going in detail to understand the truth, I thought it is applicable to put in the detail from the Bible passages.

The following passage was taken from the book of Ezekiel from the Old Testament. The Prophet Ezekiel was lived around 592 B.C. He was in Babylon as a captive. He was surrounded by the pomp of idolatry. No clue of God whatsoever. He was in his earthly temple which means the human body. Yet he received the vision of the majesty and wonder of God's glory. The greatness of God was more magnificent than what he was seeing on the earth in heathenism. He started to describe his vision right from the first chapter. He wrote it as follows:

'[1]Now it came to pass in the thirtieth year, in the fourth month, in the fifth day of the month, as I was among the captives by the river of Chebar, that the heavens were opened, and I saw visions of God. [2]In the fifth day of the month, which was the fifth year of king Jehoiachin's captivity, [3]The word of the LORD came expressly unto Ezekiel the priest, the son of Buzi, in the land of the Chaldeans by the river Chebar; and the hand of the LORD was there upon him.'

'[4]And I looked, and, behold, a whirlwind came out of the north, a great cloud, and a fire in folding itself, and brightness was about it, and out of the midst thereof as the color of amber, out of the midst of the fire. [5]Also out of the midst thereof came the likeness of four living creatures.'

'And this was their appearance; they had the likeness of a man. [6]And every one had four faces, and every one had four wings. [7]And their feet were straight feet; and the sole of their feet was like the sole of a calf's foot: and they sparkled like the color of burnished brass. [8]And they had the hands of a man under their wings on their four sides; and they four had their faces and their wings. ⁹Their wings were joined one to another; they turned not when they went; they went every one straight forward. ¹⁰As for the likeness of their faces, they four had the face of a man, and the face of a lion, on the right side: and they four had the face of an ox on the left side; they four also had the face of an eagle. ¹¹Thus were their faces: and their wings were stretched upward; two wings of every one were joined one to another, and two covered their bodies.'

'¹²And they went every one straight forward: whither the spirit was to go, they went; and they turned not when they went. ¹³As for the likeness of the living creatures, their appearance was like burning coals of fire, and like the appearance of lamps: it went up and down among the living creatures; and the fire was bright, and out of the fire went forth lightning. ¹⁴And the living creatures ran and returned as the appearance of a flash of lightning. ¹⁵Now as I beheld the living creatures, behold one wheel upon the earth by the living creatures, with his four faces.'

'¹⁶The appearance of the wheels and their work was like unto the color of a beryl: and they four had one likeness: and their appearance and their work was as it were a wheel in the middle of a wheel.'

'¹⁷When they went, they went upon their four sides: and they turned not when they went. ¹⁸As for their rings, they were so high that they were dreadful; and their rings were full of eyes round about them four. ¹⁹And when the living creatures went, the wheels went by them: and when the living creatures were lifted up from the earth, the wheels were lifted up. ²⁰Whithersoever the spirit was to go, they went, thither was their spirit to go; and the wheels were lifted up over against them: for the spirit of the living creature was in the wheels. [21]When those went, these went; and when those stood, these stood; and when those were lifted up from the earth, the wheels were lifted up over against them: for the spirit of the living creature was in the wheels.'

'[22]And the likeness of the firmament upon the heads of the living creature was as the color of the terrible crystal, stretched forth over their heads above. [23]And under the firmament were their wings straight, the one toward the other: every one had two, which covered on this side, and every one had two, which covered on that side, their bodies. [24]And when they went, I heard the noise of their wings, like the noise of great waters, as the voice of the Almighty, the voice of speech, as the noise of a host: when they stood, they let down their wings.'

'[25]And there was a voice from the firmament that was over their heads, when they stood, and had let down their wings. [26]And above the firmament that was over their heads was the likeness of a throne, as the appearance of a sapphire stone: and upon the likeness of the throne was the likeness as the appearance of a man above upon it. [27]And I saw as the color of amber, as the appearance of fire round about within it, from the appearance of his loins even upward, and from the appearance of his loins even downward, I saw as it were the appearance of fire, and it had brightness round about. [28]As the appearance of the bow that is in the cloud in the day of rain, so was the appearance of the brightness round about. This was the appearance of the likeness of the glory of the LORD. And when I saw it, I fell upon my face, and I heard a voice of one that spake.' (Ezekiel1:1-28) The above description was from the Prophet Ezekiel.

There was another prophet in the Old Testament, Isaiah the Prophet who lived around 700B.C. He wrote his vision about God in his book, Isaiah the 6th chapter.

6. '¹In the year that king Uzziah died I saw also the LORD sitting upon a throne, high and lifted up, and his train filled the temple. ²Above it stood the seraphims: each one had six wings; with twain he covered his face, and with twain he covered his feet, and with twain he did fly. ³And one cried unto another, and said, Holy, holy, holy, is the LORD of hosts: the whole earth is full of his glory. ⁴And the posts of the door moved at the voice of him that cried, and the house was filled with smoke.'

'⁵Then said I, Woe is me! For I am undone; because I am a man of unclean lips, and I dwell in the midst of a people of unclean lips: for mine eyes have seen the King, the LORD of hosts. ⁶Then flew one of the seraphims unto me, having a live coal in his hand, which he had taken with the tongs from off the altar: ⁷And he laid it upon my mouth, and said, lo, this hath touched thy lips; and thine iniquity is taken away, and thy sin purged.'

There are some more descriptions about God from the visions of Prophet Daniel. If we read the book of Daniel God revealed him many things very mysterious which will come to pass in the future about the kingdom of God. Surprisingly, the descriptions of all the Prophets are similar to one another.

In the last book of the New Testament, named 'Revelation', John the disciple of Jesus Christ explained the vision which he had seen in his spirit when he was exiled in Patmos. He lived around 70-95 AD. It is very interesting to see the following passage from the book of Revelation. The 4th chapter had similarity with the above visions of Ezekiel the Prophet, who lived around 592BC, Isaiah the Prophet 700B.C and the Prophet Daniel around 600BC.

John the disciple of Jesus Christ was bound in the prison in Patmos Island for the word of God and for the testimony of Jesus Christ. By that time all other disciples were died as martyrs. He was lonely. He was much dismayed. During that time, John saw this vision which really strengthened him. He wrote all that was shown to him in the last book of the Bible, the Revelation.

He wrote: '²And immediately I was in the spirit: and, behold, a throne was set in heaven, and one sat on the throne. ³And he that sat was to look upon like jasper and a sardine stone: and there was a rainbow round about the throne, in sight like unto an emerald. ⁴And round about the throne were four and twenty seats: and upon the seats I saw four and twenty elders sitting, clothed in white raiment; and they had on their heads crowns of gold.'

'⁵And out of the throne proceeded lightning and thundering and voices: and there were seven lamps of fire burning before the throne, which are the seven Spirits of God. ⁶And before the throne there was a sea of glass like unto crystal: and in the midst of the throne, and round about the throne, were four beasts full of eyes before and behind. ⁷And the first beast was like a lion, and the second beast like a calf, and the third beast had a face as a man, and the fourth beast was like a flying eagle. ⁸And the four beasts had each of them six wings about him; and they were full of eyes within: and they rest not day and night, saying, "Holy, holy, holy, LORD God Almighty, which was, and is, and is to come. ⁹And when those beasts give glory and honour and thanks to him that sat on the throne, who liveth for ever and ever, ¹⁰The four and twenty elders fall down before him that sat on the throne, and worship him that liveth for ever and ever, and cast their crowns before the throne, saying, ¹¹Thou art worthy, O Lord, to receive glory and honor and power: for thou hast created all things, and for thy pleasure they are and were created." (Revelation4:2–11)

Ezekiel, Isaiah and John described what they saw in their visions. All these thrilling visions were not able to describe the face of God. The light of His face was too intense to see and is unapproachable even in the visions. That is why; they were unable to see the face of God to describe, but they wrote that they saw 'as the appearance of a man.' That is the only conclusion we had.

The Bible explains Monotheism and Singular nature of Jehovah (Yahweh) God. We read God's name as "I am that I am" in Torah (Exodus 3:13 &14) It explains, God is one, and God is unified. All attributes of God are one, and together. Even though there is "One Lord," this doesn't necessarily mean there is only one God; it means that God is ONE.

The Bible also explains how man is in the image of God. If we take a human, even though he appears to be one (singular) he comprises three prominent states. (body, soul and spirit) Since God wanted to create man in "HIS image," man resembles God and vice versa. But God is so great, His wisdom is infinite. He is incomparable, Holy, Almighty and extremely powerful. Now we remember God is one, but God used the word "WE" in Genesis 1:26 '²⁶And God said, "Let us make man in our image, after our likeness: and let them have dominion over the fish of the sea, and over the fowl of the air, and over the cattle, and over all the earth, and over every creeping thing that creepeth upon the earth." And then in the next verse, God used singular word for God. ²⁷So God created man in his own image.'

Thereby we see man in three states (like a trinity) with the body, the soul, and the spirit. At our last breath we lose our life on earth but our soul continues to live because it is a living soul as God said so. Our mortal bodies turn back to dust and return to the earth (Body State) but it in the form of seed, and the spirit returns back to GOD who gave it. (Spirit State) '⁶Or ever the silver cord be loosed, or the golden bowl be broken, or the pitcher be broken at the fountain, or the wheel broken at the cistern. ⁷Then shall the dust return to the earth as it was: and the spirit shall return unto God who gave it.' (Ecclesiastes 12:7) – We are one human yet we have three stages – body, soul, and spirit. Even though we are one person we undergo three states. Similarly, there is One God but three components of God.

God is a Holy Spirit and one singular "Spirit being" which is everlasting. He is everywhere and deals with every soul. He is the creator who cares, sustains and controls. Since He created man in His own image with His own hands, He loves the human race more than anything. He did not create angels in His image. God is immortal being, God is always there as a Father God when He came in the human form in the name of "son of man" to enlighten our Spirit to give us an everlasting eternal life which we lost in the Garden of Eden.

God Himself appeared in the flesh to demonstrate His sacrificial love for us. God did not come in other forms such as animals. This is the most awesome plan to reveal Himself to His creation. God is always there on the throne as Father God (immortal) when He came as Jesus (life, word and light) while He works every where as a Holy Spirit the guide and the comforter. If we can not understand interlink of One God and His complex work in the universe and in the heaven we underestimate His power. God is awesome and His love for us is so intense.

In the Father, there is Son and the Holy Spirit; in the Son Jesus Christ there is the Father and the Holy Spirit; and in the Holy Spirit there is the Father and the Son Jesus Christ. All the three are interlinked and unified. This is why at the human creation, as stated in Torah: Genesis 1:26, God said, "Let us make man in our image." (Please note the word "Let us" in the verse). This explains Triune God in the Torah.

How God works in three phases when He is the only One God?

1. GOD the Creator, called 'The Father' is the Creator of the universe, similar to the word Al-Qadr with the meaning of 'the Power' in the Islam. God is Omnipotent, Omnipresent, and Omniscient.

2. HIS WORD / HIS ARM also called his 'Spiritual Son' / 'part of His Spirit' became flesh in the birth of Jesus, the

Son of Mary. He is the 'Living Word' and reveals God's law and will. He spoke God's promises to men, and talked in the language of human beings. (His being as the WORD is similar to the adjective 'Murid – Willing' in Muslim Doctrine.) 'Kalimatu Allah': means Word of God. Since the beginning of the world no one on earth is comparable to the birth, life and death of Jesus Christ.

3. THE SPIRIT OF GOD, or 'The Holy Ghost,' who gives help and guidance to those who believe in Him and sanctifies them. This Spirit of God is equivalent to the adjective 'Muhyi, means life-giver' in the Islam. The Spirit is like wind. When we accept Jesus Christ as our Savior we will be born with a new spirit. This is spiritual newborn. We have spiritual appetite. We start new life. The Holy Spirit enables us to do the will of God. He comforts us in all our downfalls. Romans 8:1, 9, 10, and 14: "Therefore, there is now no condemnation for those who are in Christ Jesus. [9]You, however, are not in the realm of the flesh but are in the realm of the Spirit, if indeed the Spirit of God lives in you. And if anyone does not have the Spirit of Christ, they do not belong to Christ. [10]But, if Christ is in you, then even though your body is subject to death because of sin, the Spirit gives life because of righteousness. [14]For those who are led by the Spirit of God are the children of God."

The Three Appearances of the only one God:

The three appearances of only one God: The Father, the Son/ Word and the Holy Ghost are portrayed and described as three Persons but they are in one essence God's existence. Each one is inseparable from the others; each has the same might, immortality. Father, Son and Holy Spirit are the revelation of one God. There is difference in saying, 'Father, Son and The Holy Spirit or the Holy

Ghost,' but all can be expressed by one word: God. The Father role is different and the Son role is different and the Holy Spirit role is different but altogether they all are same. To understand the concept in a simple way, it can be compared to ice, water, and vapor. Three forms are from the same substance but they differ in their appearance and functions.

Let us just assume: But this is only an illustration to explain how God can be one in three.

Ice: Father God ----- 'The Father of lights, with whom is no variableness, neither shadow of turning.' (James1:17) '[15]Which in his times he shall shew, who is the blessed and only Potentate, the King of kings, and Lord of lords; '[16]Who only hath immortality, dwelling in the light which no man can approach unto; whom no man hath seen, nor can see: to whom be honor and power everlasting. Amen.' (Timothy 6:16–17) He was a creator.

(Ice is essential in the universe)

Water: The Son of God ----- Reachable to everybody. He was born like a human, lived like a human. The Son of God is the most merciful. We need water. The water is the most amazing substance on the earth and without it; life would not be possible and is a main actor in the climate. Jesus Christ said, "I am the way, life and truth". The wages of sin is death but Jesus Christ came to give us eternal life. '[6]For unto us a child is born, unto us a son is given: and the government shall be upon his shoulder: and his name shall be called Wonderful, Counselor, The mighty God, The everlasting Father and The Prince of Peace.'(Isaiah 9:6) Jesus is mercy and grace and is a redeemer.

(Water is essential to the universe)

Vapor: The Holy Spirit ----- Like vapor spreads everywhere and is like the powerful wind. The Holy Spirit is the most powerful enabler and the comforter. We need vapor. God's Spirit spread everywhere. He reaches everybody and works everywhere. '[13]In whom ye also trusted, after that ye heard the word of truth, the gospel of your salvation: in whom also after that ye believed, ye were sealed with that Holy Spirit of promise.' (Ephesians 1: 13)

(Vapor is essential to the universe)

As we have seen how ice, water and vapor are essential to the universe to keep up Ecology, same way all the three phases of God are essential. Each phase is important as the other. One phase can not accomplish all purpose unless changing its phase.

The universe contains all three forms of one substance. All the three forms such as ice, water, and vapor are needed. All of them are important. The universe can not function without these three. From this simple truth, we can understand the three forms of one God. All the three are phases of one God to function the role of only one God.

Even though the ice, the water, and the vapor are different in form they are the same substance. Each of these harmonizes with each other. The ice melts and become water, the same water when subjects to heat can convert into vapor, it condenses to water and water freezes to ice and vice versa! Similarly, the Father, the Son, and the Holy Spirit are three in one, all the three are one! They have the same divine name, nature, essence, and authority. They are all unified and work together. Therefore, they three are in one or one in three phases. There is only One God.

The Christian religion rejects idolatry and tritheism or the belief in three Gods completely. A real believer in Christ will never keep idols or any forms or any objects except the word of God as it is written in Deuteronomy 11:18-21. '[18]Therefore shall ye lay up these my words in your heart and in your soul, and bind them for a sign upon your hand, that they may be as frontlets between your eyes. [19]And ye shall teach them your children, speaking of them when thou sittest in thine house, and when thou walkest by the way, when thou liest down, and when thou risest up. [20]And thou shalt write them upon the door posts of thine house, and upon thy gates: [21]that your days may be multiplied, and the days of your children, in the land which the LORD swore unto your fathers to give them, as the days of heaven upon the earth.'

It is so shameful to see Christians or churches whoever uses visual arts, and use of icons and symbols in worship. They are not doing according to the word of God. Actually the place where people gather to worship should be called as 'House of prayer.' In Isaiah 56:7, it is written, '[7]Even them will I bring to my holy mountain, and make them joyful in my house of prayer: their burnt offerings and their sacrifices shall be accepted upon mine altar; for mine house shall be called an house of prayer for all people." There is no word like church to describe a building where the people meet. The group of believers can be mentioned as the church.

The real sacrifices of God as mentioned in Psalms 51:17 are: '[17]the sacrifices of God are a broken spirit: a broken and a contrite heart, O God, thou wilt not despise.' And God is saying to his people in Hosea 14:1-2"Return unto the LORD thy God; for thou hast fallen by thine iniquity. [2]Take with you words, and turn to the LORD: say unto him, Take away all iniquity, and receive us graciously: so will we render the calves of our lips". It is written in the word of God that we have to love our God with all our heart, all our mind. A man commits idolatry whenever he honors or loves anything in the world such as money, power, pleasure, race, family or creature more than God. That is why it is written in Colossians3:5, '[5]Put to death, therefore, whatever belongs to your earthly nature: sexual immorality, impurity, lust, evil desires and greed, which is idolatry.'

There is ONE God in three phases. The Oneness of the Trinity of God in Christianity does not violate the Doctrine of Taw hid, and it does not mean a unity of several Gods. The Islam had mistaken the Trinity as "Father, Son, and mother Mar 'yam (Mary)" Mother of Jesus was just a human being; she was not a part of Holy trinity. God used Mary or Mar 'yam as a wrap of His gift to the world or to the human race. Mary was found as a clean vessel to be used by God to show miracle to the world. Some Christians give more regard to Mary than Jesus Christ. Jesus came as a gift to the world to give us an everlasting joy. But they give more preference to the wrap of the gift, rather than giving preference to the gift.

In the Old Testament of the Bible, the images of God fell on the earth which reveals God. They are symbols and signs of upcoming of Jesus Christ's first coming to the world. These symbols that were mentioned in the Old Testament are: The first sacrifice that was made in Eden by God to give covering to Adam and Eve, the blood of the lamb that was slain to put on the door posts (Passover), manna from above as a food in the wilderness in their journey, tabernacle, sacrifices (offerings), High priest, festivals and six cities for refuge etc.) If we refer them, we can clearly understand that these were the images of Jesus Christ. God sent many messengers and the prophets to communicate with people. But the purpose of God was not accomplished by them.

In every book of the Old Testament a different title to only one God can be seen as a key point. It reveals His character and the significance to the particular situation. It reflects Jesus Christ and His aspect of speaking with His people through that particular prophet or messenger. Finally He came to the earth Himself as a word of God to communicate and have fellowship with the mankind. The time that He had spent on the earth as a man, He understood weakness, agonies or sufferings, feelings, responsibilities, and stages of human life. And He was sacrificed to finish His purpose. Our Father in heaven is a Holy and mighty God who loved the human race even to give His life for them. He had authority to give life and take back His life. He is the only one who is able to do this impossible thing.

If He comes down with His full Glory and all His power, no man can approach Him. For example, when God came to the Mount

Sinai, people died whoever touched the mountain. In Exodus 33:18-23, when Moses asked God, "I beseech thee, show me thy glory". [20]And God said, "thou canst not see my face: for there shall no man see me, and live. [21]And the LORD said, "behold, there is a place by me, and thou shalt stand upon a rock: [22]And it shall come to pass, while my glory passeth by, that I will put thee in a cleft of the rock, and will cover thee with my hand while I pass by: [23]And I will take away mine hand, and thou shalt see my back parts: but my face shall not be seen."

As it is mentioned in 22nd verse, it clarifies that no one can see God the Father but only in the cleft of rock (Jesus Christ). Bible explains very well in many illustrations about the rock which indicates Jesus Christ. Jesus is the reflection of God. We see all attributes of God in Jesus. It was written in Deuteronomy 8:15: '[15]Who led thee through that great and terrible wilderness, wherein were fiery serpents, and scorpions, and drought, where there was no water; who brought thee forth water out of the rock of flint;' 'the rock' mentioned in preceded verse is Jesus Christ. God brought water from the rock which satisfied Israelites in the terrible wilderness. In the same way this world is comparable to the wilderness. But Jesus Christ is the rock which satisfy His children.

The fore plan of God was shown in the Old Testament. The first glimpses of God revealed to the people in the Old Testament were temporary to satisfy the flesh but the latter in the New Testament will be spiritual and forever. Jesus said, '[14]But whosoever drinketh of the water that I shall give him shall never thirst; but the water that I shall give him shall be in him a well of water springing up into everlasting life.'(John 4:14) 'And he that believeth on me shall never thirst.' (John 6:35) There are many examples in the Old Testament to give us the understanding about the rock. In Psalms 61:2; Psalms 95:1, 'the rock' specified in these verses is God.

In the New Testament, Jesus said in Mathew 7: 24-25; Luke 6:48. '[24]Therefore whosoever heareth these sayings of mine, and doeth them, I will liken him unto a wise man, which built his house upon a rock: [25]and the rain descended and the floods came, and the winds blew, and beat upon that house; and it fell not: for it was founded upon a rock. [26]And every one that heareth these sayings of mine, and doeth them not, shall be likened unto a foolish man, which built his house upon the sand: [27]And the rain descended and the floods came, and the winds blew, and beat upon that house; and it fell: and great was the fall of it.' (Mathew 7:24–27)

We have many references in the Holy Bible about the rock. [4]And did all drink the same spiritual drink: for they drank of that Spiritual Rock that followed them: and that Rock was Christ.' (1Corinthians10:4) [33]As it is written, Behold, I lay in Sion a stumbling stone and rock of offence: and whosoever believeth on him shall not be ashamed. (Romans 9:33)

All these above references explained us that Jesus Christ is the Rock. If Jesus Christ did not come to the world, we might not see God. But now we had seen Him in person. God is not an unknown any more. We saw all the divine characteristics in Jesus.

In Hebrews 1st chapter, 1–3, we see how God remarkably stated about Jesus Christ that "He is brightness of His glory and express image of His person. God, who at sundry times and in divers manners spoke in time past unto the fathers by the prophets, [2]Hath in these last days spoken unto us by his Son, whom he hath appointed heir of all things, by whom also he made the worlds; [3]Who being the brightness of his glory, and the express image of his person, and upholding all things by the word of his power, when he had by himself purged our sins, sat down on the right hand of the Majesty on high"

All the above scriptural references indicate that Jesus is the proof of God's existence in front of human eyes. Jesus came to intercede for man, so that; man can approach the Father only through Jesus Christ. The Spirit from God is Jesus. He came in the human flesh. He belongs to all the human beings. But He was unlike the human beings in having attributes of God. He was Mercy and Truth. He was holy even in the flesh. He lived pure life when He came to the earth. His name was the word of God. It explains us why it was written in the Old Testament that God's word is pure as silver refined seven times.

Jesus came and stayed in the world for a short time to accomplish the things which He can not accomplish in the form of the Spirit. As we all knew that God is a Spirit being. He demonstrated His love and showed in deeds. Jesus in the human flesh was limited to only short period of time. He stayed in the world thirty three and half years. That is the reason, after His ascension to heaven, He sent His Spirit to be a comforter. Whoever enters into the kingdom of God could recognize Him. He is same but he is in His glory.

The Holy Spirit is like a vapor that spreads everywhere in the universe, the Holy Spirit serves, (comforts and guides) lives in whoever is born again with the Spirit of God.

How can we reason it when we say Jesus Christ is divine? We have full evidence to believe the truth about Jesus Christ that He is divine. Let us look into His life on the earth from birth to His ascension.

A new bright star in the sky appeared where He was born. His birth was proclaimed by angels to Mary, and later with foster father Joseph. An angel foretold His name to Mary as Jesus and Immanuel. (Mathew gospel 1:21-23) Then an angel appeared to shepherds abiding in the field, keeping watch over their flock by night. And lo, the angel of the Lord came upon them, and the glory of the Lord shone around them: and they were sore afraid. And the angel said unto them, Fear not: for, behold, I bring you good tidings of great joy, which shall be to all people. For unto you is born this day in the city of David a savior, which is Christ the Lord. (Luke Gospel 2:9-11) And in 13th and 14th verses of same chapter, and suddenly there was with the angel a multitude of the heavenly host praising God, and saying, " Glory to God in the highest, and on earth peace, a good will toward men."

There came wise men from the east to Jerusalem for they had seen the star. Star led them to the place where Jesus was born. They brought him gifts. When Herod heard these things he called wise men privately and inquired of them diligently what time the star appeared. Herod told them to come back after they go and worship Jesus. Wise men left to Bethlehem as the star led them, they presented their gifts and worshipped baby Jesus. (Mathew Gospel 2:12) Herod was plotted to kill baby Jesus. So their return to Herod was forbidden. They were warned of God in dream that they should not return to Herod. They departed into their own country another way.

An angel appeared to Joseph in a dream, saying, arise, and take the young child and his mother, and flee into Egypt, and be thou there until I bring thee word, for Herod will seek the young child to destroy him.(Mathew Gospel 2:13) The same chapter 19th verse, when Herod was dead, behold, an angel of the Lord appeared in a dream to Joseph in Egypt, saying, arise, and take the young child and his mother, and go into the land of Israel: for they are dead which sought the young child life.

When He was fasted for 40 days and 40 nights in the wilderness, and wild beasts were with Him. Satan came and tempted and He was victorious over Satan. And Satan left Him, behold angels came and ministered him.

Just before Judas Iscariot came with chief priests, elders and captains of the temple came to betray Him, he was in an agony. He knew future event (crucifixion). All His disciples were sleeping, at that moment, there appeared an angel and strengthened Him. (Luke Gospel 22:43)

When He gave up His spirit on the cross, there was darkness over all the earth. Sun was darkened and earth was quaked. When He was risen from dead on the third day, there was a great earth quake: for the angel of the Lord descended from heaven, and came and rolled back the stone from the door of the tomb and sat upon it. His countenance was like lightning, and his raiment white as snow:

and for fear of him the keepers of the tomb did shake, and became as dead men. And the angel answered and said unto the women, Fear not ye: for I know that ye seek Jesus, which was crucified. He is not here: for He is raised, as he said. Come; see the place where the Lord lay. And go quickly, and tell His disciples that He is risen from the dead: and behold, he goeth before you into Galilee: there shall ye see him: lo, I have told you." (Mathew Gospel 28:2-7)

At the time of His ascension into the heaven, again two angels in white apparel appeared to the people who were standing and gazing. "Ye men of Galilee, why stand ye gazing up into heaven? this same Jesus, which is taken up from you into heaven, shall so come in like manner as ye have seen him go to heaven.(Acts1:10-11) We see frequent intervention of angels in all turns of His life. When He was baptized in Jordan, people around Him heard a voice from heaven, saying, "Thou art my beloved Son in whom I am well pleased." (Mark Gospel] Mathew Gospel 17:5) and also when he was transfigured on a mountain. His disciples saw and heard same words from heaven.

Some people try their best to bring some baseless ideas that Jesus Christ never said that He is God. Those people are not realizing how the prophecies and promises concerning Christ which were fulfilled in His birth, works and death at his first advent. We are looking forward for unfulfilled prophecies and promises to be fulfilled at His second advent. Lord Jesus Christ pointed out those in His days, yet some people rejected him. He came from woman as it was written in Genesis 3:15. Jesus Christ defeated Satan. Even there is a full evidence of his divinity was shown in His existence in the world, yet people rejected Him. Imagine if he claimed directly that He is God that came down, do anybody believe him?

His birth, His life and His works are the clear evidence that Jesus Christ is high above all. We read at least thirteen times intervention of angels in every turn of His life.

The God Father, As the Son Jesus Christ, and the Holy Spirit (His Spirit) considered as one, can be compared as a person who have body, soul, and spirit considered as one person. We mentioned God as the power or first Spirit Being who is beginning and ending. He is described as FATHER GOD. The same GOD exhibited as SON in human form as JESUS CHRIST (Savior, Immanuel means God is with us) to reach human race whom He had created. And the same GOD came as HOLY SPRIT to live in human race. The Holy Bible explains only one God. The concept of the Holy Bible is very strict Monotheism and it explains there is only one God and He made man in His likeness.

The Miracles of Jesus and
His Divine Power from the Bible

Jesus Christ came as the son of man and performed public miracles with a multitude of witnesses. There is a wealth of historical documentation from contemporaries in the New Testament and contemporaries of Jesus early church. Especially in the four Gospels, we see His humanitarian compassion for the poor and unfortunate. These four Gospels convey good news to four corners of the earth which indicates Jesus belongs to the whole world.

Jesus Christ (Emmanuel) proved He was fully divine and fully human. Immanuel means "God is with us". Jesus came to be with us in order to forgive our sins, heal diseases and raise the dead, to show us He is the Master of the creation. He knew hearts of men, and proved "life" is in His hands. He is the perfect image of God. The images of God, which were portrayed in the scriptures, were fulfilled in Jesus. We see the confirmation in the following references of the New Testament.

Colossians 1:15-19: "[15]Who is the image of the invisible God, the firstborn of every creature: [16]For by him were all things created, that are in heaven, and that are in earth, visible and invisible, whether they be thrones, or dominions, or principalities, or powers: all things were created by him, and for him: [17]And he is before all things, and by him all things consist. [18]And he is the head of the body, the church: who is the beginning, the firstborn from the dead; that in all things he might have the preeminence. [19]For it pleased the Father that in him should all fullness dwell; but He made such a sacrifice to come and live with mankind. [20]And, having made peace through the blood of his cross, by him to reconcile all things unto himself; by him, I say, whether they be things in earth, or things in heaven.'

When he came to the world, he was masterful in art of being and accomplished the things that God only can do. God had shown himself in the human form of Jesus to the world but the misery of humanity is some people could not believe this mystery and rejected him." A few attributes of God were clearly explained in the following passages from the Gospels:

Gospel of Matthew 9:2– 7: '[2]And, behold, they brought to him a man sick of the palsy, lying on a bed: and Jesus seeing their faith said unto the sick of the palsy; Son, be of good cheer; thy sins be forgiven thee. [3]And, behold, certain of the scribes said within them, this man blasphemed. [4]And Jesus knowing their thoughts said, wherefore think ye evil in your hearts? [5]For whether is easier, to say, Thy sins be forgiven thee; or to say, Arise, and walk? [6]But that ye may know that the Son of man hath power on earth to forgive sins, (then saith he to the sick of the palsy,) Arise, take up thy bed, and go unto thine house. [7]And he arose, and departed to his house. [8]But when the multitudes saw it, they marveled.'

In this above passage Jesus proved to the world that He has the authority to forgive the sins. In addition to that, there is one more amazing characteristic to notice is that He knew the thoughts of man. To whom it is possible to know the thoughts of the human? It is possible only to God. It shows us that Jesus is not a mere man but God in the flesh that is why He is able to forgive the sins, and knew the hearts of the people.

The passage in Gospel of Matthew 20:29-34 gives us an understanding that He was able to give sight to blind. Not only that, His compassion is beyond the limit.

'²⁹And as they departed from Jericho, a great multitude followed him. ³⁰And, behold, two blind men sitting by the way side, when they heard that Jesus passed by, cried out, saying, Have mercy on us, O Lord, thou son of David. ³¹And the multitude rebuked them, because they should hold their peace: but they cried the more, saying, Have mercy on us, O Lord, thou son of David. ³²And Jesus stood still, and called them, and said, what will ye that I shall do unto you? ³³they say unto him, Lord that our eyes may be opened. ³⁴So Jesus had compassion on them, and touched their eyes: and immediately their eyes received sight, and they followed him.'

Jesus had the power to heal. If He said one word the blind might have been healed but He was so compassionate and touched their eyes and gave them the sight!

Jesus miracle right after the 'Sermon on the mount' was healing a leper. In two chapters, 5-7, the Sermon on the Mount was so wonderful. The people were so impressed. At the end of the 7th chapter, in the last two verses, starting from 28th verse it says, '²⁸And it came to pass, when Jesus had ended these sayings, the people were astonished at his doctrine: ²⁹For he taught them as one having authority, and not as the scribes.

The people might be amazed of His sayings, such as "⁸Blessed are the pure in heart for they shall see God! ²⁸Whosoever looketh on a woman to lust after her hath committed adultery with her already in his heart.⁴⁴Love your enemies, bless them that curse you, do good to them that hate you, and pray for them which despitefully use you, and persecute you;" Whoever heard these sayings might have thought who could live up to that extent. But we see in the next chapter of Mathew Gospel, Jesus healed a leper and proved through Him impossible thing are possible. Those days' lepers were cast out and despised of their own community. They can not hide the disease. It makes a person so low. By healing the leper Jesus did three fold regain to the person. First He killed the disease, secondly He repaired the damage done to his body, and thirdly He had brought him back into the society.

Let us look into the Gospel of Mathew 8:1-5; "¹When He was come down from the mountain, great multitudes followed him. ²And, behold, there came a leper and worshipped him, saying, Lord, if thou wilt, thou canst make me clean. ³And Jesus put forth his hand, and touched him, saying, I will; be thou clean. And immediately his leprosy was cleansed. ⁴And Jesus saith unto him, See thou tell no man; but go thy way, shew thyself to the priest, and offer the gift that Moses commanded, for a testimony unto them."

In this passage Jesus touched even discarded, outcast leper and healed him. He showed such a compassion and love.

There is another most wonderful thing that everybody has to know is Jesus has command over the creation. In Gospel of Mark 4:37- 41: '³⁷And there was a great storm of wind, and the waves beat into the ship, so that it was now full. ³⁸And he was in the hinder part of the ship, asleep on a pillow: and they awake him, and say unto him, Master, cares thou not that we perish? ³⁹And he arose, and rebuked the wind, and said unto the sea, "Peace, be still." And the wind ceased, and there was a great calm. ⁴⁰And he said unto them, "why are ye so fearful? How is it that ye have no faith?" ⁴¹And they feared exceedingly, and said one to another, what manner of man is this, that even the wind and the sea obey him?'

Even though the creation was under the subjection of Jesus Christ, He never misused His authority instead we see His care, love, and gentleness, Jesus was not weary or angry when the disciples woke Him up from His rest. We need to acknowledge that God is the controller of the universe. The same power we see in Jesus Christ.

When we read the following passage in Gospel of John 5:16-21, there was safety in the presence of Jesus Christ. '¹⁶And when even was now come, his disciples went down unto the sea, ¹⁷and entered into a ship, and went over the sea toward Capernaum. And it was now dark, and Jesus was not come to them. ¹⁸And the sea arose by reason of a great wind that blew. ¹⁹So when they had rowed about five and twenty or thirty furlongs, they see Jesus walking on the sea, and drawing nigh unto the ship: and they were afraid. ²⁰But he saith unto them, "it is I; be not afraid." ²¹Then they willingly received him into the ship: and immediately the ship was at the land whither they went.'

When the disciples received Jesus into their ship, they reached their destination. This is miraculous! What a wonderful assurance in Jesus!

There is power even in His garments. The Gospel of Mark 5:25 – 34, shows his marvelous cognition even though he was in the human form. Here in this passage we read '²⁵And a certain woman, which had an issue of blood twelve years, ²⁶And had suffered many things of many physicians, and had spent all that she had, and was nothing bettered, but rather grew worse, ²⁷When she had heard of Jesus, came in the press behind, and touched his garment. ²⁸For she said, if I may touch but his clothes, I shall be whole. ²⁹And straightway the fountain of her blood was dried up; and she felt in her body that she was healed of that plague, and sayest thou, Who touched me ³⁰And Jesus, immediately knowing in himself that virtue had gone out of him, turned him about in the press, and said, Who touched my clothes? ³¹And his disciples said unto him, Thou seest the multitude thronging thee? ³²And he looked round about to see her that had done this thing. ³³But the woman fearing and trembling, knowing what was done in her, came and fell down before him, and told him all the truth. ³⁴And he said unto her, Daughter, thy faith hath made thee whole; go in peace, and be whole of thy plague.'

Nobody ought to tell Him. He knew the hearts of the people. John Gospel 2:24, 25, it says, 'But Jesus did not commit Himself unto them, because He knew all men. And needed not any should testify of man: for He knew what was in man.'

There is another incident which was written in the same chapter that Jesus knew before Nathaniel came to Him. We read this in John

Gospel 1:43–51, it is written, "⁴³On the morrow he was minded to go forth into Galilee, and he findeth Philip: and Jesus saith unto him, follow me. ⁴⁴Now Philip was from Bethsaida, of the city of Andrew and Peter. ⁴⁵Philip findeth Nathaniel, and saith unto him, we have found him, of whom Moses in the law, and the prophets, wrote, Jesus of Nazareth, the son of Joseph. ⁴⁶And Nathaniel said unto him, Can any good thing come out of Nazareth? Philip saith unto him, Come and see. ⁴⁷Jesus saw Nathaniel coming to him, and saith of him, Behold, an Israelite indeed, in whom is no guile! ⁴⁸Nathaniel saith unto him, whence knowest thou me?

Jesus answered and said unto him, Before Philip called thee, when thou wast under the fig tree, I saw thee. ⁴⁹Nathaniel answered him, Rabbi, thou art the Son of God; thou art King of Israel. ⁵⁰Jesus answered and said unto him, "Because I said unto thee, I saw thee underneath the fig tree, believest thou? Thou shalt see greater things than these." ⁵¹And he saith unto him, "verily, verily, I say unto you, ye shall see the heaven opened, and the angels of God ascending and descending upon the Son of man." Jesus made it clear that He belongs to heaven and He came down to the earth to accomplish the things.

Even greater thing He did. He had authority bring back dead to life. In the Gospel of John, 11th chapter, Jesus raised Lazarus from His tomb in the town of Bethany. Jesus had the power to give life back! No one on earth have power to give life, except God." Jesus Christ proved this solid truth while he was on the earth. God ever exists. He is same forever.

It is written, 'Jesus Christ is the same yesterday, today, and forever.' Hebrews 13:8.

I had many proofs in my life that Jesus Christ is unchanged. For the glory of God I would like to share one of my personal experiences about my mother that testifies to this real truth. This particular incident made me to trust Him forever. My parents shared this truth with many people in their life time.

My mother was the first one of her family to accept Jesus Christ as her personal Lord and Savior. At that time my father had no trust in Jesus. At the time of my mother's acceptance she was pregnant for the fifth time and I was about two years old. On the third month of her gestation period, I was running around and abruptly fell on her lap. The next day she had fever and severe abdominal pain. The doctors in those days could not correctly diagnose her because she was pregnant. My mother's temperature remained high so my father took her to a well known hospital in a nearby city and had her admitted into the hospital. My aunt stayed with my mother to look after her even though there were frequent family visits. My mother's condition remained the same and remained in the hospital for three months. My mother was properly diagnosed when a specialized doctor from Australia visited the hospital and was referred to examine my mother's condition.

She was diagnosed with a severe infection; there was pus in-between her womb and thigh. The twenty-four weeks fetus had to be removed to drain the pus. The doctors operated on my mom, it went smoothly. During that time my father was at home with us. At that time, we were three kids; that night he humbled himself before God, fasted and prayed without sleeping. He confessed his sins, and cried out to God saying, "O God, the God of my wife to whom she prays please hear my cry. If you are the real God save my wife that I may know you are God alone on this earth."

Early the next morning my father received a message from the hospital that my mother died, the doctors declared her death. When my father heard the news he lost all faith in God and set out to the hospital to make further arrangements. My aunt requested the hospital to put the body in a separate room instead of the morgue until my father would arrive.

As my aunt was waiting for my dad's arrival, she heard a soft voice of my mother and saw my mother's body slowly moving. She was frightened and ran to the nurses' desk and told them what she saw. The nurses surprised, came and checked my mother; they removed the wrap that covered her body and saw my mother's eyes were opened. The nurses checked my mother's vitals and saw they were normal; the room began to flood with astonished doctors and nurses.

My mother told them she heard a voice asking her to turn around so that they can give her an injection, she saw a flash and a needle, but did not feel any pain. When she turned around to see who the person was, there was no one there, except a cloth on her face. Then she called out her sister. My mother's testimony was amazing to anyone and everyone who heard it! At that time my father had finally arrived, he was speechless when he saw my mom's room with full of people and my mom was alive. Then he began to praise God and said how real and true Jesus is because of the answered prayer!

Not only did God answer my father's prayer, much to my parents and the doctors surprise the twenty-four weeks fetus had a heartbeat. Even though there were no incubators or ventilators during that time, they provided the best medical care within their reach to the baby boy, and he survived. God performed miracles one after the other. My father's faith grew strong in the Lord. My mother later on had four more children. God's wonderful works made my parents strong in faith.

They started a ministry in their home and the assembly was blessed with about four hundred believers. My brother, who was twenty four weeks fetus miraculously survived, is not a handicap. In fact, he is now blessed with a wife and two children. He is a testimony to our wonder-working, all powerful God, the God, the "Jesus Christ who is the same yesterday, today, and forever." If you want to know more about the miracles of Jesus read the Gospels in the New Testament. In John Gospel 21:24-25, John testified, "[24]This is the disciple which testifieth of these things, and wrote these things: and we know that his testimony is true. [25]And there are also many other things which Jesus did, the which, if they should be written every one, I suppose that even the world itself could not contain the books that should be written. Amen."

However, in many incidents Jesus told the people not to spread fame or focus on only the miracles. (Luke 6:26) Jesus did not want fame. His focus was that people should know Him as the Son of God. This is what His emphasis was on: He does not belong to the world. He came from above and belongs to the eternal kingdom of heaven. Jesus' influence came not from wars, political power or wealth or advertisement. His compassionate words and actions influenced human race and challenged the Truth. The purpose of Jesus came to this world is the kingdom of God should be within everybody's reach. Please read the following verse from John Gospel what he had promised.

John 6:40: "This is the will of him that sent me, that everyone which seeth the son, and believeth on Him, may have everlasting life: and I will raise Him up at the last day." In this verse Jesus clarified, who He is. He gave assurance that He will give everlasting life, and raise them at the last day to those whoever believes in Him. What an assurance in Jesus words! Whoever, reject this kind of assurance will suffer the consequences and never forgive themselves.

Out of the three forms of one God the reachable form is Jesus Christ. God came into this world in the form of a human being. Since He was God in person, revealed His immense characteristics. Actually he is a combination of virtues. A perfect person that has ever walked on this planet earth is only Jesus Christ. His character influenced and changed many lives in the world that great multitudes have followed Him.

Many people died as martyrs for the truth. Many people are willing to suffer their life or give their life for Him. Why? Here is the answer. His love is greater than the death. They have tasted His love. Jesus' teachings were authoritative and made profound impressions on people's lives. For example Jesus Christ's Sermon on the Mount in Matthew 5:5: "Blessed are the meek: for they shall inherit earth," was followed by Karam Chand Gandhi. This teaching enabled him to win India's independence from Britain without any war. Jesus Christ has changed numerous lives because of His love and trustworthiness. Actually He changed the course of history. The most wonderful thing is He attracted me and changed my life.

The Miracles of Jesus (Isa) in the Noble Qur'an

In the Noble Qur'an, Jesus had honorary titles. Jesus peace be upon Him is a wonderful, humble messenger of God who came down and revealed God's word to the people. In the Qur'an, it says, His birth was unique and angel came to Mary to tell that she will be getting faultless son which will happen by the Spirit of Allah. He will come as a sign from God. He came to confirm that which was before Him of the Torah. He had spoken to the mankind when he was in cradle. He did miracles. The Muslims believe that He was raised up by Allah unto Himself. He still lives there with Allah in heaven. He was honored by Allah.

Let us read from the Qur'an to confirm the above summary.

In the Qur'an Mary-19; (Part -16) in 19, the Angel said: "I am only messenger of thy Lord that I may bestow on thee a faultless son." And in the Family of Imran-3 (Part – 3) 45-50. "[45]And remember when the angel said: Jesus, son of Mary, illustrious in the world and the hereafter, and one of those brought near [46] He will speak unto mankind in His cradle and in his manhood, and he is of the righteous. [47] She said: my Lord! How can I have a child when no mortal hath touched me?"

He said: so. Allah createth what He will. If He decreeth a thing, He saith unto it only: be! And it is. [48]And He will teach him the

Scripture and wisdom, and the Torah and the Gospel. [49]And [make him] a messenger to the Children of Israel, [who will say], 'Indeed I have come to you with a sign from your Lord in that I design for you from clay [that which is] like the form of a bird, then I breathe into it and it becomes a bird by permission of Allah. And I cure the blind and the leper, and I give life to the dead – by permission of Allah. And I inform you of what you eat and what you store in your houses. Indeed in that is a sign for you, if you are believers. [50]And I come confirming that which was before me of the Torah, and to make lawful some of that which was forbidden unto you. I come unto you a sign from your Lord, so keep your duty to Allah and obey me.' Here Jesus stressed the point 'obey me.' He clarified whom everyone has to obey.

Muslims give reverence to Jesus. But they do not recognize the words of the angel to Mary that He is faultless. It is impossible to a human being to be faultless. They could not identify His life – giving authority. They compare Jesus with Adam who has no authority whatsoever. Yet Muslims believe that Jesus will return to the earth on the end days to judge all the people by their deeds and give rewards accordingly.

Adam and Jesus in the Noble Qur'an

In Suraht'Ali Imran 3:59, Sahih International, it says 'Indeed the example of Jesus to Allah is like that of Adam. God created Adam from the dust then He said to him, "Be" and He was. This reference about Adam and Jesus to Allah is needed thorough research because the real truth is uncertain in this reference. Allah did not say, "Be" to the potter's clay of black mud altered when He made Adam but He breathed into him His Spirit.' To clarify this concept of Adam's creation, let us go further into the Qur'an to search the truth of Islam.

The explanation of the birth of Adam in Islam is continued as follows: "Verily, We created man of potter's clay of black mud altered" And remember when thy Lord said unto the angels: "Lo! I am creating mortal out of Potter's clay of black mud altered. So when I have made him and breathed into him of my Spirit, do ye fall down, prostrating yourselves unto him" [Surah15:26-28, 29]

And in the detail of Adam's creation, The Prophet said, "Allah created Adam in HIS IMAGE, in His complete shape and form sixty cubits (about 30 meters) in height. (30 meters is almost 98feet) [Sahih Bukhari, volume 8, book74, and number 246] God made Adam, out of clay. It was indicated that Adam was earthly. He was from the dust but in the image of God. Because of God's breath which was blown into Adam, thence, the life in the mankind is continuing. But the body decays into the dust when we die. Adam lived for 930 years on this earth and died. Adam's body was decayed after he died. When the human race is continuously multiplying with same pattern why Allah gave revelation about Jesus and His birth? Because, Jesus birth and life were different from all other human beings even though He was born as a human.

Now let us read, how Jesus was born? Jesus Christ was born of Virgin Mary. He grew in her womb as a normal child. He did not come instantaneously with life, when they blew the Spirit into Mary as it was written in the Qur'an, Jesus was born to Mary even though no mortal hath touched her. An angel came and said, "O Mary! Lo! Allah giveth thee glad tidings of "a word from Him, whose name is the Messiah, Jesus." Though He was a word from Allah, He was born as a son of man. But Jesus was not born because of one word 'Be.' His body was not decayed like Adam. Allah raised Him to Himself as it was written in Surah 19:33. His body was raised and was ascended to heaven. According to the Islam Jesus went alive to the heaven. There is huge difference in between Adam and Jesus. Adam died but Jesus went alive to the heaven according to the Noble Qur'an.

If we discuss about their birth the only resemblance is, Adam and Jesus both were in the 'form of man.' The concept of human creation explains us that Jesus Christ, even though "Spirit from God" when He came as a 'son of man' in the flesh, (as a human) He resembles Adam in the form of man. This explains as "in the likeness of Adam". Jesus Christ lived on the earth for a while as a human just like Adam, even though He is "the Spirit of God." Adam was the first living being on the earth made from the potter's mud altered but Jesus came as the "word from God" or Spirit from God in the human form to reveal the truth and told the people to obey Him and after He finished the purpose of Allah. Then He went back to the heaven.

Adam and Jesus both had no physical father. We read from the Qur'an, that Adam was created from potter's mud altered and God blew His breath into it and it became the first man Adam. We also read how Jesus was born? Jesus was born to Virgin Mary. This sentence gives us the explanation that Adam and Jesus are the same in the way how they both were born without any physical father. The difference was that Adam came as a mortal it says in the Qur'an, Lord said unto the angels: "Lo! I am creating mortal out of the Potter's clay of black mud altered." But Jesus came when no mortal touched the Virgin Mary. Here in the concept of their birth we are able to understand mortal verses immortal. God said that He was creating mortal out of clay and made Adam whereas Jesus was born without the mortal touch.

Let us further continue to search in the Noble Qur'an about the first man Adam. Adam was deceived by Satan, Adam went astray. Then his Lord chose him, and turned to him with forgiveness and gave him guidance." [Qur'an 20:121-122]

God said, "So he (Satan) misled them with deception." [Qur'an 7:22]

God said to Adam, "Get you down (upon the earth), all of you together, from Paradise, some of you are an enemy to some others. Then, if there comes to you guidance from 'Me,' whoever follows My Guidance shall neither go astray, nor fall into distress and misery." [Qur'an 20:123] The mankind has a long history of committing mistakes and forgetting.

They said, "Our Lord! We have wronged ourselves. If you forgive us not and bestow not upon us Your Mercy, we shall certainly be of the losers." [Qur'an 7:23]

Adam realized that he was a loser. God sent him down from the paradise. Allah forgave him but not kept him there in the paradise or not sending him back to the world the second time to judge the people. There was no significance in his life that we could talk about. Hence there is no need to follow Adam, since he is not coming to the world the second time to judge all the people.

It is quite clear that "Jesus Christ is the Spirit from Holy God as it was written in [Nisa 4, 24:171] He was faultless as the angel specified at His birth. He overcame all the temptations even though He was in the human form. Jesus was a conqueror of the sin and is willful to deliver people from their sins. He is alive in the heaven to come second time to the world as a judge to all the nations. He lives forever. According to the Islam, He was not died. But we read this verse in the Qur'an in Sura Maryam 19:33: "And peace is upon me the day I was born and in the day I shall taste death, and the day I will be raised alive." He tasted the death and was raised alive.

The Hadith, Sahih Muslim, book 1, number 287 is clear that when Christ, peace be upon him, returns to govern the people. The Prophet Muhammad said: "By Him in whose hand is my soul, the son of Mary will approach the al-Rawhâ pass (between Mecca and Medina), to perform Hajj, Umrah, or both." Every one should realize how important Jesus Christ is in the sight of God's plan. Jesus could not be compared with Adam.

If Jesus did anything against Allah, or if He taught against Allah, or if He did not accomplish the purpose of Allah, Allah might not had chosen Jesus to come back again the second time to the world to rule and pay wages according to the deeds of all the people. Because of all these reasons, we understood that, what Jesus said and taught were right in the sight of Allah. This is the main reason, why, everybody has to follow Jesus. Whereas Adam was mislead by the Satan. God said to Adam, "Get you down upon the earth all of you from paradise; some of you are enemy to some others [Qur'an 20:123] There is vast difference in between Adam and Jesus. We have to notice the difference that Allah sent Adam down from the paradise but raised Jesus to be with Him.

The inference from these verses is that Jesus has authority to save souls as the Muslims believe He will come to kill (Dajjal) Antichrist. The Prophet Muhammad had trust in Jesus that He could save him from the coming dangers. That is why he said, "By Him in whose hands is my soul, the son of Mary."

If one pays attention to what Allah says about Jesus, it is interesting to notice that He is similar to Him by whom He was sent to the world. Jesus is the Spirit from God but in the human form. Jesus created clay birds and breathed life in exactly the same way that God did when He created Adam. God made Adam as a mortal out of Potter's clay of black mud altered and He breathed His life of breath into Adam. [Surah 15:28-29] The same way, Jesus in His childhood made birds out of clay and breathed life into them!

This only makes sense in light of, Jesus being God's very own Spirit whom he had sent to become incarnate from the Virgin Mary. At the very least, this shows that Jesus possesses the very same life-giving Spirit of God. This divine quality was possible only to Jesus. He could 'create' and 'to give life.' Did any one come across that kind of divine entity in the history of the world who could bring life to an object or to the dead? Out of all the prophets, only Jesus was born faultless, led pure life. No other prophet did such actions. Therefore the position of Jesus is unique and can not be compared to others. Adam was never did any miracles, but Jesus did miracles in which He gave the life. It is possible only to God to give the life.

The Muslims argue that, both verses in the Qur'an. 3:49 and 5:110 say, 'that Jesus breathed life into the clay birds by the permission of Allah as Moses did. Moses was different from Jesus in performing the miracles. Here is the difference that the people should know. Whenever Moses was not able to solve the problem with Israelites, he approached God and God instructed him to solve the problem and he did it accordingly. And God told Moses to take help from Aaron his brother because he needed help. Moreover, Moses made a mistake in obeying God. When God told him to talk with the rock, he hit the rock. Because of his disobedience, God punished him from being entered into Canaan, whereas Jesus never made any mistake.

In the Qur'an it was written, Jesus talked when He was in the cradle. And when He was a boy, He made clay birds. He did not ask Allah to give him permission to give them life. Jesus did the miracle instantaneously when he was just a boy. Whenever Jesus performed miracles, He instantly did them without waiting upon God. The phrase that Jesus made clay birds did demonstrate that Jesus worked in perfect accordance with God, never acted independently from the Divine will. Again by doing this, Jesus fulfilled the will of God. That is the reason, Allah was pleased with Jesus. It is very well understandable that whatever Jesus taught was right in the sight of Allah. Because of all these reasons Allah was instructed that everybody has to follow Jesus and those who does not choose to follow Jesus are against Allah.

Some people have wrong notion that Allah sent Jesus only for the Israelites. If Allah did so, why, He is sending Jesus the second time to judge the whole world at the end time and He is coming to judge everybody and will give wages according to everybody's deeds. Please notice the word 'everybody's deeds.' He does not belong to one nationality. He judges everybody on the earth. The Noble Qur'an and the Holy Bible are very clear that Jesus will be coming to give wages according to the deeds of all the people. If God separates the messengers for the Israelites and the Arabians, He might send Jesus the second time also, only to the Israel nation to judge them. But God is sending Jesus to the whole world. It proves His sovereignty. This warns everybody to be careful and follow His teachings.

Jesus confirmed the Torah and brought the Gospel (the good news) to the whole world. That is the reason why God is sending Jesus the second time to the earth to judge all the people according to His teachings. There is no other way, except to follow Him to be in obedient with Allah. There is no other path to the eternity rather than Jesus.

Therefore, 'the difference in between Adam and Jesus' is very huge and there is least to be compared of. Adam and Jesus were different in their purpose and the life. There is no significance in Adam's life. There are no teachings of Adam whereas everybody has to follow teachings of Jesus as Allah confirmed them in the Qur'an. Jesus is alive to come back. This confirmed that Jesus is there in the heaven for ever. He said that even before the creation He was there.

And His words are true. That is why everybody is looking forward for His second coming.

He will be coming on the clouds with the angels. Whoever is disobedient to His teachings and are not following Him will be punished by Allah as it was written in the Qur'an. No other aid or supporter could help them out except Allah. The verse 173 says, "Then to those who believed and did good deeds, He will pay their wages in full and by His munificence, give them more, and those who hated (worshipping Him) and were proud, He will inflict a painful punishment; and they will not find for themselves other than ALLAH, any supporter or any aide.

Adam and Jesus Christ
in the Holy Bible

Adam and Jesus are alike in that each of them was the first of its kind. From Adam came certainty the death while from Jesus came the hope of the resurrection. Let us discuss about their birth and life according to the Holy Bible.

According to the Holy Bible, Adam was the first man of the mankind. In other words he was the father of all the generations on the earth. If we look into the first book Genesis of the Bible, there is a great deal of description of the creation. God made Adam in the image or likeness of Him. This image is found in the fact that man is personal, rational and moral being. Man is triunity and is made up of body, soul and spirit. God gave him sovereignty over the earth crowned him with glory and honor, and put him into the Garden of Eden to dress it and to keep it. He gave Adam dominion over all the animal creation (serpent also comes under this) and He subdue the earth for man.

God put the test of obedience by commanding him not to eat the fruit of only one tree. This is written in Genesis 2:16-17, '16And the. LORD God commanded the man, saying, "Of every tree of the garden thou mayest freely eat: 17But of the tree of the knowledge of good and evil, thou shalt not eat of it: for in the day that thou eatest thereof thou shalt surely die."

The further explanation is continued in Genesis 3:1-20. We knew the rest of the story that Eve listened to Satan; she ate the fruit, and gave to Adam. He yielded to Eve, ate the forbidden fruit that was not for him or her to have. In other words Adam committed covetousness. Covetousness is idolatry according to the word of God. (Colossians 3:5) Adam had guilty of murder. God told him, "thou shalt not eat of it: for in the day that thou eatest thereof thou shalt surely die." Now according to God's words, Adam was chose to be disobedient, covetous and was a murderer. He killed himself, not bodily but spiritually. He never accepted the truth that he disobeyed. He put all the blame on Eve. He was not even repented of his sin. He was left with dead spirit which was disconnected from God.

His body was alive but his soul was darkened and spiritually he was dead. God cursed them, and their progeny for their disobedience. '¹⁷And unto Adam God said, "Because thou hast hearkened unto the voice of thy wife, and hast eaten of the tree, of which I commanded thee, saying, Thou shalt not eat of it: cursed is the ground for thy sake; in sorrow shalt thou eat of it all the days of thy life; ¹⁸Thorns also and thistles shall it bring forth to thee; and thou shalt eat the herb of the field; ¹⁹In the sweat of thy face shalt thou eat bread, till thou return unto the ground; for out of it wast thou taken: for dust thou art, and unto dust shalt thou return.' Thus the first man Adam, even though God had created him as a perfect man and had given a pleasant place and kingship, he could not keep it. He inclined towards Satan and fell into the sin. The consequences were the curse and the death.

Adam and Eve were put out from the Garden of Eden to outside. They lost the close relationship with God. They lost their glory. Since we are their progeny, we also lost it. "²³For all have sinned, and come short of the glory of God." (Romans 3:23) Adam was earthy; he was made out of the clay. He inclined towards the earthly thing and he could not withstand the temptation and was a victim to Satan.

In 1 John 2:15-17. It says, "¹⁵Love not the world, neither the things that are in the world. If any man loves the world, the love of the Father is not in him. ¹⁶For all that is in the world, the lust of the flesh, and the lust of the eyes, and the pride of life, is not of the Father, but is of the world. ¹⁷And the world passed away and the lust thereof: but he that doeth the will of God abided for ever." Adam did not do the will of God. Hence he could not inherit the everlasting life. Adam was mentioned in the Bible very few times. His years were limited and he was died and again never rose again.

On the contrary to Adam, Jesus is entirely different. Jesus was born of the Virgin Mary according to the Scripture and lived according to the Scripture, died on the cross and rose again according the Scripture. We all knew about His life on the earth through the Gospels. Jesus did wonderful miracles. He has power to give life, raised people from the dead. Jesus Kingdom is not of this world. He fulfilled what God wanted Him to do. He came to save the people from the curse and the death.

John the Baptist testified about Jesus Christ in John 3:31. "³¹He that cometh from above is above all: he that is of the earth is earthy, and speaketh of the earth: he that cometh from heaven is above all". (John 3:31)

The purpose of Satan was to defeat Jesus Christ. Jesus had power to withstand all kinds of temptations and was victorious. Luke Gospel 4:1-13 from the Bible, is written as follows: Jesus Christ was fasted for forty days and forty nights, Satan knew that Jesus was in physically weakened state. At that time Satan came to tempt Him. Jesus temptations were more severe than Adam's. Yet Jesus had power to withstand all kinds of temptations and He was victorious.

The Satan tempted Jesus Christ in four physical aspects. The first temptation was a very basic need of a person. The Satan tempted Him by knowing that He was in hunger. Yet Jesus rebuked the Satan by the Scripture quotation. The bodily appetites were subdued by His spiritual strength. The second temptation was about 'His power.'

Jesus never disobeyed God. He did not misuse His divine power. He did not fall for wealth, splendor, power, or earthly glory. He was victorious over all the temptations and resisted the devil with the Scriptures.

Jesus was sent to the world for the special purpose by Father. He was obedient to every command of God to be an example to the mankind. God was pleased by Jesus and His accomplishments thereby Jesus became a mediator in between God and the human. Only through Him the human race can go to God.

Therefore being justified by faith, we have peace with God through our Lord Jesus Christ: '⁹Much more then, being now justified by his blood, we shall be saved from wrath through him. ¹⁰For if, when we were enemies, we were reconciled to God by the death of his Spiritual Son, much more, being reconciled, we shall be saved by his life. ¹¹And not only so, but we also joy in God through our Lord Jesus Christ, by whom we have now received the atonement. Now we have a privilege to call God as our heavenly father.' (Romans 5: 9-11) What we lost in Adam we regained through Christ.

The main difference in between Adam and Jesus Christ is: Adam sinned against God and lost paradise; where as Jesus obeyed God and pleased Him and earned authority to grant paradise to those whoever believes in Him. In John Gospel 6:28-29. '²⁸Then said they unto him, what shall we do, that we might work the works of God? ²⁹Jesus answered and said unto them, this is the work of God that ye believe on him whom he hath sent.' God came in the human form as a son. He is considered as Son of God.

He had same authority as God has. It is clearly stated in John 5:21-24, '²¹For as the Father raiseth the dead and giveth them life; even so the Son also giveth life to whom he will. ²²For neither doth the Father Judge any man, but he hath given all judgment unto the Son; ²³that all may honor the Son, even as they honor the Father. He that honoreth not the Son honoreth not the Father that sent him. ²⁴Verily, verily, I say unto you, He that heareth my word, and believeth him that sent me, hath eternal life, and cometh not into judgment, but hath passed out of death into life.' Those who needed life should come to Jesus Christ. The death was transmitted to every one from Adam our first father. To be delivered from it, every one should come to Jesus. Those who believe in Jesus has no judgment but will inherit the eternal life.

In the New Testament, Paul had revelation to write this to Corinthian church to explain the significance of Jesus Christ with that of Adam. It is written in 1Corinthians15:21, 22&43-49.

'²¹For since by man came death, by man came also the resurrection of the dead.

²²For as in Adam all die, even so in Christ shall all be made alive?

⁴³It is sown in dishonor; it is raised in glory: it is sown in weakness; it is raised in power:

⁴⁴It is sown a natural body; it is raised a spiritual body. There is a natural body, and there is a spiritual body. ⁴⁵And so it is written, the first man Adam was made a living soul; the last Adam was made a quickening spirit. ⁴⁶Howbeit that was not first which is spiritual, but that which is natural; and afterward that which is spiritual.

⁴⁷The first man is of the earth, earthy; the second man is the Lord from heaven.

⁴⁸As is the earthy; such are they also that are earthy: and as is the heavenly, such are they also that are heavenly.

⁴⁹And as we have borne the image of the earthy, we shall also bear the image of the heavenly.'

Jesus Christ had authority to give same life to those who believe in Him. Being a deity, after His departure from the world He sent His Holy Spirit to live in us to enable a believer to live victorious life. A believer also can defeat Satan only through the cross where He conquered and crushed the Satan. He bore the sins of all the people. Jesus was buried to bury the sins of all the people. He rose again to live in a believer. This is the power of God with which a believer lives the life of Christ Jesus.

Was Jesus Really Crucified or Not?

In the Qur'an, Surah Al-Nisa 4:157: We read the verse "They said, "indeed we have killed Jesus Christ, the Son of Mary, and the Ambassador of God: actually they did not kill nor crucify him. ----"

And in Sura Maryam 19:33: In the revelation of Jesus, it says, "And peace is upon me the day I was born and in the day I shall taste death, and the day I will be raised alive."

Those above verses in the Qur'an are very much understandable that, Jesus was tasted death and was raised again. So Jesus was born to Mary (Maryam), tasted death and rose again. If the Muslims believe those above verses are really from Allah, there should be no change or twist in His words. Allah's words in the above verse are very simple so that even simple can understand. If any one interpret differently or twist His words they are imposed to terrible punishment from Allah. The people should remember the most important fact that, 'God never change or twist His words.'

If anybody reads with a notion that these statements came as a revelation from Allah, It really makes a person to stop for a moment to think about the fact. Allah is truthful God. How these two contrasting statements could came into existence in the Qur'an? These two statements have diversified meaning in which we read, "indeed we have killed Jesus Christ and we did not kill nor crucify." And what is the meaning of "taste death and will be raised alive?" It had created a perplexing situation to people to understand the truth. It presented to the world that Allah changes His ideas as a double minded. Allah never is double minded. Somehow these two statements were misinterpreted. Is God double minded? No!!! Not. The word of God says, "A double minded man is unstable in all his ways". (James 1:7.) Can God change His words? Can God says one thing and does another thing? No never!!! God knew past, present and future and He knew the ending in the beginning.

There in the Torah, the book of Numbers 23:19, it says, 'God is not a man, that He should lie; neither the son of man, that He should repent: hath He said, and shall He not do it? Or hath He spoken, and shall He not make it good?'

The Muslims believe it is impossible for the favorite of God, or a prophet to die on the Cross without any protection. While that may seem true, man must understand God's predestinated plan and His thoughts are different from our own thoughts and plans. God is not a man to neither lie nor deceive; He is Holy and is a God of truth and love. God loves us with a sacrificial, everlasting and unconditional love beyond our finite comprehension.

It may seem senseless to some people for a Holy God to leave His heavenly throne to come down to the earth and die for sinners like us. But because of His love is so intense He did so, in order for us to obtain relationship with Him and life abundance unto the eternity. God created us as living souls. He does not want us to be condemned unto the eternity. A father or mother on this earth tries their best to live for their children and do whatever sacrifice they can do for them. Even though they are earthly and temporary (do not have life guarantee on this earth) strive to give their life for their children. God had created us in His own image as His sons and daughters for a definitive purpose. Then, how much more our God could care us?

According to the Qur'an we read about an event where an individual was crucified, but the identity of the person was not confirmed. Why should we ignore this kind of fact? Let us search the truth.

The Gospel of John19:17-18, 25-27, tells us about the person on the cross. It states, 'Jesus went out, bearing his own cross, to the place called 'The place of a Skull', which in Aramaic is called Golgotha. There they crucified him, and with him two others, one on either side, or Jesus between them. [25]But standing by the cross of Jesus were his mother and his mother's sister, Mary the wife of Cleophas, and Mary Magdalene.[26]When Jesus saw his mother and the disciple whom he loved standing nearby, he said to his mother, "Woman, behold, your son!" [27]Then he said to the disciple, "Behold, your mother!" And from that hour the disciple took her to his own home.' This is the third word Jesus spoke while he was upon the cross. In this context, we could see Jesus personally talked with his mother and the disciple John; these two people were the direct witnesses for the clarity to the fact that Jesus was upon the Cross.

The crucifixion of Jesus Christ is the real purpose of God to this world. This shows God's real love towards the human race. Ignoring such a fact is objection to God's decision.

Even though there are very direct statements from Allah in the Qur'an that 'Jesus tastes death' and 'indeed we have killed Son of Maryam and Ambassador of God', yet some of the Muslims are assuming that God tricked the Jews and sent someone who looked like Jesus to be crucified to save Him. This kind of assumption is a serious rebellion to God and insulting Allah by saying He deceived the people. Allah is not a deceiver. They are insulting Allah that He changes His words and He tricks the people. The very act of 'deceiving' is against God's attributes.

We should not believe without fact or confirmation from the history. God gave us wisdom to be vigilant to analyze the facts instead of ignoring them. Linking Jesus crucifixion with Pontius Pilate represents the incident that took place during Roman Empire. This fact was proved by the history. About 20 years later after the crucifixion, Tacitus, a Roman historian, wrote a book surveying the history of Rome. He described about Nero, the Roman emperor how he punished early Christians. While writing about the persecution of early Christians, he wrote that their originator, Christ, had been executed in Tiberius' reign by the governor of Judea, Pontius Pilatus (Annals 15; 44, emp.added)

Tacitus was not a Jesus Christ's follower to write and verify Jesus Christ's crucifixion. He wrote it because this was a historical fact.

Let us proceed the history how it took place? Under the Roman law, any one who claimed to be a king was guilty of rebellion against emperor. The normal punishment was crucifixion. But the crucifixion couldn't take place until the Roman governor Pontius Pilate gave the final order for it.

Pontius Pilate before delivered Jesus to the crucifixion, said unto Him, "Art thou the King of the Jews? Jesus answered, "My kingdom is not of this: if my kingdom is of this world, then would my servants fight, that I should not deliver to the Jews: but now is my kingdom not from hence." (John 18:33) These are all historical evidences of Jesus Christ's crucifixion. We cannot deny this historical truth. As per the Qur'an we have to consider the Gospels. We should discern whether the Gospels came earlier or the Qur'an? History reveals that the Qur'an was written later after more than 700 years. There was a gap of at least 600 years in between Jesus and Muhammad.

The four Gospels (Matthew, Mark, Luke, and John) contain a great deal of historical information about Jesus' birth, miracles, death, resurrection, and ascension, thus confirming the crucifixion as a fact. These four different authors came to the same conclusion because they were eyewitnesses of Jesus Christ. Their written work was also similar because all the Scripture was given by inspiration of God. If we accept the condition of the law stating if two or three eyewitnesses for a certain event, are enough to confirm the event to be factual and true according to the law.

In the Torah- Deuteronomy 17:6, it was written, "⁶At the mouth of two witnesses, or three witnesses, shall he that is worthy of death be put to death; but at the mouth of one witness he shall not be put to death. This is the reason why we take the four Gospels to be factual and true. I have taken this verse from the Torah, since in the Qur'an – Al-Maidah 5:68 & Surah10:94, it says, A Muslim has to uphold the Old Testament, the Torah and the Gospels and has to accept it.

Al-Maidah 5:68 "Say, "O people of the Scripture you are standing on nothing until you uphold the Law (Torah, the Gospel and what has been revealed to you from your Lord." And surely we have given Law of Moses, Old Testament (The Torah) so do not hesitate to accept it.

Allah stated, "So if you are in doubt, O Muhammad, about that which 'We' have revealed to you, then ask those who have been reading the Scripture before you, then ask those who have been reading the Scripture before you." (Surah10:94).

Allah had directed Muhammad to ask his doubts, those who had been reading the Scriptures before him. Because of this main reason, it is important to take into consideration of the four Gospels. The four Gospels were preceded Muhammad. If they were corrupted, Allah might not direct him in this way. Therefore, we have to take into consideration the Torah, the Scripture and the four Gospels. Especially, the four Gospels were directly from four eye witnesses. When we read them we understand the fact that all of them were coincided with each other. It encourages us, when we come to know that they were harmonized with each other even though they were written by the four different authors. The different authors came up with the same material since they were written by the inspiration of God. This very fact really astonishes the reader of the Gospels.

Jesus Christ personally, told His disciples about upcoming events such as His death and His resurrection. His direct communication with His disciples reveals it in Mark Gospel 10:33–34, "Saying, Behold, we go up to Jerusalem; and the Son of man shall be delivered unto the chief priests, and unto the scribes; and they shall condemn him to death, and shall deliver him to the Gentiles: [34]And they shall mock him, and shall scourge him, and shall spit upon him, and shall kill him: and the third day he shall rise again." Jesus foretold the upcoming things to His disciples and those events took place within a short period of time. If Jesus is a deceiver, Allah never had chosen Him to be the judge to the whole world on His second return.

Jesus foretold the truth about His death in the Scripture and to His disciples by saying, "The Son of Man must suffer many things and be rejected by the elders and chief priests and scribes, and be killed, and on the third day be raised. And He said to all, "If anyone would come after me, let him deny himself and take up his cross daily and follow me." (Luke 9:22-23; Mark Gospel 9:31; Luke Gospel 9:22; and John Gospel 12:32-33.) All most all authors of the Gospels were witnessed this truth.

His death and the resurrection took place just as He told them. Unless Jesus was sure, He can not self prophesy His death and resurrection. If it was a lie, Jesus might have lost His title (Speech of Truth). Allah's noble messenger Jesus was not a coward to escape from the truth. Jesus Christ came to the world to confirm the Torah and fulfill the prophecies which were written about Him. Allah is not a liar to change His words!

There is a historical and logical truth in how the disciples followed Jesus Christ. They stood very firm as His witnesses. The Qur'an even testifies to the faithfulness of the disciples and called them examples to be followed. Why would the disciples follow Jesus even when it cost them their lives if they wanted to promote a lie? The disciples knew Jesus to be the truth and were able to faithfully follow Jesus Christ even to the point of death, because of the truth that found in Him and the eternal life promised to them in Jesus Christ. Al most all His disciples were the martyrs. They realized how faithful and truth full Jesus was. That is why they were not hesitated to spare their lives for His name sake.

Some Muslims say Allah would never punish one person for someone else's sin. God is our creator and our heavenly father who wanted us in right direction unto eternity. If our children go astray, as their parents we agree to suffer for them to bring them back to right path. Our heavenly father loves us more than we love our children, because He created us in His own image. That is why He suffered for us.

But why does Jesus (Allah's Spirit according to the Noble Qur'an) has to die? How did He bare our sins to save us? Why God has to humble Himself and became man and came to this world and died for us? Is this possible to God?

When I am trying to answer this question, I am always reminded of an incident that happened between my father and me when I was four years old. I remembered my dad always wore a white, iron-pressed, clean, and spotless suit before he went to work. I loved my dad so much that I always wanted to go to be with him. He told me very gently that I couldn't and had to stay at home. But, I remembered on a particular day I did not listen to him; I snuck out of the house and started to run after him. My eyes were completely focused on my dad that I did not pay any attention to what was in front of me--an open sewage under the road. Running even faster towards my dad, who now was just a few feet away, I fell into the sewage making a huge "thump" sound. I was covered in filth and dirty water and I was not able to reach my dad. I was sunken in the sewage. I was unable to come out of the sewage and I began to cry very loudly, when suddenly arms that seemed so familiar and loving, picked me out of the sewage. It was my father! He began to console me, took me home, and gave me a bath ridding the filth I was covered in. My father, without thinking twice, neglected his own clean white suit (that I stained) by picking me out of the dirty sewer and put me on him to carry me home. He stained his clothes and washed me clean instead.

The same way, God saw us in the sewage of sin and the filthiness of the world that stained our spirits. Psalmist compared sin as a horrible pit and miry clay. The lusts of the world always have strong hold on the people. The world with all kinds of attractions draws us into it. For certain we do not belong to this world. We were driven out from the paradise (the Eternal kingdom) because of our forefather Adam's mistake. Adam could not withstand by himself when he had done the mistake. As human beings we are weak. Even though we try our best by ourselves, we still fall into it. The more we try the more we fall into it. We needed a strong hand to pull us out.

That is the reason, why Psalmist wrote these words, "²He brought me up also out of a horrible pit, out of the miry clay, and set my feet upon a rock, and established my goings. ³And he hath put a new song in my mouth, even praise unto our God: many shall see it, and fear, and shall trust in the LORD." (Psalms 40:2-3) If a person fell in a horrible pit or miry clay, a very strong person has to come to pull him or her from it and willing to stain Himself.

It is written in 2Corinthians 5:21 − 21. "For he hath made him to be sin for us, who knew no sin; that we might be made the righteousness of God in him." The important fact for this is we cannot approach the Holy God with our filthiness. We must be spotless and pure inside first; resembling the God's holiness.

Washing our hands and feet physically does not rid the sin from our conscience. Therefore man cannot wash his own sin away, but someone greater than him or her and the one who is capable of pull and pick us up from the "sewage of sin", can wash us pure. This is why God himself as a part of HIS SPIRIT (Jesus Christ) came down to the earth to give us a new covering or in other words a new spirit with a sacrifice.

And it is true as we refer in Isaiah 46:9, 10. "Remember the former things of old: for I am God, and there is none else: I am God, and there is none like me, Declaring the end from the beginning, and from ancient times the things that are not yet done, saying, My council shall stand and I will do my pleasure." That is the will of God and His pleasure to save His children.

In the beginning God gave man two signs of a sacrifice and covering. It can be seen in the beginning of the creation in Genesis

3rd chapter. When Adam committed the first sin towards God; shame was revealed to him. '7And the eyes of them both were opened and they knew that they were naked; and they sewed fig leaves together, and made themselves aprons to cover themselves.' When God called him, Adam said, "10 I heard thy voice in the garden, and I was afraid, because I was naked; and I hid myself." It explains us that, what they made themselves with leaves could not cover them properly. Adam and Eve's self efforts could not cover them fully. The next verses in the same chapter, tells us that God gave them clothes with animal skins for complete protection. Same way our efforts to do good deeds are not sufficient to stand in front of God. He had the Master plan for our lives. Whatever God does for us is perfect.

In this situation, the Most Merciful and the Most Compassionate God revealed His love to Adam. God Himself made coats of skin clothing to Adam and Eve. This was the first sign that God revealed to the humanity that He will give them a new covering with a sacrifice. God did this because Adam and Eve lost the privilege of the eternity by their disobedience.

The first attempt of God in saving Adam and Eve is He killed an animal. The life of an animal was sacrificed and the blood was sprinkled. This was the first and foremost sign we see how God gave them the protection. This is the first sign of sacrifice. The life needs to be taken off to make skin coats for their complete protection but blood is the life. Now we understand that God did the sacrifice to get them the skin coats. Their physical shame was recovered. The first covering was physical and was the forerunner for the second which was spiritual.

Some people don't agree with the concept that human beings are born as sinners. I have three children, each one about two years apart. I observed their response when their next sibling was born. Since the newborns require more attention than a two year-old, sometimes the other child would come by the newborn and reveal jealousy in their actions and facial expressions. Each older sibling would respond in a similar manner to the newborn when he/she was receiving more attention than the other. Their responses are instinctively driven even at a young age. The thoughts, words and deeds of the man are always sinful. '⁵And God saw that the wickedness of man was great in the earth, and that every imagination of the thoughts of his heart was only evil continually.' (Genesis 6:5)

In the Gospel of Matthew 12:33, Jesus stated, "³³Either make the tree good and its fruit good, or make the tree bad and its fruit bad, for the tree is known by its fruit." Since Adam and Eve both ate from the tree of the knowledge of good and evil we have the innate nature of knowing between good and evil and can instinctively sin even at a tender age even though we do not realize that we are sinning. But again, the children at a very young age forget their jealousy in an instant. That is how we should be! But adults keep grudges, never forgive each other.

Lord Jesus Christ being so compassionate said to His disciples, "Truly, I say to you, unless you turn and become like children, you will never enter the kingdom of heaven." (Matthew 18:3) Even though children are born with a sinful nature they do not realize the difference between good and evil until they reach an age of accountability where they are able to distinguish the both by their conscience. And until we reach the age of accountability we are not going to be judged. God is very compassionate. He knew that we inherited our qualities from our first father Adam.

The Bible says, 'For all have sinned, and come short of the glory of God.' 1John 1:8: 'If we say we have no sin, we deceive ourselves, and the truth is not in us.' In the Gospel of Mark 7:20-23, it is written, 'And he said, 'What comes out of a person is what defiles him. For from within, out of the heart of man, come evil thoughts, sexual immorality, theft, murder, adultery, coveting, wickedness, deceit, sensuality, envy, slander, pride, foolishness, All these evil things come from within, and they defile a person." Because of the sinful nature of human beings, the world is corrupted. There is no safe place to live in this world.

The Islam stands on the Gospel and the Torah according to the Sura Al-Māʾidah 5: 68. If we read, 5:68, it says, 'Say, "O people of the Scripture you are standing on nothing until you uphold the Law (Torah, the Gospel and what has been revealed to you from your Lord." And surely we have given Law of Moses, Old Testament (The Torah) so do not hesitate to accept it. Let us see what the Torah says about Moses law.

In the Torah, God gave Moses Law and instructions of five burnt offerings and sacrifices. Law is like a mirror, when we look into the mirror we see our faults. Nobody can be perfect in front of the law. It constantly reminds our mistakes and punishment. In our lives, many times law clarifies that we come short in fulfilling the divine law. The law always judge and punish. So in the Old Testament period of time the burnt offerings and the sacrifices were needed to be perfected.

In these five offerings, burnt sacrifice should be a male without any blemish. These sacrifices had to be made and only the high priest could only enter into the holy place to offer up the sacrifices every year for his sins and for the people's sins. God saw the service of offering up the sacrifices, even when done perfectly it could not make man perfect when pertaining to his conscience. Man only appeared good outwardly but inwardly his heart was still impure. This was the second sign of sacrifice which foretold a greater and permanent sacrifice that was going to be made.

God said, "'Behold, all souls are mine; as the soul of the father, so also the soul of the son is mine: the soul that sinneth, it shall die." (Ezekiel18:4) Once God utters it never changes. Righteous God demands righteousness. He is Holy. God wanted to cleanse the human conscience and spirit to resemble His holiness.

While we are on this earth, God wants us to be His habitation, and when we die He wanted us to live with Him forever in His holy kingdom. This is possible only through God who created us in His image! Who can be perfect according to the law, unless the creator shows us mercy? He is the only one who is efficient in doing so. The capable and the perfect one is only God. In order for 'a Will' or 'a Testament' to be in full effect the Testator has to die.

We can question how come Jesus was there, when the first covenant or 'the will' was made? Jesus Christ was there in God when He created Adam and Eve. God said, "Let us make man in our image" (Genesis 1:26-27) and in John Gospel Jesus said these words. "And now, O Father, glorify thou me with thine own self with the glory which I had with thee before the world was." (John 17:5) '[58]Jesus said unto them, verily, verily, I say unto you, Before Abraham was, I am.' (John 8:58) Theses words of Jesus clarified the truth that He was in God even before the creation. Jesus was the only one who is declared by God as faultless and is capable of doing such a great act to redeem all the creation.

He offered Himself as the sacrifice which gives us permanent protection and it is Spiritual. He was the Lamb of God who was blameless through the Eternal Spirit, in order to purge and cleanse our conscience from the evil works to serve the living God. For by this one offering Jesus has forever perfected those who are sanctified in His Holy Blood. (Hebrews chapters 9 &10) This sacrifice would not only cover all of man's sins but create in man a new and contrite spirit.

The New Testament book, Colossians, talks of how the Old Testament law observances were abolished in Christ. Since the law was the shadow of Christ, a righteous life can be lived when we live in the grace of God that was shown upon the cross.

He came to earth to fulfill the written scripture in the Old Testament. There is a trace of explanation that the people are not able to understand. There is difference in between the law and the grace. There is none that can perform all the law without a trace of fault or mistake. That is why to perform all the law we should need grace because of our inability to observe the law up to full measure. Even if we make a little deviation from the law we are deserved the punishment.

Now when the grace is offered all our weaknesses are covered. God our creator knew our weakness and inability to accomplish His divine standard and He came to the world in the form of the human. Galatians 4:4, 5: "But when the fullness of the time was come, God sent forth his Son, made of a woman, made under the law, [5]To redeem them that were under the law, that we might receive the adoption of sons.' In Philippians 2:6-8, it is written, "[6]Who, being in the form of God, thought it not robbery to be equal with God: [7]But made himself of no reputation, and took upon him the form of a servant, and was made in the likeness of men: [8]And being found in fashion as a man, he humbled himself, and became obedient unto death, even the death of the cross.' Now He knew personally the life of the human in the world.

Jesus Christ who is above all the mankind was able to fulfill and take man's sins upon Himself. Jesus committed no sin, nor was any guile found in His mouth; when reviled, He did not revile in return; when suffered, He did not threaten. He was the Lamb of God and the perfect sacrifice to take the sins of the human race. So Jesus went to the cross to be sacrificed.

The truth of the cross which was prophesied in Psalms 85:10. It is written as follows: '[10]Mercy and truth are met together; righteousness and peace have kissed each other.' This was fulfilled in the sacrifice of Jesus Christ. Through His sacrifice, Jesus made a way for the human race to reach God through reconciliation; only His holy blood made this way not our good works. He left His throne and suffered for us. He is way above but we are below. This explains us the Grace which means we are not at all worthy to receive such a great gift the eternal life through His sacrifice. That is the reason it is very difficult to some people to believe this fact that God Himself took the form of man to come to this world and sacrificed His life.

God showed unconditional love but some people are reluctant to accept it.

The significance of the cross can be explained as follows: Cross is t –shaped structure with vertical stake which stands out for "I" (self) and the law. "I" selfishness and our deeds or our self efforts were crossed out. It is crossed out with horizontal beam, which represents grace to forgive our sins and it is the symbol of the Christianity where Jesus Christ accomplished all the Scripture.

Jesus Christ put an end to all the burnt offerings and sacrifices. A high priest no longer has to come in between God and the man instead there is only one official mediator (Jesus) and He is our high priest. He always intercedes for our weaknesses. What a great plan of God! God knew that the human is weak and frail and are vulnerable to make mistakes since the beginning of the creation. Yet He removed all the sacrifices or sprinkling of the blood. No more obstacles to communicate with God. He gave us privilege to communicate with God through Him.

This evidence can be seen in Matthew Gospel 27:50 and 51. '[50]Jesus, when he had cried again with a loud voice, yielded up the ghost. [51]And, behold, the veil of the temple was rent in twain from the top to the bottom; and the earth did quake, and the rocks rent.' Dear reader please notice the veil of the temple was rent in twain from top to bottom, indicating there is no veil in between man and God through Jesus Christ.

Even before He was sacrificed His life on the cross, He told His disciples about His body and His blood. In Luke Gospel 22:19-21, '[19]And Jesus Christ took bread, and gave thanks, and broke it, and gave unto them, saying, "This is my body which is given for you: this do in remembrance of me. [20]Likewise also the cup after supper, saying, and this cup is the New Testament in my blood, which is shed for you. [21]But, behold, the hand of him that betrayeth me is with me on the table." He put an end to the animal sacrifices for the redemption of the sins.

By His own sacrificial blood which He shed, He entered into 'the Holy Place' and offered it to obtain the Eternal redemption for us. He laid His life down and shed His blood for the human race. God made His Spirit (Jesus Christ) who had no sin to be sin for us so we might be made righteous in Him. Moreover, He died and rose again! He conquered the death so we can have the eternal life as well! Those who believe on Him will defeat the second death (death of the Spirit) and will rise up or resurrected to inherit the Eternity.

This great sacrifice of God was foretold in the Old Testament of the Holy Bible. It was written by many prophets. Since it was a divine plan, it was revealed ahead of the time to the prophets and it was fulfilled. Here below I mentioned some of the prophecies which were written in the Old Testament.

Isaiah the prophet in 700 B.C prophesied Jesus Christ's death in Isaiah Chapter 53.

'¹Who has believed our report? And to whom has the arm of the LORD been revealed? ²For He shall grow up before Him as a tender plant, And as a root out of dry ground. He has no form or comeliness; and when we see Him, There is no beauty that we should desire Him. ³He is despised and rejected by men, A Man of sorrows and acquainted with grief. And we hid, as it were, our faces from Him; He was despised, and we did not esteem Him. ⁴Surely He has borne our grief. And carried our sorrows; yet we esteemed Him stricken, Smitten by God, and afflicted. ⁵But He *was* wounded for our transgressions, He was bruised for our iniquities; the chastisement for our peace *was* upon Him, and by His stripes we are healed.

⁶All we like sheep have gone astray; we have turned, every one, to his own way; and the LORD has laid on Him the iniquity of us all. ⁷He was oppressed and He was afflicted, yet He opened not His mouth; He was led as a lamb to the slaughter, and as a sheep before its shearers is silent, so He opened not His mouth. ⁸He was taken from prison and from judgment, and who will declare His generation? For

He was cut off from the land of the living; for the transgressions of 'My' people He was stricken.

⁹And they made His grave with the wicked—but with the rich at His death, Because He had done no violence, nor was any deceit in His mouth. ¹⁰Yet it pleased the LORD to bruise Him; He has put Him to grief. When you make His soul an offering for sin, He shall see His seed, He shall prolong His days, and the pleasure of the LORD shall prosper in His hand. ¹¹He shall see the labor of His soul, and be satisfied.

By His knowledge 'My' righteous Servant shall justify many, For He shall bear their iniquities. ¹²Therefore I will divide Him a portion with the great, And He shall divide the spoil with the strong, Because He poured out His soul unto death, And He was numbered with the transgressors, and He bore the sin of many, and made intercession for the transgressors.' (Isaiah 53)

King David prophesied in Psalms 22:16-18. '¹⁶For dogs have surrounded Me; The congregation of the wicked has enclosed Me. They pierced My hands and My feet; ¹⁷I can count all My bones. They look and stare at Me. ¹⁸They divide 'My' garments among them, and for My clothing they cast lots.' (Psalms 22:16-18)

The Book of Zachariah prophesied in Chapter 11:12-13; 12:10 and Zachariah 13:6. '¹²Then I said to them, "if it is agreeable to you, give me my wages; and if not, refrain.' So they weighed out for my wages thirty pieces of silver. ¹³And the LORD said to me, 'Throw it to the potter'—that princely price they set on me. So I took the thirty pieces of silver and threw them into the house of the LORD for the potter." (Zachariah 11:12-13) In 12:10, it is written, "¹⁰And I will pour on the house of David and on the inhabitants of Jerusalem the Spirit of grace and supplication; then they will look on Me whom they pierced. Yes, they will mourn for Him as one mourns for His only son and grieve for Him as one grieves for a firstborn.' '⁶And one will say to him, 'What are these wounds between your arms?' Then he will answer, "Those with which I was wounded in the house of my friends." (Zachariah 13:6)

All of these chapters and the verses indicate and foretold how Jesus Christ will suffer on the Cross of Calvary. All the prophecies of those prophets were true and were fulfilled. How can we deny the writings of these many prophets? If one single prophet wrote, some people may not take it into consideration according to Deuteronomy 17:6, but these prophecies were written in different time periods by different authors. This is such concrete evidence that the Torah and the Old Testament contain the Messianic prophecies; they are the portrayed images of God in the heaven. The life of Jesus Christ and the events took place in accordance with the Old Testament predictions.

Every activity of Lord Jesus Christ was accomplished according to the Scripture.

Now we knew why God had chosen Jesus Christ to be a just judge and ruler to come second time to the world. In John 10:17, Jesus said, "Therefore doth my father love me, because I lay down my life, that I might take it again. No man can take it from me, but I lay it down of myself. I have power to lay it down, and I have power to take it again. This commandment have I received of my Father." These words of Jesus Christ came true in His crucifixion. Therefore, God gave authority to Jesus Christ as a just ruler at the end of the world, because God was so pleased for His accomplishment and His loyalty.

Even though, Jesus Christ experienced human life on the earth His love was divine. He was not like any other prophet as some people think of. He never got sick. He did not have any wives or children or focused on the material gain, rather He was moved with compassion for the human race. He was faultless. It is possible only if He came as 'a part of God' or 'Son of God.' He became a son of man in the flesh and came down to the earth to save His creations by laying His life on the cross in order to save them. Since sin is the cause of death, victory over the death cannot be won unless the one who is sinless is willing to die for the human race. Jesus is the only one who was born faultless and lived pure and holy.

The last seven words or seven phrases of Jesus on the cross have a very great significance and indicate the completion. The sixth phrase was "It is finished," tells us He finished the purpose of His coming so that now we can become righteous and spotless in Him. He finished all the sacrifices and put an end to them. The last words of the SAVIOR were "It is finished." No starting of any new teachings. No changes in the plan of God because His plan is unchanged. That's what happened on the cross. It is finished. If Jesus was not suffered on the Cross, how these last seven words of Jesus Christ uttered on the Cross came into existence? Those seven words had great importance with such a great meaning in them.

The announcement at the birth of Jesus Christ by Gabriel the Angel to Mary, Joseph (foster Father of Jesus) and also to shepherds was fulfilled. "[10]And the angel said unto them, "Fear not: for, behold, I bring you good tidings of great joy, which shall be to all people. [11]For unto you is born this day in the city of David a Savior, which is Christ the Lord. [12]And this shall be a sign unto you; ye shall find the babe wrapped in swaddling clothes, lying in a manger. [13]And suddenly there was with the angel a multitude of the heavenly host praising God, and saying, [14]Glory to God in the highest, and on earth peace, good will toward men." (Luke Gospel 2:10-14) The heavenly plan of His birth was fulfilled on the earth. He finished everything which is necessary to save the mankind from the eternal damnation.

The prophecy of 'Jesus Christ's death' in the Qur'an, Surah Al Nisa 4: 157: 'Indeed we have killed Jesus.' and Sura Mary'am 19:33: 'I shall taste death and day I will be raised,' were fulfilled in the crucifixion of Jesus Christ. Jesus Christ died on the cross and He rose from the dead and ascended into the heaven. The Crucifixion was the historical event. And it was confirmed by His disciples and the two angels from the heaven. Because of all the above facts the crucifixion is the will of God. No one can deny this truth unless Satan blinds them.

The Resurrection of Jesus Christ from the Dead

Even Muslims accept the fact that Christ is alive and they are expecting for His second return to the earth. Not even one passage or text in the Qur'an denies the resurrection of Jesus from the dead. A revelation about Jesus Christ was written in the Qur'an, Surah -Maryam 19:33.

"Blessed I am, the day I was born, the day I die and the day I will be sent alive from the dead." [Surah Maryam 19:33]

In the Qur'an al- Imran 3:55, it says, 'Behold, Allah said, "O ISA (JESUS) I will take you and raise you to myself and clear you of those who disbelieve and I will make those who follow you are superior to those who disbelieve till the day of resurrection." Here in this statement Allah clarified the fact of 'Resurrection.' by saying, "I raised you to myself." The word 'Resurrection' came because Allah raised Jesus from the dead. In the same way there will be a resurrection day for all the people when Jesus comes in the end days.

These two statements are very clear in stating and confirming that Jesus died and rose again. There is no resurrection without the death. Dear reader, have you thought about this statement seriously? This fact has been made a lie later on in the Islam by misinterpretation that Jesus was not crucified. It is the enemy's work to falsify God's truth to bring eternal damnation to mankind. If Jesus was not resurrected from the dead, then there is no hope to anybody to be resurrected from the death.

The Satan is blinding the eyes and hearts of the people, even though there are so many proofs of His death and resurrection. We have to yield to the truth and think about a moment, why Pontius Pilate ordered to guard the grave of Jesus? He would not have guarded it if any one other than Jesus Christ was buried. It clarifies the truth that it was the body of Jesus Christ that was in the grave. Now the grave is empty and is a witness to the people that He was raised. Since He was resurrected, we have the hope that we also will be resurrected.

Jesus Christ whose name is "Speech of Truth" told His disciples in Mark Gospel 10:32–34. '32 And they were in the way going up to Jerusalem; and Jesus went before them: and they were amazed; and as they followed, they were afraid. And he took again the twelve, and began to tell them what things should happen unto him. He foretold them about His suffering, the crucifixion and the resurrection.

In 700B.C Isaiah the Prophet was revealed about the death and victory of Jesus Christ. It is written, "He will come and swallow up death in victory". (Isaiah 25:8) The Death had no power over Him. What a great truth! The prophecy was foretold many years ahead and it was fulfilled.

According to the Gospels, on the third day after the crucifixion there were two angels of the Lord who descended from the heaven to the tomb of Jesus, and said, "Fear not ye: for I know that ye seek Jesus, which was crucified. He is not here: for he is risen." God with His infinite wisdom kept the two angels to reveal the truth. Dear Reader, has anyone in any part of the world that had ever been resurrected? There is no one. It is difficult to believe this unique thing unless the angels clarify the truth. That is why God sent His angels. Lord Jesus Christ is the only one who was resurrected and ascended to the heaven.

We can not suspect or misinterpret the two statements in the Qur'an al- Imran 3:55 and Sura Mar'yam 19:33, because the two angels from the heaven clarified crucifixion and resurrection of Jesus Christ.

"Blessed I am, the day I was born, the day I die and the day I will be sent alive from the dead." [Surah Mar'yam 19:33]

'Behold, Allah said, "O ISA (JESUS) I will take you and raise you to myself and clear you of those who disbelieve and I will make those who follow you are superior to those who disbelieve till the day of resurrection." [Qur'an al- Imran 3:55]

He was able to resurrect because He has the power to give life and take life as a Savior, bringing hope to the whole world. Jesus had the power. The people are so weak in understanding the impossible things of God. God knew it. That is the reason God sent the two angels to confirm the truth.

The empty sepulcher is the evidence that He had risen. Usually, graves are full of bones, but His tomb is empty.

In Ephesians 4:10, Paul wrote to Ephesians' church that '10He that descended is the same also that ascended up far above all heavens, that he might fill all things.' This verse shows us that there is a proof regarding Jesus Christ's crucifixion and resurrection. After Jesus Christ was resurrected, He appeared for forty days in his heavenly body; He showed off his nailed pierced hands and feet to over five hundred witnesses including the disciples.

In the Gospel of John 20:24-29, we read about His disciple Thomas who doubted Jesus Christ's resurrection; Jesus reappeared to Thomas and a room full of witnesses, showing them His pierced hands and feet.

If we read the passage, it is written: "24But Thomas, one of the twelve, called Didymus, was not with them when Jesus came. 25The other disciples therefore said unto him, we have seen the LORD. But he said unto them, except I shall see in his hands the print of the nails, and put my finger into the print of the nails, and thrust my hand into his side, I will not believe. [26]And after eight days again his disciples were within, and Thomas with them: then came Jesus, the doors being shut, and stood in the midst, and said, Peace be unto you. [27]Then saith he to Thomas, reach hither thy finger, and behold my hands; and reach hither thy hand, and thrust it into my side: and be not faithless, but believing. [28]And Thomas answered and said unto him, My LORD and my God. [29]Jesus saith unto him, Thomas, because thou hast seen me, thou hast believed: blessed are they that have not seen, and yet have believed. Believe him and you will be blessed."

After the resurrection of Jesus Christ, there were ten distinct appearances. All were recorded in the Scripture: Jesus appeared to Mary Magdalene (Mark 16:9-11; John 20:11-18), to the women returning from the tomb with the angelic message (Mathew 28:8-10), to Peter. (Luke 24:34). To the Emmaus disciples (Mark 16:12; Luke 24:13_32). To the disciples but Thomas was absent at that time. (Mark 16:4; Luke 24:26-43; John 20:19-25)

The next Sunday night, when Thomas was there, Jesus appeared them again as we read in the above paragraph. Then He was appeared to seven disciples beside the Sea of Galilee. (John 21) Later He appeared to the Apostles and 'above five hundred brethren and to James.'(Mathew 28:16-20; Mark 16:15-18; 1Cor 15:6; 1Cor 15:7) He appeared to His disciples when they were at their evening meal. (Mark 16:19-20; Luke 24:44-53) At the time of His ascension to heaven from the mount called Olivet. (Acts1:3-12)

Jesus appeared in different places, at different times to different people. Even after His ascension into the heaven, Jesus Christ appeared in His glory to Stephen, (Acts7:54-56) '[55]But he, being full of the Holy Ghost, looked up steadfastly into heaven, and saw the glory of God, and Jesus standing on the right hand of God, [56]And said, Behold, I see the heavens opened, and the Son of man standing on the right hand of God.'

Saul who was persecuting the disciple of Jesus Christ on his way to Damascus he saw Jesus and heard His words then the entire course of his life was changed. He saw Jesus as a bright light and heard His voice. This incident made Saul to change his attitude towards Jesus and His mission. He became one of His apostles. This experience of Paul is a direct evidence for the people to understand who Jesus Christ is. The direct communication of Jesus Christ to Saul resulted in Saul's conversion to Paul. We could read the incident from the book of Acts 9:1-9.

'9.[1]And Saul, yet breathing out threatening and slaughter against the disciples of the Lord, went unto the high priest, [2]And desired of him letters to Damascus to the synagogues, that if he found any of this way, whether they were men or women, he might bring them bound unto Jerusalem. [3]And as he journeyed, he came near Damascus: and suddenly there shined round about him a light from heaven: [4]And he fell to the earth, and heard a voice saying unto him, "Saul, Saul, why persecutest thou me?" [5]And he said, "Who art thou, Lord?" And the Lord said, "I am Jesus whom thou persecutest: it is hard for thee to kick against the pricks." [6]And he was trembling and astonished said, "Lord, what wilt thou have me to do?"

And the Lord said unto him, "Arise, and go into the city, and it shall be told thee what thou must do." And the men which journeyed with him stood speechless, hearing a voice, but seeing no man. [8]And Saul arose from the earth; and when his eyes were opened, he saw no man: but they led him by the hand, and brought him into Damascus. [9]And he was three days without sight, and neither did eat nor drink.' Later Saul converted as Paul and became an apostle.

Again Paul saw Jesus at Corinth (Acts 18:9-10) and then in the temple at Jerusalem. (Acts 22:17-21), again at Jerusalem. (Acts 23:11) and in another vision. (2 Corinthians 12:1-4)

Lastly in the New Testament, Jesus Christ appeared to John when he was in Patmos Island. He had heavenly visions and he was a witness what he had seen. He wrote in the book of Revelation, that '[12]And I turned to see the voice that spake with me. And being turned, I saw seven golden candlesticks; [13]And in the midst of the seven candlesticks one like unto the Son of man, clothed with a garment down to the foot, and girt about the paps with a golden girdle. [14]His head and his hairs were white like wool, as white as snow; and his eyes were as a flame of fire. [15]And his feet like unto fine brass, as if they burned in a furnace; and his voice as the sound of many waters. [16]And he had in his right hand seven stars: and out of his mouth went a sharp two-edged sword: and his countenance was as the sun shineth in his strength.'

'[17]And when I saw him, I fell at his feet as dead. And he laid his right hand upon me, saying unto me, "Fear not; I am the first and the last: [18]I am he that liveth, and was dead; and, behold, I am alive for evermore, Amen; and have the keys of hell and of death."

All the other prophets such as Adam, Abraham, Moses and Muhammad were dead but Jesus Christ alone arose from the dead. He is the only one who was resurrected from the death in the entire world history. We can confirm this truth from the four Gospels, and the prophecies of the Scriptures. Christ is alive. He will come back.

Paul analyzed about the resurrection of Christ in a letter to Corinthian church in 1Corinthians15:17-26. '[17]And if Christ be not raised, your faith is vain; ye are yet in your sins. [18]Then they also which are fallen asleep in Christ are perished. [19]If we have hope in Christ only for this life, we are of all men most miserable. [20]But now is Christ risen from the dead, and become the first fruits of them that slept. [21]For since by man came death, by man came also the resurrection of the dead. [22]For as in Adam all die, even so in Christ shall all be made alive. [23]But every man in his own order: Christ the first fruits; afterward they that are Christ's at his coming. [24]Then cometh the end, when he shall have delivered up the kingdom to

God, even the Father; when he shall have put down all rule and all authority and power. ^{25}For he must reign, till he hath put all enemies under his feet. ^{26}The last enemy that shall be destroyed is death.'

Jesus Christ is the first one of all the people to destroy the death. Every one whoever believe in Him will be in the same order. This confirms the truth of the Resurrection.

The Ascension of Jesus
Christ to the Heaven

In the Qur'an al- Imran 3:55: 'Behold, Allah said, "O ISA (JESUS) I will take you and raise you to myself and clear you of those who disbelieve and I will make those who follow you to superior to those who disbelieve till the day of resurrection." This is Allah's statement. He gave this statement until the resurrection day. There should not be any disbelief to anybody until the day of resurrection to follow Jesus Christ because He was the first one who was resurrected from the dead.

As per the Qur'an, the resurrection of the people will take place at the end of the world, until then, everybody has to follow Jesus Christ. Dear reader! When we had this many evidences, why do we have to disbelieve? Do you disbelieve it? If anybody disbelieves Allah's statement, he or she is dishonoring Allah. Are you following ISA (JESUS)? If you disbelieve this statement and are not following Jesus, you are neglecting Allah's words. If you follow Jesus you will become superiors on the day of resurrection because Allah has said this statement as per the Qur'an. Allah never changes His words. We should not change Allah's words.

Jesus Christ's ascension to the heaven (Miraj) was witnessed by eleven disciples outside the city near Bethlehem. This can be seen in the Gospels- the Holy Scriptures. As we have mentioned in the previous chapter, Jesus appeared for forty days to the people from the day of His resurrection until His ascension to the heaven.

Before Jesus ascended into the heaven, he gave His last sermon to the disciples. The sermon focused on His second coming as well as the task of the great commission: to go out into the world, preach the gospel of salvation, and to make all people followers of Christ, and to baptize them in the name of the Father, the Son, and the Holy Ghost. This describes (The Triune God). These are the words of Jesus Christ. He told them these words before He was ascended. If Allah did not accept this fact or not pleased with the teachings of Jesus Christ, He might not send Jesus back second time to judge the whole world.

John Gospel 14: 25 & 26: Jesus said, "[25]These things I have spoken to you while being present with you. [26]But the Helper, the Holy Spirit, whom the Father will send in My name, He will teach you all things, and bring to your remembrance all things that I said to you."

Before His ascension Jesus told them, In Acts 1: 8, Jesus said, "'[1]ye shall receive power when the Holy Spirit has come upon you, and you will be my witnesses in Jerusalem, Judea and Samaria and to the uttermost part of the earth." Luke Gospel 24:49-51. [49]And, behold, I send the promise of my Father upon you: but tarry ye in the city of Jerusalem, until ye be endued with power from on high. [50]And he led them out as far as to Bethany, and he lifted up his hands, and blessed them. [51]And it came to pass, while he blessed ---them, He was parted from them, and carried up into heaven."

The Coming of the Holy Spirit, the Comforter & His Significance in the Holy Bible

―――――〜∾〜―――――

In the Old Testament, the Holy Spirit is revealed as a divine person. He comes upon whom He will, apparently without reference to conditions in them. The Prophets in the Old Testament wrote revelations of God when the Holy Spirit came upon them. The Old Testament is full of the prophecies about Jesus Christ or the images of God. After Jesus came to the world, He personally revealed the eternal things. Until then nobody knew the details of the Eternal kingdom.

The pre told prophecies in the Old Testament are all about Jesus and the fore plan of God. When the time was fulfilled He presented Himself to the world and spent His time with the human and fulfilled all that was written about Him. After His ascension to the heaven, the people needed a guide or a helper (comforter) in their daily life.

In the New Testament, Jesus Christ at the close of His ministry, He promised that the Holy Spirit would come to abide in them. On evening of His resurrection He came to the disciples in the upper room and breathed on them saying, "receive ye the Holy Spirit" (John 20:22) but He instructed them to wait before beginning their ministry until the Spirit should come upon them. (Luke 24:49; Acts 1–8)

In a few days after His ascension to heaven, on the day of Pentecost the Holy Spirit came upon them. 'When the day of Pentecost arrived, they were all together in one place. ²And suddenly there came from heaven a sound like a mighty rushing wind, and it filled the entire house where they were sitting. ³And divided tongues as of fire appeared to them and rested on each one of them. ⁴And they were all filled with the Holy Spirit and began to speak in other tongues as the Spirit gave them utterance. ⁵Now there were dwelling in Jerusalem Jews, devout men only from every nation under heaven. ⁶And when this sound was heard, the multitude came together, and were confounded, because that every man heard them speaking in his own language.' (Acts 2:1-6) This was the mile stone to remember that Jesus commissioned to evangelize the world. (Mathew28:18-20:Mark16:15-18; Luke24; 47-48; John20:21-22)

Jesus did not wait for 600 years to send the Holy Spirit, the Comforter. He neither had left them alone nor forsaken them without sending the Comforter. And it also came to pass the prophecy of the Prophet Joel, "I will pour out in those days of my Spirit upon all flesh and they shall prophecy" (Joel 2:28-32) He did not deviate from His promise.

After the disciples received the Holy Spirit, they were empowered from above! They could not stop preaching the Gospel. Peter was just an ordinary fisherman. When he preached the Gospel, many people were convicted of their sins. Let us read this passage in Acts 2:38-41. Peter preached only a few simple words, "Repent, and be baptized every one of you in the name of Jesus Christ for the remission of sins, and ye shall receive the gift of the Holy Ghost." With this message many accepted Jesus Christ as their personal savior, and were received the gift of the Holy Spirit. ⁴¹Then they that gladly received his word were baptized: and the same day there was added unto them about three thousand souls.' This is the evidence of the Holy Spirit. It proved the fact that He convicts people about their sins.

After Pentecost the Holy Spirit was imparted to such as believed, in some cases by the laying on of hands of those who already received the Holy Spirit. (Acts 8:17; 9:17) Peter's experience in the conversion of Cornelius (the Gentile in Acts 10) it became clear that Jew or Gentile were to be saved on same conditions and the Holy Spirit was to be given to those who met the one essential condition of trust in Jesus Christ.

Without the Holy Spirit there is no (spiritual) understanding about the fulfillment of the Scripture in Jesus death, resurrection, and they could not understand about the Holy Spirit which Jesus promised them. But when they received the Holy Spirit after Jesus was glorified then they remembered Jesus' promise concerning the Holy Spirit as we read in Luke Gospel 24:49-51. We see the promise of Lord Jesus Christ that was fulfilled in the lives of His disciples. Even these days, lives of the believers witness the faithful promise of Jesus Christ.

Why Jesus Christ has to send the Holy Spirit or the Comforter to His believers? What is the need of His Spirit and His significance? As I mentioned earlier, the people needed a Comforter in His bodily absence. Jesus' other name is Emmanuel (God is with us) He did not want to leave the people without help or guidance.

Jesus Christ as a loving Savior never left them comfortless. Before Jesus left, He told them they would receive the Holy Spirit as a Comforter. He mentioned these terms to make His disciples understand that He was not leaving them lonely. Jesus Christ mentioned the term 'the Holy Spirit the Comforter' in two chapters of John Gospel 14 & 16.

This is one of the seven names of the Holy Spirit. He told His disciples in a simple manner that they could understand. Whoever receives His Spirit shall surely understand the purpose of His Spirit that was sent into a believer. The New Testament distinguishes between having the Spirit which is true to all believers, and being filled with the Holy Spirit. It is another Christian privilege. Jesus said that He needed to depart before the Holy Spirit the Comforter could come. He wanted His disciples to be sealed and bonded by the Holy Spirit, so that they would be capable of perceiving His guidance and continue to do His ministry.

A real believer could understand the great significance of the Holy Spirit or the Comforter through his or her life experience.

Let us see Jesus' statements, concerning the Comforter the Holy Spirit. (John Gospel: 14:16-18, 26; 16:7-8) Please notice the explanation of Jesus Christ about the Comforter.

1. The Comforter or helper will abide with you forever (John 14:16)
2. But the Comforter which is the Holy Spirit whom the Father will send in my name. (John 14:26)
3. For if I go not away, the Comforter will not come unto you: but if I depart, I will send Him unto you. (John 16:7)

Comforter: Greek Parakletos meaning one called alongside to help; thus a helper, a consoler. It is translated 'advocate' in 1 John 2:1, "an advocate with the Father." Christ Jesus is the Christian's Paraclete with the Father when the Christian sins; the Holy Spirit is the Christian's indwelling Paraclete to help His ignorance and infirmity, and to make intercession. (Romans: 8:26-27)

Here is the summary of characteristics of the Holy Spirit if we view the words of Jesus Christ, regarding the Holy Spirit. The references from the Scriptures are quoted below:

1. 'He will glorify me' (John 16.14)
2. 'He will bear witness to me' (John 15.26)
3. 'He will convince the world concerning sin because they do not believe in me' (John 16. 8-9)
4. 'He will take what is mine and declare it to you' (John 16.14)

5. 'He will bring to your remembrance all that I have said to you' (John 14.26)

The believers consider that Jesus Christ's teachings are true since He is 'the speech of Truth.' We need to understand that whoever does not support His teachings are against Him. The verses specified above are a clear understanding to be seen about the nature of the Holy Spirit. The only essential thing is that we have to go forward to receive Him. When we receive Him, the work of regeneration is the first inward work of the Holy Spirit that takes place; this work is called being born again. Once any one receives Him, and then His Spirit will perform full accomplishment in him /her.

His Spirit which a believer receives has seven names in the Holy Bible.

The seven names are as follows: 1.The Spirit of Holiness. 2. The Eternal Spirit. 3. The Comforter. 4. The Spirit of Truth. 5. The Spirit of His son. 6. The Spirit of power, love and sound mind. 7. The Anointing Spirit.

Now Let us discuss about those seven names of His Spirit to understand the truth how important is His Holy Spirit:

1. <u>The Holy Spirit means the Spirit of Holiness</u> (Romans1:4) Jesus, '⁴And declared to be the Son of God with power, according to the Spirit of holiness, by the resurrection from the dead': He lives only in a holy habitation. Once He enters, He enables a person to live a holy life to be His son and daughter to be with Him in His holy city. '¹⁵But as he which hath called you is holy, so be ye holy in all manner of conversation; ¹⁶because it is written, Be ye holy; for I am holy.' (1Peter1:15–16).

2. <u>The Eternal Spirit:</u> The Holy Spirit that we receive from God is the Eternal Spirit. It is clearly explained in 1Corinthians 2:12–14. '¹²Now we have received, not the

spirit of the world, but the Spirit which is of God; that we might knoweth the things that are freely given to us of God. [13]Which things also we speak, not in the words which man's wisdom teacheth, but which the Holy Ghost teacheth; comparing spiritual things with spiritual. [14]But the natural man receiveth not the things of the Spirit of God: for they are foolishness unto him: neither can he know them, because they are spiritually discerned.' (1Corinthians 2:12-14). That is why, even a well educated or learned person can not understand the spiritual things, unless He is born again spiritually, receiving the Eternal Spirit to teach him. Whoever receives the Eternal Spirit can understand the Eternal things. (Hebrews 9:14) '[14]How much more shall the blood of Christ, who through the Eternal Spirit offered himself without spot to God; purge your conscience from dead works to serve the living God?' He purges our conscience to be fit into eternal kingdom. He teaches us to understand the eternal things. He guides us to discern the things to differentiate the earthly things and the heavenly things and helps us to concentrate or focus on the things which are Eternal.

3. <u>The Comforter:</u> (John 14:16-18) '[16]And I will pray the Father, and he shall give you another Comforter, that he may abide with you for ever; [17]Even the Spirit of truth; whom the world cannot receive, because it seeth him not, neither knoweth him: but ye know him; for he dwelleth with you, and shall be in you. [18]I will not leave you comfortless: "I will come to you." Jesus told His disciples that 'The Spirit of truth' comes as a Comforter to dwell in us and shall be in us. He is the one who comforts us. [5]And hope maketh not ashamed; because the love of God is shed abroad in our hearts by the Holy Ghost which is given unto us.' God's great plan of sending His Spirit as a Comforter reveals His infinite wisdom and

immeasurable love towards them who are obedient to Him and they are His children.

He comforts us in many ways.

First of all, He comforts us as a Savior. If a person saves another person, the person who saves never leaves that person until the person is safe and secure. In the same way, the Holy Spirit comforts those who accepts Jesus as their personal savior. God sent the comforter or His Holy Spirit to comfort those who are saved from the Eternal damnation.

Then secondly, He cares us like a father. He loves us as a father. (Hebrews 12:6) '6For whom the Lord loveth he chasteneth, and scourgeth every son whom he receiveth.' He knew how to make us come to His high standard to be called as His son or His daughter and his love is persistent and consistent. He comforts us with the divine love which is infinite, immeasurable, and countless. It is an unexpected and unconditional love.

He comforts us as a mother. Holy Spirit as a comforter punish us as a father and takes us into His loving arms as a mother (Isaiah 66:13) '13As one whom his mother comforteth, so will I comfort you; and ye shall be comforted in Jerusalem' (Jerusalem means His house. In other words it is 'a group of believers' whom we call as a fellowship).

He comforts us as a brother or a family member. (Mathew 12:48-50) '48But he answered and said unto him that told him, who is my mother? And who are my brethren? 49And he stretched forth his hand toward his disciples, and said, behold my mother and my brethren! 50For whosoever shall do the will of my Father which is in heaven, the same is my brother, and sister, and mother." He comforts us as a family member.

He comforts us as a friend. John 15:15. '15Henceforth I call you not servants; for the servant knoweth not what his lord doeth: but I have called you friends; for all things that I have heard of my Father I have made known unto you." He comforts us as a friend. We can go to Him at any time. We have a privilege to talk with him as a dear friend. He will reveal future things and heavenly things to us. I had such a privilege to testify that He is my closest friend that I ever had. He revealed my father's death when he was in a far away country. The next morning, I got a call that my father died. Not only this, He revealed me many, many things even before they were happened.

He is our faithful witness and He comforts us as our Prince. (Revelation 1:5-6) "⁵And from Jesus Christ, who is the faithful witness, and the first begotten of the dead, and the prince of the kings of the earth.⁶And hath made us kings and priests unto God and his Father; to him be glory and dominion for ever and ever. Amen." We have such a great comfort that one day we will be risen from the dead just like Him. He comforts us as our Prince who gives us full safety unto eternity. Unto him that loved us, and washed us from our sins in his own blood, He was dead but he was raised. In the same manner, we also will be raised.

Lastly, He is our Bridegroom. The group of believers considered as His Bride. The Bridegroom will come for his Bride. (Revelation 19:7 and 21:2) "²And I John saw the holy city, New Jerusalem, coming down from God out of heaven, prepared as a bride adorned for her husband."

That's how He loved us with full divine love and comforts us in all aspects of our life. By having the Holy Spirit or His Spirit as a comforter we get all comfort.

4. <u>The Spirit of the Truth:</u> (John16:13) '¹³Howbeit when he, the Spirit of truth, is come, he will guide you into all truth: for he shall not speak of himself; but whatsoever he shall hear, that shall he speak: and he will shew you things to come.' This is such a clear message to understand His plan of salvation and sanctification to enter into His kingdom. Day by day He tells us the coming things, leads us and guides us.

5. <u>The Spirit of His Son:</u> "⁶And because ye are sons, God hath sent forth the Spirit of his Son into your hearts, crying, Abba, Father.⁷Wherefore thou art no more a servant, but a son; and if a son, then an heir of God through Christ.'(Romans 8:6-7) Even though, Father chastens us we have a Spirit of His son to go boldly to his feet to ask him whatever we have needed. We have the promise of Jesus, '²⁴whatsoever ye shall ask the Father in my name, he will give it you. ²⁵Hitherto have ye asked nothing in my name: ask, and ye shall receive, that your joy may be full.' (John 16:24-25) This is such a privilege. We are in no lack of anything except that we have to ask only according to His will. We received all these privileges by having "The Spirit of His Son." We have such a freedom and have every right to go to Father for all our needs. Moreover, in God's plan of redemption, the believer transforms into the image of His son to inherit His Kingdom.

6. <u>The Spirit of Power, the Love and a Sound mind.</u> (11Thimothy 1:7) '⁷For God hath not given us the Spirit of fear; but of power, and of love, and of a sound mind. When we receive His Spirit we boldly give witness about Lord Jesus and the marvelous things that he had done for us. We will have his love poured in us even to love our enemies. And we will have sound mind in all kinds of situations. No fear will enter into us. This Spirit enables us to live boldly in such a fearsome world.

7. <u>The Anointing Spirit:</u> (John 2:27) '²⁷But the anointing which ye have received of him abideth in you, and ye need not that any man teach you: but as the same anointing teacheth you of all things, and is truth, and is no lie, and even as it hath taught you, ye shall abide in him. In our life time we will be safe by having anointed Spirit, which has power to lead us and guide us from false prophets or false Christs, wrong doctrines and teachings.

If we want to see, talk, or to be in touch with God and guided by God, our spirit should be in alliance with the Spirit of God, His Holy Spirit. It is only possible through His Spirit because God is a Spirit being. It is such a great privilege to those who accept Jesus Christ as their Lord and Savior. Because He clearly explained how His Spirit works in us. II Corinthians 3:17 states, "Now the Lord is the Spirit" There is a relationship between the Spirit and the Lord, and both are said to dwell in the believer. (Romans 8:9-11). Galatians 2:20 says, "Christ lives in me." And in Acts 16:6 -7, it states that 'the Holy Spirit and the Spirit of Jesus are the same.'

There is much more to understand the abundant life that we receive through His Spirit which He promised to send on His followers. So far we came to know a very least, not even a glimpse of it from our discussion. It is all the inward work of the Holy Spirit in a believer to sanctify and to protect to have an abundant life in full measure unto the eternity.

The inward work of the Holy Spirit in a believer and living holy are a bit complicated to those who do not know the complexity of the human personality.

The Personality of the Human according to the Holy Bible

The complexity of the human personality is very unique in the sense that God made man in His own image or in His likeness. Many people may wonder how this Holy Spirit works in a person.

The mystery of the creation of the human in the image of God is clearly explained in the Holy Bible. God made man in His own image and in His likeness so that he could have unbroken fellowship and communion with the loving and holy God. God is very holy.

In the Old Testament God told Moses that none could see Him and live. In Hebrew 12:14, it is written, '14Follow peace with all men, and holiness, without which no man shall see the Lord' also in 1Peter 1:16, the word of God says, "Be ye holy; for I am holy." Jesus in His sermon on the mount in Mathew 5:8, said, "Blessed are the pure in heart: for they shall see God." Because of this divine nature of holiness of God, Adam and Eve were cut off from God when they sinned against Him.

According to the Christianity God made Adam. He made a doll with the mud and blew into it His Spirit then man became a living soul. The Spirit of God imparted the life and the trace of His Spirit into the human race whereas the animals were not made in that manner. God made the rest of the creation only by His word. He wanted man in His likeness to commune with him. God with His infinite wisdom made man as a triune like Him. If we retrieve the reference from (Genesis1: 26–27) we understand that how man was made in the image and likeness of God. In this concept man was made with the body, the soul and the spirit.

The first man Adam and Eve were made in His image and were very near to Him. They had very close relationship with God. But it was a tragic incident in which Adam and Eve lost the connection with the Holy God. We have been discussing about this topic in the previous chapters how the same relationship had been rectified by our compassionate God by sacrificing His only begotten son, Jesus Christ. He came to redeem us by His own blood. We have been discussed it that before He left the world, He promised of 'the Holy Spirit.'

Now let us discuss about how a man in the body can receive the Holy Spirit and how the Holy Spirit could impacts the life of a person?

Before we proceed to know the significance of the Holy Spirit, we should know that how we were created in the image of God? And how can we be guided by Him? Or how 'the Spirit of God' works in us? Since God is a Spirit Being we should be like Him to coordinate with Him. Because of this reason we were created with the physical body and the spiritual body.

The human was made up of three components, such as the body, the soul and the spirit. There are quite a few references from the Holy Bible to understand the terms, 'body, soul and spirit.' We could see the difference among these three in these below quotations.

'[12]For the word of God is quick, and powerful, and sharper than any two-edged sword, piercing even to the dividing asunder of soul and spirit, and of the joints and marrow, and is a discerner of the thoughts and intents of the heart.' (Hebrews 4:12) Through this verse we are able to understand that the soul, the spirit and the body responds with the word of God and functions accordingly.

'¹¹Therefore I will not refrain my mouth; I will speak in the anguish of my spirit; I will complain in the bitterness of my soul.' (Job 7:11) Job in the Bible was expressing his suffering from all the three components his body, spirit and soul.

These above references clearly indicated three components of the human. It comprises two parts. One is a physical body system and the other is a spiritual body system. Now let us proceed to know the functions of our physical body and the spiritual body.

1. <u>The Physical Body:</u> The physical body is one of the components of a person. It has different organs to do the different functions to achieve its role. The physical body receives the traits and characteristics from the biological parents and from their generations. The body is the part of a person and identity of a person but is not all of a person. The body can be killed. It has organs, many parts to function as a whole and accomplish the tasks and the wishes of a person. It has five senses with which the physical body can function. Only with the physical body we are able accomplish the things and enjoy in this world.

Once the body is killed, it can not function. As long as the body is alive, the soul and the spirit dwell in it. The body has five senses. The body works with these five senses according to the influence of the spirit in the body. If the spirit is inactive of the spiritual things the body becomes dominant in fulfilling its desires rather than pleasing God. If a spirit is in alliance with the Holy Spirit of God it is in connection with the eternal things. It influences the body towards the eternal things and the body uses all its desires to please God.

Once the body dies we do not see it again with our physical eyes. The dust goes back to the dust as per the word of God and it is true. There are so many opinions and concepts about the death of the physical body.

There are four main theories about the death.

1. The Ending of a Person: In this theory there is no difference to an animal and the man. They believe that the human born like an animal and live in this world and die like an animal. They think man was evolved from a unicellular organism by evolution. But there was not even a simple evidence of super or special generation came out from the mankind since many years. Those who believe this concept are atheists. They do not believe that there is a super natural power, God. In the holy Bible the Palmist wrote that ''The fool hath said in his heart, there is no God. Corrupt are they, and have done abominable iniquity: there is none that doeth good.' (Psalms 53:1)

2. The Deliverance of the Soul from the Body: Some people believe that as long as a soul lives in a body it has no freedom to go wherever it wishes. But once it leaves the body it can go freely according to its wish. There is no evidence for this concept because whoever died never came back to the people to tell that they are very happy after they die or after they left the body. There is no evidence of such incidents.

3. The Incarnation: There are so many beliefs in this concept. Some believe, if they do good works they will be born in a higher level of life in the next birth. And some others believe if some one dies immediately they enter into any available lively form whether animal or human, which about to conceive to become a new birth. They may end up into any lively form like monkey, dog, butterfly, bird or human whatever is available and that too according to their good and bad deeds in the preceded birth. According to this theory we should see a better moral society. But the present society is not

morally better than the people of previous generations. The people even trying their best they are not advancing morally. So this concept is also far away for the truth.

4. The Maha Niryanam: In the Maha Niriyanam a soul merges into the Supreme soul. And never be born in the world. The soul goes into the vast universe. They neither have any proof of nor some evidence of it.

But the Bible or the word of God teaches in a different way about the Death.

There are two the most definitive concepts about the Death in the holy Bible.

1. The death of a person means, the soul temporarily leaves the body. This is the physical death of a person and is the first death or temporary death. The temporary death of the body was explained in the Bible in a very simple manner.

2. Secondly, all the trinity of a person such as the body, the soul and the spirit which are condemned by God will face the Death which is Second Death. The Bible says there will be a final judgment by God. Whoever is condemned by God will face the Second Death which is forever.

According to the Christianity, there is no condemnation in Jesus Christ. There is an eternal assurance in Jesus Christ. Hence the believers don't face 'the Second death.'

The physical death according to the holy Bible is explained in three ways. It is compared to a seed, vapor and sleep.

1. The Seed: There is an explanation in the Bible about the seed of wheat or corn. It was explained in detail. '[37]And that which thou sowest, thou sowest not that body that shall be, but bare grain, it may chance of wheat, or of some other

grain: [38]But God giveth it a body as it hath pleased him, and to every seed his own body.' (I Corinthians 15:37–38) And Jesus Christ said, "[24]Verily, verily, I say unto you, except a corn of wheat fall into the ground and die, it abideth alone: but if it dies, it bringeth forth much fruit."(John 12:24) It explains the simple fact that any seed has to die to give the life again. If a wheat seed is sown only the wheat plant will come out of it. If a corn seed is sown the corn plant comes vice versa. The life of that plant is embedded in the seed. Through this example it is clear that if a person dies the same person will come out of it. No animal or plant will come from the human.

2. <u>The Vapor</u>: The holy Bible says about the human life in a very meaningful way. [14]Whereas ye know not what shall be on the morrow. For what is your life? It is even a vapor that appeareth for a little time, and then vanisheth away. (James 4:14) The waters from the water sources they evaporate and come back again as waters. The waters which were evaporated never came back as milk, honey or other things. The man's death can be explained in the same way. The human dies temporarily and again the same person will be coming back on God's appointed time.

3. <u>The Sleep</u>: Lord Jesus Christ in John Gospel 11:11 went to raise Lazarus who was dead and had lain in the grave for four days. "[11]And after that he saith unto them, our friend Lazarus sleepeth; but I go, that I may awake him out of sleep." Lazarus came out alive from the grave with the power of His words. This incident was written in the Gospels. If a person is in a deep sleep he or she can not know any thing what is going on around them. In the same way our body sleeps for sometime until Lord comes. Again the same body will rise up.

All these above examples reveal the truth that one day everyone will rise up with the same body.

Jesus Christ is an example. He died and was kept in the grave. He rose again on the third day with glorious body. His tomb was empty. Even The angels testified the truth that he had raised. That is the reason Jesus Christ clarified the Truth in John Gospel 11:25, '25Jesus said unto her, "I am the resurrection, and the life: he that believeth in me, though he was dead, yet shall he live." There is no one on the earth that defeated the death except Lord Jesus Christ. Not every one in the world has a hope of the eternity. Many people have a question of what happens after we die. This question is bothering the people throughout the ages.

Along with the physical body, there is a spiritual body. The physical body dies but it will rise up as a spiritual body when Lord comes. As it is written in 1Corinthians 15:44, "44It is sown a natural body; it is raised a spiritual body. There is a natural body, and there is a spiritual body.'

The spiritual body comprises the soul and the spirit.

The second component of the human is the soul. It plays such a great role in the human. As God declared man as 'a living soul,' it means the soul lives forever.

2. <u>The Soul:</u> When God gave His breath, man became a living soul. The 'Life' came from God and is continuing in the mankind. The Soul is a real person or inner personality but the identity is only with the Physical body. The soul is the real person varies from person to person in intellect to think, emotions and will power to say yes or no to respond. So the soul is the seat of the affections, the thoughts, images, the desires, emotions, and the will of man. The soul is the individuality of a person so as the physical body. The soul can not be killed by any means but soul is in the

hands of God. Once a person is born, his or her soul is there forever.

The soul influences the body. The soul has will power to lean on either way, body as well as the spirit. Only according to its will, the soul is influenced by the spirit. The soul is not satisfied until it reaches its serenity. The soul attains serenity only when it is under the control of the Spirit of God from where it gets discernment to weigh the earthy things and the heavenly things. Since the soul came to the human with the breath of God, it never satisfies even it achieves the things of the world in full measure. That is the reason we come across many suicides of young famous and rich people in this world. Even though they achieve earthly excellence, they still have lack in their lives and they were not satisfied. They craved for some thing which they could not understand and their life on the earth.

Here below are some of the quotations to understand what the soul is meant for a person. We read in Mathew 11:28-29, '[28]come unto me, all ye that labor and are heavy laden, and I will give you rest. [29]Take my yoke upon you, and learn of me; for I am meek and lowly in heart: and ye shall find rest unto your souls.' In this verse Lord Jesus Christ is inviting every one whoever wanted to have the rest for their souls. He gave full assurance to give rest to our souls.

Jesus Christ's soul was exceedingly sorrowful in His human form because the people were not recognizing for what purpose He came to the world. Even though this eternal plan of God was foretold in the scripture, yet the people could not recognize the plan of His coming to the world. He came to the world to bear all the sins of the mankind to make sinful man into a pure and holy person so that he will be fit to enter into the holy abode of God. Jesus knew that 'this very act' which is very difficult for His holiness and sinless ness, and at the same time He was separated from the word 'Holy God' at the moment when He bore the sins of all the people on the cross and it was unbearable and gruesome. Because of that reason His soul was extremely sorrowful. It is written, '[38] then saith he unto them, "My soul is exceeding sorrowful, even unto death: tarry ye here, and watch with me." (Mathew 26:38)

3. <u>The Spirit:</u> The spirit is the third component of the human. As we knew that God breathed into Adam's nostrils, there came life. Along with it, the Spirit of God also was imparted to Adam. All the generations inherited the same spirit which was given by God to communicate with God and to be connected with Him since God is a Spirit being.

Our spirit is the source of God's Spirit which has the power to control our body and the soul. God's Spirit is holy but when sin entered into man's spirit, it became unholy ceased to receive message from God. Thence there was no communication with the Spirit of God. Man was ceased to hear God's voice. And was not able to see Him or walk with Him. In other words there is a huge barrier in between God and the man. The spirit was dead to the spiritual things or the heavenly things. It became unholy, and dead to be in communion with God when sin entered into the first man Adam. He was disconnected from God.

The dead spirit can be recharged or revived by either the influence of the Holy Spirit or the Unholy Spirit.

The spirit has three parts: the Conscience, the Worship and the Intuition.

1. The Conscience: The Conscience is the moral responsibility. It is the inner voice which says right or wrong on every turn of our life. But as we neglect or reluctant to that voice, eventually our inner ears to hear that voice become handicapped or become deaf.

2. The Worship: The inner eyes have longing to see God or to know about God and there is passion for Him. How can I

find God? There is a desire to commune with God. Hope towards unseen in helpless conditions, expecting help from a super power (God) for a miracle to happen in life. Some people want to find God in nature, buildings, place or rituals etc. Because of the thirst for the true peace, love and joy. (These are the fruits of the Spirit)

3. The Instinct or Intuition: All of a sudden we see an unexpected person coming into our house, say a family member or a friend, even though not visible to our physical eyes. In a few minutes we see that person knocks at the door, we see it in our soul with communication, only when we led by the Spirit. The instinct thoughts are such as "get up and go from here or to go and see so and so or let me find out how my sister is doing" This type of instinct thoughts for a special purpose are conveyed only through the spirit in our soul. I have this kind of experience many times in my life. When a person's spirit is in complete alliance with the Holy Spirit then only he or she will come to know God's consciousness. It makes the person to act right in front of God.

Here are some references from the Holy Bible for the understanding and to clarify the word 'the spirit.'

There is a proverb in the Bible. 'The spirit of man is the candle of the LORD, searching all the inward parts of the belly.' (Proverbs 20:27) The candle of the Lord what God gave to our first parents was put off by Satan because of 'the will' which they had. Their candles were put out. But it is possible only to God to light it. Psalmist says, '28for thou wilt lights my candle: the LORD my God will enlighten my darkness.' (Psalms. 18:28)

In the personality of the human only the spirit could understand the inspiration of God. It is written in the Bible, '8but there is a spirit in man: and the inspiration of the Almighty giveth them understanding.' (Job 32:8)

In 1 Corinthians 2:11, it says, '[11]For what man knoweth the things of a man, save the spirit of man which is in him? Even so the things of God knoweth no man, but the Spirit of God. It explains why we need our spirit to be kept pure and holy so that God's Holy Spirit come in contact with our spirit. If we have the Spirit of God we come to know the spiritual things."

It is a must to understand the concepts of the human creation to understand the real purpose of the human creation. God created Adam and Eve in His image and gave them dominion on all of His creation. Man was created in innocence, placed in a perfect environment. He commanded them not to eat the fruit of the knowledge of good and evil, thou shalt not eat of it: for in the day that thou eatest thereof thou shalt surely die."(Genesis 2:17) Here we noticed the warning of God, 'thou shalt surely die.' They both did eat it and disobeyed God. But now they came to know the good and the evil.

As per the commandment of God, they both were dead spiritually and their soul was darkened and their body was defiled. In that way Adam and Eve were sinned against God and they had threefold downward fall.

They lost connection with God. The sin that they committed became a barrier in between God and the man. Since God is holy there is no place for the sin in front of God. They were driven out from the Paradise. God was out of their sight. The punishment of the sin is death as God said so. As per His word, the consequences are the physical death and the spiritual death. But the life that God had given was preserved in an unseen way because of His grace. The same concept we already discussed in the aspect of our physical body.

The death became universal. Every one dies, some as a fetus who are not being born, some as little children, old, low, great, good, bad, rich and poor. There is no difference or the age limit for the death. Whoever is born has to die. The sin of the first man and the woman brought this universal effect to all of their generations.

The one judgment of God by sending them away from Him came upon all the men as an Eternal condemnation. It is continued from them unto all the generations. We all are carrying the same traits. It is written, '23For all have sinned, and come short of the glory of God.' (Romans 3:23)

God by being known the future of the human, He had His plans to save us from the Eternal damnation. Our creator, our Father who made us loved us and He is rich in His mercy. His grace is so abundant.

It is written in the holy Bible, "1And you were dead in the trespasses and sins 2in which you once walked, following the course of this world, following the prince of the power of the air, the spirit that is now at work in the sons of disobedience- 3among whom we all once lived in the passions of our flesh, carrying out the desires of the body and the mind, and were by nature the children of wrath, like the rest of mankind. 4But God, being rich in mercy, because of the great love with which he loved us, 5even when we were dead in our trespasses, made us alive together with Christ—by grace you have been saved." (Ephesians 2:1-5)

Yet, some people are not aware of the grace of God and are not realizing that the people are the living temple of God. The Satan which put off the candle of light which God kept in the human race by deceiving Adam and Eve. They gave chance to the Satan by not believing the words of God. The same thing is happening through out the history of the mankind. It is written, "4In whom the god of this world hath blinded the minds of them which believe not, lest the light of the glorious gospel of Christ, who is the image of God, should shine unto them." (11Corinthians 4:4) God said, "16Know ye not that ye are the temple of God, and that the Spirit of God dwelleth in you? 17If any man defile the temple of God, him shall God destroy; for the temple of God is holy, which temple ye are."(1Corinthians 3:16-17) In these stated verses from the holy Bible, it clearly explains us that our spirit was dead, our minds were blinded and our body was defiled.

Every one ought to stand before the judgment seat of God. As He is our creator every one has to give account to God for the things that were done by him/her. It is written that, '[10]For we must all be made manifest before the judgment-seat of Christ; that each one may receive the things done in the body, according to what he hath done, whether it be good or bad.' (11Corinthians 5:10)

Here we have a question. How every one's works could appear to God? The word of God is very clear to make us understand this concept. In Jeremiah 17:1, God says, "[1]The sin of Judah is written with a pen of iron, and with the point of a diamond: it is graven upon the table of their heart, and upon the horns of your altars." Guilty stains by sinful thoughts, words and deeds; whatever we do everything is being recorded. When man is able to grasp the sound waves how much more God could do? He could do unimaginable things. In the above verse, God said, it is graven upon the table of our hearts. That is why the heart that was not repented, not forgiven or not cleansed is not inhabited by the Holy Spirit of God. He could not live in a filthy place. Instead the evil spirits come and live in it.

Those guilty stains should be washed out and be cleansed. The only solution that could reverse this terrible condition is 'the holy blood of Lord Jesus Christ,' which cleanses our trespasses, sins and purges our conscience. In Hebrews 9:14, we read, '[14]How much more shall the blood of Christ, who through the Eternal Spirit offered himself without spot to God, purge your conscience from dead works to serve the living God?' Because of this wonderful act, a sinner can be cleansed and worthy enough for the habitation of the Holy Spirit.

Then the Holy Spirit comes and lives in our spirit to renew or regenerate the dead spirit. Then we could hear Him clearly. It will reverse its direction and we will become a new person with new faculties. The conscience once dead will become sensitive. Now a vast difference will occur. We feel miserable for a sinful thought or to tell a lie. It is very difficult to deceive others. Gradually we lose our selfishness. If we do anything wrong in the sight of God we will be restless until we confess, repent and determine not to do it again. We try to spend more time with God. There is a hunger for God's word, longing to know about the Eternal things.

It is possible to any person; any background any nature, any community, any character and any nation. The same result will occur. They will become stronger and stronger day by day with the nourishment of the word, prayer and fellowship. The miraculous deed of this transformation of man is only possible to God who is a Spirit Being. Hence by giving us the spirit, God gave us a privilege to interact with His Holy Spirit to transform us into His likeness so that we will be fit for His presence by regaining all three downward fall of a person.

The following verses from the word of God are the examples to explain this concept more clearly. '¹⁶Know ye not that ye are the temple of God, and that the Spirit of God dwelleth in you?'(1 Corinthians 3:16) '¹⁹What? know ye not that your body is the temple of the Holy Ghost which is in you, which ye have of God, and ye are not your own?' (1 Corinthians 6:19)

The factors like biological inheritance, physical environment, culture, socialization, group experience, and unique individual experience are also play a role on a person's life but the influence of the word of God, prayer, fellowship and especially power of the Holy Spirit plays major role and it convicts the believer instantaneously from falling into the sin. The life of a person will turn into different direction which leads his/her unto the eternity. There are so many believers with their life changing experience became as witnesses of Jesus Christ to others.

There are so many life examples: Starting with Jesus' disciples, they became so powerful and their lives were changed when they filled with the Holy Spirit. As we read in the other chapters of this book, Saul changed to Paul. Once he was against to Jesus Christ but he committed his life to Christ. My brother was an alcoholic, smoker. Now he is a faithful witness of Jesus Christ. Who could change the lives in such a way? The new beginning of the believer starts by the indwelling of the Holy Spirit. It is possible only to the creator. I mentioned in this paragraph only a few examples but there are vast majority of people of different back grounds were changed and are the witnesses of Christ. This is only through the influence of the Holy Spirit.

There will be a fresh start when we reborn into a spiritual family. We start hearing His voice and feel His presence wherever we are. By my experience I truly say it is such a joy, unspeakable and full of glory. Our intuition power will be increased. We will get the Spiritual gifts such as healing power, prophesying, teaching the word of God--and we discern the things which are not of God etc. These gifts are all from the Holy Spirit. We will become new creatures. '17Therefore if any man be in Christ, he is a new creature: old things are passed away; behold all things are become new. (2 Corinthians 5:17)

The newborn is separated from the world and become a member of the spiritual family. Slowly the believer grows with the word of God, prayer, fellowship and taking part in the Holy Communion. Eventually attains the image of Christ. If the spirit is connected with the Holy Spirit, then there is communication with God and to the heavenly things and the life will be led by God. The result is, the person who is led by God have pure conscience and do good deeds and keeps the body undefiled. The soul will be brightened and the spirit remains holy. There is longing to do the will of God. All the three components of a person will be in accordance with God and fit to live with God in His abode.

If the spirit of a person is influenced by the evil spirit then the life of a person will be led by the evil or Satan. Or a person can lead his or her life by the desires of the flesh and the soul. If our Spirit is not able to hear the voice of the Holy Spirit, it will be influenced by the soul and the body. In this aspect the spirit is not that guides the soul and the body. The bodily desires with the emotions of the soul influence our life without any discernment. As long as a person lives in sin he or she can not feel the presence of God, can not enjoy His power, and can not hear His voice.

In addition to those he or she is unable to enjoy His true peace. The result of it is the pride, selfishness, self will, anger, jealousy, thoughts of bitterness, hatred and all kinds of evil nature. Then all the trinity of a person such as the body, the soul and the spirit condemned for ever, will face the Death which is the Second Death. The Bible says there will be a final judgment by God. Whoever is condemned will face the second death. This Eternal condemnation first came in the Garden of Eden. It is continuing in the humanity to face the Eternal damnation.

Some people don't believe that there is Satan and evil spirits. But according to the Holy Bible, we do have a clue that God made the earth and other creation before the creation of the present earth. We never know how many times He made the creations.

In Genesis 1:2, before the creation there was the earth which was merged in waters and there was darkness all over. It was void and without form. The Bible is the only resource where there are some hints that angel Lucifer with his angels was cast down when he rebelled against God. (Isaiah 14: 7-17; Ezekiel 28:12; Isaiah 45:18; Jude 1:6; Revelation 12:9) Because of these references from the Bible there is a scope to believe the divine judgment interpretation on the status of the Old Earth. (Genesis 1:2) There is no clue to grasp the time period how long the earth was under the waters and was in the darkness. The Scripture gives no data for determining how long ago the universe was created. Later in 9th and 10th verses, God cleared the earth by His word to dry and named it as the earth. He created man on the sixth day in His image as triune like Him.

As we are analyzing the facts, we have a question why Satan was there at that time to deceive Adam and Eve in the Garden. As there are references from the word of God which were mentioned in the above paragraph we could come to an understanding that the Satan Lucifer was there on the doomed earth with his angels. And He pursued the human whom God had created in His own image to be His companions. Satan tried his best to take the human along with him to the Eternal damnation which is the Second death.

The first parents of all the nations or the human race were reluctant to the commandment of God and ate the forbidden fruit which was the cause of death. They were attracted by looking the tree that was good for food, and that it was pleasant to the eyes, and a tree to be desired to make one wise, Eve took of the fruit thereof, and did eat, and gave also unto her husband with her; and Adam did eat. The same way the generations of them are doing the same thing in the world. Instead of hearing the voice of God they are inclining their ears to the Satan by having desires which are against to God. Yet the love of God was not ceased.

The first attempt of God in saving Adam and Eve was, He killed an animal. The life of an animal was sacrificed and the blood was sprinkled. This was the first and foremost sign we see how God gave them the protection. This is the first sign of sacrifice. Life needs to be taken off to make skin coats for their complete protection but the blood is the life. Now we understand that God did sacrifice to get them skin coats. Their physical shame was recovered. The first covering was physical and was the forerunner for the second which was spiritual. Jesus Christ came to the world and put to an end to the sacrifices. He offered His sinless blood to cleanse our sins. His blood is the only source to cover from the punishment and cleanse the sinner so that the Holy Spirit of God comes and lives in the human.

When our spirit is sensitive to the Holy Spirit, our soul will be coordinating accordingly to the influence of the Holy Spirit and the body will be guided by the soul of that particular person. The physical body does the things by the discipline applied by our soul influenced by the Holy Spirit. The attitudes, desires, way of thinking will be changed. The result of it is the pure conscience and full worship for God. The spiritual talents and gifts that were enhanced by the Holy Spirit will be used for God's glory.

God never force any person to love Him or to come to Him. He gave us free will. As we knew even Adam and Eve were given freedom to choose or to decide whether to obey God or disobey. They acted according to their own will. Yet the plan of God in creating the human race was not changed. His love for the human was not ceased. He is lovingly inviting all the people to come to have relationship with Him to talk and walk with Him and enter into His kingdom to be with him forever.

This is the main purpose of God in making the human in His image or in His likeness. God is triune and so is the human. The holy Bible explained very well why God said; now let us make man in our image, after our likeness: and let them have dominion over the fish of the sea, over the fowl of the air, and over the cattle, and over all the earth, and over every creeping thing that creepeth upon the earth.(Genesis 1:26)

He did not give the privilege to the angels to rule the coming kingdom of God. His purpose was never changed. God who is our creator made us in His image to be His sons and daughters to reign with Him forever.

The evidence and the accomplishments of the Holy Spirit as a True Divine Entity according to the Holy Bible

There are plenty of the evidences and the accomplishments of the Holy Spirit in the believers starting from the departure of Jesus Christ until this day. Lord Jesus Christ promised that the Holy Spirit will come upon those who believe in Him. He knew how much the Holy Spirit was needed to the believer to be guided and comforted in this world.

It is impossible to a person to live separately from the evil walk of this world and to appear holy in the presence of God without the guidance of the Holy Spirit. We ourselves just like Adam and Eve, have no strength to resist the devil and lusts of the human flesh. But once we receive the Holy Spirit, we shall see the difference in our lives. There are many evidences to prove that there is a great deal of difference in the people's lives after they received the Holy Spirit.

Let us start with the evidence of the Holy Spirit from the New Testament. Early church Apostle Peter one of the disciples of Jesus Christ, after receiving the Holy Spirit he did many miracles. He gave powerful messages even though he was a fisherman. Here there is one illustration from the Bible in the book of Acts 5:1-6. It shows the power of the Holy Spirit. We will be able to understand how the Holy Spirit guides and reveals the things to the believers.

5.'¹But a certain man named Ananias, with Sapphira his wife, sold a possession, ²And kept back part of the price, his wife also being privy to it, and brought a certain part, and laid it at the apostles' feet. ³But Peter said, Ananias, why hath Satan filled thine heart to lie to the Holy Ghost, and to keep back part of the price of the land? ⁴Whiles it remained, was it not thine own? And after it was sold, was it not in thine own power? Why hast thou conceived this thing in thine heart? Thou hast not lied unto men, but unto God. ⁵And Ananias hearing these words fell down, and gave up the ghost: and great fear came on all them that heard these things. ⁶And the young men arose, wound him up, and carried him out, and buried him.' (Acts 5:1-6)

In this above narration, Peter the disciple of Jesus Christ came to know the truth that the couple hide some money and lied to the Apostles. The Holy Spirit revealed Peter that Ananias lied about the money. Otherwise there was no other way to find out their lie.

In Acts 5:14-16, 'Peter the disciple of Jesus preached.¹⁴And believers were the more added to the Lord, multitudes both of men and women.¹⁵Insomuch that they brought forth the sick into the streets, and laid them on beds and couches, that at the least the shadow of Peter passing by might overshadow some of them.¹⁶There came also a multitude out of the cities round about unto Jerusalem, bringing sick folks, and them which were vexed with unclean spirits: and they were healed every one.' This was not because of Peter's own strength but because of the Holy Spirit.

The second example is whoever receives the Holy Spirit could do even greater things as per Jesus' promise. As it is written in the Bible whoever touched Paul's clothes, were healed because of the power of the Holy Spirit.

Lord Jesus Christ knew how much help we are needed in His absence. He was in this world as an Emmanuel (God is with us). Then in His absence, He sent His Holy Spirit to live in us and so that His work is being continued and done until He receives us to Him.

Jesus Christ promised that He never leaves us alone in our journey as a believer. Jesus promised to give us the power of the Holy Spirit, to make us His sons and daughters, to be His disciples and to do even greater things than He did. Since then, numerous miracles were happened and are still happening among the believers. These days too, the Holy Spirit is doing His powerful things, guiding and leading the believers in all kinds of situations.

Only those who are born again Christians are being lead and guided by the Holy Spirit. It is true. I experienced such things in my life too. Let me share a simple incident with you. Once I went to a city for a particular purpose. I stayed a few days in my friend's house. I completed the work but my friend requested me to extend my trip, so that I can attend her brother's wedding. My friend planned to reserve bus tickets for three of us. Her colleague and I agreed to go to the wedding with her. Early in the next morning, I had a dream in my sleep that I was going in a train heading to my father's house instead of traveling with my friends in the bus. I woke up and told my friends about my dream at that night. They laughed and said, "No! No! You will be coming with us. Let us get ready to go to reserve the bus tickets." We all got ready to go out to the bus station.

We were about to lock the door to go to the bus station. Postman came to the door and delivered a telegram. We all three were stunned. My brother gave me a telegram. "Father is serious, start immediately." I was so sad. My friends said, "Please do not worry, let us first go to the train station and try our best to buy a ticket for you so that you will be going to your father's house. That same day was a festival day. It was very hard to obtain a seat without reservation. Luckily, I was able to purchase a train ticket. Finally, I got into a seat in the train heading to my father's house.

My friends reminded my dream and were astonished. That's how the Holy Spirit reveals us the upcoming things. Such a privilege to the true believers of Christ! [13]Howbeit when he, the Spirit of truth, is come, he will guide you into all truth: for he shall not speak of himself; but whatsoever he shall hear, that shall he speak: and he will shew you things to come.' (John 16:13)

I had seen many miraculous things with my own eyes. My father was diagnosed with liver failure in his forties. One God servant, Bakht Singh, laid his hands upon my father and prayed for him in the name of the Father, the Son and the Holy Ghost, and my father was healed right away and lived eighty-seven years with sound health without any intervention of doctors. God has done several miracles in my family, and has revealed upcoming events through dreams (visions) and He talks directly through the Holy Bible.

We feel the presence of God in many ways. We may hear still soft voice in our ears. He gives us instantaneous guidance; sometimes we get sudden understanding of new truth. If there is any difficult situation to face, He may wake you up to spend time with Him on your knees to get strength to be strong. Same thing happened to me before I lost my second daughter.

Many people do not take part of this wonderful blessing because they are spiritually blind and are on their own efforts to reach the kingdom of God.

Dear reader, every religion teaches us to do good works to get into the heaven, but in whatever "good works" we do, we can never attain God's righteousness, because God is the most holy. Only through His Holy Spirit we will be living holy not with our own effort. Mankind is always weak and prone to fall in the spiritual walk. Only if He gives His righteousness, then we will be righteous. That is the reason; God hath sealed us by His own Spirit to change us into His image or likeness from glory to glory. Once we might be useless and hopeless but when his Holy Spirit comes and dwell in us we will be changed into his likeness and useful to many.

It is written in 2 Corinthians1:22 and 3:18, '22 who hath also sealed us, and given the earnest of the Spirit in our hearts. 18 But we all, with open face beholding as in a glass the glory of the Lord, are changed into the same image from glory to glory, even as by the Spirit of the Lord.'

It is an endless effort for a man to attain His holiness. It is only by the grace of God and the help through the Holy Spirit we are able to be holy to enter into the heaven. "[8]For it is by grace you have been saved, through faith — and this is not from yourselves, it is the gift of God — [9]not by works, so that no one can boast." (Ephesians 2:8-9)

Thus we need the Holy Spirit to attain the holiness; He is our guide, helper and the comforter. Only those who are sealed by the Holy Spirit are able to lead a holy life. You already had read the complete plan of God in sending His son and His spirit into our heart. Jesus said in John 16:7: '[7]Nevertheless I tell you the truth; it is expedient for you that I go away: for if I go not away, the Comforter will not come unto you; but if I depart, I will send him unto you.' And He did it.

In order for us to receive the Holy Spirit all we have to do is to believe by faith that Jesus Christ came to the world to save sinners, only His blood can cleanse a sinner. It is a wise thing to be obedient to confess and repent for the sinful life. Jesus Christ has already done everything for us to obtain the eternal life! He has fulfilled the will of the Most Holy God. The Holy Spirit continues to do His work until the second return of Jesus Christ. The secret is the group of the believers whoever believe in Him are His body. As we are His body the Holy Spirit who lives in us makes the body of Christ as pure as He is.

The coming of the Holy Spirit and His Significance according to the Noble Qur'an

In the Noble Qur'an, we see that Gabriel is the Holy and Honest Bearer of Revelations. Gabriel considered as the Holy Spirit. This information we read from the Qur'an 2:97.

Here below are the verses from the Qur'an: These references are indeed talking about the angel Gabriel. In 2:97 'Say, "Anyone who opposes Gabriel should know that he has brought down this (Qur'an) into your heart, in accordance with God's will, confirming previous Scriptures (The Torah), and providing guidance and good news for the believers." Here it seems that angel Gabriel has power to enter into a person's heart.'[16:102] Say: "The Holy Spirit hath revealed it from thy Lord with truth, that it may confirm (the faith of) those who believe, and as guidance and good tidings for those who have surrendered (to Allah)"

[26:192-193] And lo! It is a revelation of the Lord of the worlds, which the True Spirit hath brought down. [Pickthall] In the Qur'an the angel Gabriel was mentioned as the true spirit)The following verses are directly taken from the Qur'an and are also talking about the angel Gabriel.[2:87] 'We gave Moses the scripture, and subsequent to him we sent other messengers, and we gave Jesus, son of Mary, profound miracles and supported him with the Holy Spirit. Is it not a fact that every time a messenger went to you with anything you disliked, your ego caused you to be arrogant? Some of them you rejected, and some of them you killed.'[2:253]

'These messengers; we blessed some of them more than others. For example, GOD spoke to one, and we raised some of them to higher ranks. And we gave Jesus, son of Mary, profound miracles and supported him with the Holy Spirit.' [19:17-19] 'While a barrier separated her from them, we sent to her our Spirit. He went to her in the form of a human being. She said, "I seek refuge in the Most Gracious, that you may be righteous." He said, "I am the messenger of your Lord, to grant you a pure son." (Here in this verse angel Gabriel mentioned that He is the messenger of Lord to grant Mary a pure son)

All these above phrases from the Qur'an tell us that the Holy Spirit is angel Gabriel. Gabriel can not live in every human being. The angels are the spirits but there is no evidence of living in the human. There are some angels that sinned against God. There is evidence that God did not spare when angels sinned against Him.

In all these verses in the Quran, there is no intimate connection of God with our Spirit. According to the Qur'an, we human beings are from the dust and clot of a blood. There is no scope of getting holiness. Hence every Muslim has to go through the hell fire to be cleansed. Then they ask the prophets for help. With the help of the Prophet Muhammad a good person will go to the paradise but bad person will end up in hell fire. But the prophet himself had no surety to go to paradise. He relied on Jesus for the rescue of his soul.

[5:110] 'GOD will say, "O Jesus, son of Mary, remember My blessings upon you and your mother. I supported you with the Holy Spirit, to enable you to speak to the people from the crib, as well as an adult. I taught you the scripture, wisdom, the Torah, and the Gospel.'

In the above verse Allah sent Jesus with the scripture, wisdom, Torah and the Gospel. He taught the people with demonstration. He came to confirm the previous Scripture.

But the Qur'an [2:97] Say, "Anyone who opposes Gabriel should know that he has brought down this (Qur'an) into your heart, in accordance with God's will, confirming previous scriptures, and providing guidance and good news for the believers." Here in this preceding verse Gabriel came to confirm the previous scripture. He brought into the hearts of the people as per the Qur'an. But the people need to understand the previous scripture which is the Torah and the Old Testament.

The angel Gabriel brought the Qur'an into the hearts of the people. How the people could coordinate with the angel Gabriel. When angel Gabriel brought Quran to Muhammad he was frantic with fear and attempted suicide. Muhammad said, "O Kadija (his wife), I see light, hear sounds and I fear I am mad." When the prophet himself was so frightened with the angel Gabriel, how every person could get the Qur'an into their hearts by the angel Gabriel?

If angel Gabriel is the Holy Spirit, could he dwells in a person? Is there any evidence that he dwells in the heart of any one? The Muslims believe that the prophet Muhammad saw angel Gabriel (Jibreel) a few times. When angel Gabriel visited the prophet Muhammad he was afraid. But we never had a record saying that angel Gabriel lived in the Prophet Muhammad or any other person in the world. God did not create angels in His image to live in the human. But God created mankind in His likeness.

In the Islam a believer can not walk with God in a daily life because God is very distant. Instead of explaining that God made man in His likeness, it was deviated from the concept by saying that the human was made with many states of 'Self.' In Islam there is no coordination of man with God or walking with God in daily life or hearing His voice. There is no such explanation in the Islam.

The Personality of the Human according to the Islam

The Islam is based on the Bible to begin with the Adam as the first human who was created by God in His likeness.

There are two theories in the Islam: 1. Adam the first man was made in the image of God or in His likeness.

Narrated Abu Huraira, the companion of the Prophet Muhammad: The Prophet said, "Allah created Adam in HIS IMAGE, sixty cubits (about 30 meters) in height. When He created him, Allah said (to him), 'Go and greet that group of angels sitting there, and listen what they will say in reply to you, for that will be your greeting and the greeting of your offspring." Adam (went and) said, '(Peace be upon you).' They replied, '(Peace and Allah's Mercy be on you).' So they increased 'wa Rahmatullah' The Prophet added, 'so whoever will enter Paradise, will be of the shape and picture of Adam.

Abu Huraira reported Allah's Messenger as saying: Allah, the Exalted and Glorious, created Adam in His own image with His length of sixty cubits. So he who would get into the paradise would get in the form of Adam, his length being sixty cubits, then the people who followed him continued to diminish in size up to this day. (Sahih Muslim, book 040, number 6809)

According to the above narration, the prophet Muhammad explained that Allah created Adam in His image. When Adam disobeyed, Allah sent him out of the Garden of Eden. In the (Qur'an 7:19-22; 20:121-122) Allah said, "And you Adam, dwell in the garden, you and your wife, and eat of whatever you two want; but do not approach this tree, for then you would be transgressors."

Then Satan whispered to the two, to reveal to them their private parts, which had been concealed from them; "your Lord only prohibited you from this tree lest you two become angels, or you become immortals." And he swore to them, "I am an advisor to you." Thus he led them by false hopes: when they tasted of the tree, their private parts became evident to them, and they began to sew together leaves from the garden over them. Then their Lord called to them. "Did I not forbid you from that tree and tell you Satan is an open enemy to you?"

2. The second concept of human creation is that 'Man' is born in a natural state of purity.(Fitrat al Islam)
3. The Islam believes that human beings have within them the ability to leave this state of nature into something unnatural. This potential to do what is unnatural and harmful to the "Self" is based on mankind's free will. Thus in order to return to the natural state of purity, man must gain control over the potential for wrong within him. Taking advantage of the free will through the use of the intellect man can apply revelation in choosing what is right and thus reawaken the recognition of fitrah in him.

Muslims believe that although man is not born evil, he is vulnerable to evil stimuli or external sources of misguidance.

This property of the human constitution, to be vulnerable to wrong, is intrinsic to man. The emotional and biological impulses of man are not inherently evil, but are susceptible to such evil stimuli. Thus they need to be controlled and directed in accordance with divinely prescribed laws so that the "Self (nafs)" can be transformed into the highest level of spiritual achievement. [xl]

According to the Qur'an, all psychological phenomena originate in the Self. The Self is essence of man, and is often referred by one of four terms in Arabic.

1. Qulb (heart)
2. Ruh (soul)
3. Nafs (desire nature) personality and behavior
4. Aqi (intellect/reason)

Each of these signifies a spiritual entity. According to some explanations there are two words in Arabic: Nafs (soul) and Ruh (spirit) In the Quran 17:85, they will ask thee concerning the spirit, say: The spirit is by command of my Lord and of the knowledge ye have been vouchsafed but little. It explains that the spirit is a separated thing. The spirit shapes up according to the deeds that were done by the body.
There are several states of the Self.

1. Lower Self- Qur'an 12:53. "Yet I do not exonerate myself; for the self is certainly compulsive with evil unless my Lord has mercy; for my Lord is most forgiving, most merciful." This Self is prone to lower aspects of the Self, representing negative drives in man.
2. The self – reproaching Self – Qur'an 75:2. "And I swear by the accusing self." This state corresponds to the Self when it becomes aware of wrong – doing and feels remorse.

167

3.   The peaceful Self– Qur'an 89:27-28. "O tranquil soul, "return to your Lord, pleased and accepted." This is the state of inner peace and happiness, when you feel satisfied and content in yourself. This is the state that aiming to achieve.

The state of 'the Self' is dependent on many different faculties and powers. Thus the Islamic personality is influenced by a variety of factors including: biological inheritance, physical environment, culture, socialization, group experience, and unique individual experience.

Therefore in the Islam, only through the self, one has to do the good deeds and obey divine laws. This concept was failed since the beginning. Even the great prophets committed mistakes. Adam was the first man made by God in His image, in purity and innocence. Yet he could not stand firm on God's command even though God warned him the consequences. God used Moses to lead all His people yet Moses committed mistakes. All most all the prophets committed sin except Jesus.

In the Islam the Prophet Muhammad said that Adam was created in the image of God but it was not explained why God created Adam in His image or in His likeness. The Qur'an could not stand on the point in which the human is in the image of God. It did not explain why God was mentioned as plurals "We" in some of the statements? Why God made man in his likeness? What is the purpose of God in creating the human in His likeness? Why God did not make the angels in His image or in His likeness? There are many question marks that yet to be answered in the Qur'an.

The Life experience of the Prophet Muhammad as a comforter

The Muslims believe that God sent Muhammad as a comforter. Was the Prophet Muhammad a Comforter to the whole world that Jesus Christ promised to send?

Most of the people are getting into confusion about this matter. Jesus Christ promised before His ascension that He would send the Holy Spirit, the Comforter to live in a believer. According to the Bible, this promise of Jesus Christ was fulfilled within the seven days. The Holy Spirit came upon them on the day of Pentecost which was right after seven days of His ascension. According to the Bible, Jesus did not wait more than 600 years to send the Comforter to His disciples or whoever believes in Him. There was almost 600 years gap in between Jesus and Muhammad.

Muhammad was a shining example to his people. His house, his dress, his food– they were characterized by a rare simplicity. So unpretentious was he that he would receive from his companions no special mark of reverence, nor would he accepts any service from his slave that he could do for himself. He tried his best to look after his community. But Muhammad was not able to be in all the places at the same time, since he was in his human body limits. He could not comfort all the nations and all the people. Muhammad made wars to conquer other kingdoms. But Jesus did not want to fight or revenge.

Muhammad changed his laws when the situation changed. As per the Islam, he was not supported by the Holy Spirit to do miracles, raise dead to life as Jesus was.

Jesus and Muhammad should be alike if Jesus sent Muhammad as a Comforter. But Jesus and Muhammad didn't have much in common even outside of physical characteristics. When it comes to the character and actions, the two men were the worlds apart. The Prophet Muhammad went through many difficult situations with wives and associates. Especially with his wife, Aisha he had suspicions. When he came to know the truth that she was innocent, then he came up with revelations. He did not understand how much she had suffered and had mental agony in those kinds of situations. His wife could not get comfort. She was sent to her parent's house until the resolution. It was specifically written in Hadiths that she wept and cried. If he was a Comforter or the Holy Spirit that was sent after Jesus, he might not bring those kinds of situations.

Muhammad himself did not know the future things. At times he needed a comforter. He was not able to sense when his food was poisoned. And he ate the poisoned food and got sick He could not heal his sickness. He died with the sickness. How can we compare Muhammad to the Holy Spirit or the Comforter? When he himself faced so many problems and was needed a comforter for his life situations? There was no such thing that he had lived in other human being since he was another human. Only God's Spirit has ability to interact with all kinds of the people in their spirit.

However, we must realize it is impossible for one person to comfort everyone in the whole world. Man with the physical body is not a divine spirit that can interact within another individual. Thus a one universal human comforter is unrealistic. Man cannot live forever and can not exist everywhere thus he cannot be reachable at all times to every person that has lived on the planet earth.

It should not be an argument but we need to search for the truth. We need to go through the history if there was any evidence of the things that the Prophet Muhammad came to know the inner ideas of a person or the heart of the people or the heart of other person. Let us search for an example of life situation in the Prophet Muhammad's life to prove if there is any evidence that Prophet Muhammad lives in a person to be a Comforter or whether he knew what was in the heart of a person.

At times, Muhammad was very desperate in his life situations. Now let us think for a moment how any one could believe that Muhammad was a Comforter that Jesus promised before His ascension? Muhammad was dead, He was not raised from the dead or he did not ask Allah to send any Comforter to the believers. He lived 63 years and he was in the human form. Hence it was impossible for him to comfort the entire world in his life time.

Then we have a question! How a Muslim is guided through his life time without any Comforter? There is no comforter to the Prophet Muhammad nor did he send any Holy Spirit after he left. So the ultimate help is only the Qur'an. A Muslim has to understand the Qur'an. Many people do not even read the Qur'an. Because of this reason most of the Muslims follow the Islam through generations without even discerning the truth in it. Qur'an is the only guidance to a believer but very few people will read it. The Islam teaches that the Muslim has to follow the Qur'an, fear Allah and fight for Allah.

Muslims believe that Jesus Christ will come in the end days to judge and to give wages according to the deeds of the people. Because of this reason, Muhammad relied on Jesus for his redemption or his soul to be saved in the end days.

The Hadiths say, that the coming of Isa (Jesus) will be a glad tiding to the Muslims who stood firm and fought for the cause of Allah and did not succumb to the temptations of the Dajjal. There is no help to individual believer to be victorious over the temptation of the Dajjal until Jesus comes. There is no support of the Prophet to the believers because he himself relied on Jesus to come to rescue him.

A Muslim has to stand firm and keep fighting for the cause of Allah. The Islam is encouraging to fight for Allah. Especially there are some sects without any spiritual knowledge involve in fighting, killing others and killing themselves. The destroyer Satan made all his ways to destroy and make people to perish without accomplishing the purpose of Allah why He sent them to the world. They have no clear vision in the Qur'an, why God made man in His image or in His likeness?

In the Islam there is no comforter or the Holy Spirit to support the everyday life of a believer. They have no belief of the Holy Spirit living in a person. Thus there is no conviction. It is so sad to see how the people follow their own traditions and religion without even any discernment. Allah is sending back Jesus to judge all the people. Why Allah is sending Him as a judge to rule? They could not try to discern the truth that Allah was impressed and was pleased by His teachings and His life on the earth. Allah knew the best. Jesus is the only one who is capable of righteous judgment.

The prophet Muhammad taught the spiritual exercise. Muhammad could not save his own soul. Even though he followed all the spiritual exercise he relied on Jesus for his soul to be saved. So the final rescue for the souls is to rely on Jesus. But the Muslims gave high priority in the Spiritual exercise since they believe the Spiritual training in the Islam is more important to stand firm.

The Way of the Muslim life - the Spiritual Exercise

Let us now cast a glance at the mechanism of the spiritual training which the Islam has laid down for preparing the individuals and the society for this purpose. A study of the Holy Qur'an will show that every aspect of its teachings is directed towards the creation of this spiritual condition of God-fearing in every action of the believers.

The Islam affirms that man is inherently good and that sin is not truly a barrier that separates man from God. The Muslims have no guarantee of being saved. But the Spiritual training in the Islam is more important to stand. It consists of 7 fundamental beliefs and it is built on 5 pillars.

Every Muslim has to believe in 7 fundamental beliefs.

1. Belief in God (Allah).
2. Belief in angels.
3. Belief in God's prophets (Adam, Noah, Abraham, Moses, Aaron and David.)
4. Accepting there will be a Last Day.
5. Belief in the divine measurement of human affairs.
6. Belief in life after death.
7. Belief of Hell and Heaven.

The spiritual system of the Islam rests on five pillars. Faith, Prayer, Zakat, The fast and Pilgrimage (Hajj)

The first is faith in God: God is only one. He is distant and unknown. His relationship with human is that of Master/slave. As per writings of the Qur'an, Allah does not offer any assurance of salvation. The people who practice the Islam persistently should have faith and do good things. According to a recent Islamic article, hope is explained as one deed of the heart and to have a constant hope in the kindness, generosity and favors of Allah Almighty. Allah the Almighty says that "paradise is not obtained by your wishful thinking nor by that of the people of the scripture." "Moreover it was said, Faith is not wishful thinking, but rather, it is what is instilled in the heart and proven by good deeds." When the Prophet Muhammad was asked, "Which Muslim has the perfect faith?" He answered; "he who has the best moral character." (Tibrani)

For a believer Allah alone is His Master, Sovereign and Deity; seeking His pleasure is the aim of all his endeavors; and His commands alone are the commands that are to be obeyed. This should be a firm conviction, based not merely on the intellect, but also on acceptance by the will. The stronger and deeper this conviction, the more profound a man's faith will be.

The second is prayer (Salat) which, brings man into communion with God five times a day, reviving His remembrance, reiterating His fear, developing His love, reminding man of the Divine Commands again and again, and thus, preparing him for obedience to God. These prayers are not to be offered individually but it is obligatory to offer them in congregation so that the whole community and the society may be prepared for this process of spiritual development. It is a tool of individual as well as social training in the path of spiritual elevation in the Islam. The prayers are memorized and uttered in Arabic. They memorize, recite the same prayers.

The five prayer times are set and specific: at dawn, noon, afternoon, sunset, and night fall. The Kabah is the building towards which Muslims face five times a day, everyday, in prayer. This has been the case since the time of the Prophet Muhammad over 1400 years ago. The Prophet Muhammad proposed a solution that all agreed to–putting the Black Stone on a cloak, the elders of each of the clans held on to one edge of the cloak and carried the stone to its place. The Prophet then picked up the stone and placed it on the wall of the Kabah. It is a cubical building in the courtyard of the great mosque at Mecca. The Muslims regard this as House of God.

If we refer Sahih Bukhari, volume 2, the book of Hajj, chapter 56; H.No – 675, 'Umar said, "I know that you are a stone and can neither benefit nor harm. Had I not seen the Prophet (pbuh) touching (and kissing) you, I would never have touched and kissed you". People pray facing towards Kabha indicate unity in their prayer and also it shows Allah is a God who dwells locally. The Muslims parade around Kabah and offer animal sacrifices. Often the Muslim men pray at Mosques while women are expected to pray at home. Muslim women may pray at Mosques, but in the rear of the prayer hall. (Behind men)

The third is Zakat which develops the sense of monetary sacrifice, sympathy and cooperation among the Muslims. There are people, who wrongly interpret Zakat as a mere tax although the spirit underlying Zakat is entirely different from that which lies at the root of a tax. The real meaning of Zakat is sublimity and purification. By using this word, the Islam desires to impress on man the real value of Zakat which is inspired by a true love of God, that the monetary help he renders to his brethren will in fact, purity and benefit his soul.

The fourth is fasting (Saum) which, for a full month every year, trains a man individually and the Muslim community as a whole, in piety and self-restraint. Enables the society, the rich and the poor alike, to experience the pangs of hunger, and prepares the people to undergo any hardship to seek the pleasure of God.

The fifth is Hajj (Pilgrimage) which aims at fostering universal brotherhood of the faithful as the basis of worship of God. Hajj is an act of Worship – not tourism or promenade – which requires a physical and spiritual preparation. It is obligatory for every Muslim to perform Hajj once in his or her life time, unless financial or physical disability. It is a station of renewing Iman (belief) as many other stations where the sins are wiped out by forgiveness and where faith, trust, and love of Allah, His Messengers, and the believers increase. The pilgrim gets purified and comes out of his sins like a newborn baby.

It is a school of training for Taqwah – consciousness of one's duties towards Allah, good character and discipline like in the other schools of the pillars of the Islam. In Hajj, we learn how to develop the Spirit of Unity. It is an annual Muslim convention attended by the Muslims from different horizons, colors, races, and tongues etc they exchange ideas and news and celebrate their unity in faith and diversity in culture. They meet in their center-point Makkah (Qiblah.)

The Qur'an tells us to be in continuation with the Torah, the blood is the atonement of souls according to the Torah. But some Muslim doesn't believe in the concept of the sacrifices for the atonement of the sins rather they do the sacrifices because this is the way to achieve Allah's pleasure. Allah will give glad tidings to the doers of good. Together we can fulfill the obligation for which this Ummah is created. Without making the sacrifices the revival of the Islam will only remain a dream. This is the way to achieve Allah's pleasure. This is the way of the Prophet Abraham (Ibrahim) and the Prophet Muhammad.

The Surah al-Hajj verse 37 says: It is neither their meat nor their blood that reaches Allah, but it is the piety from you that reaches Him. Thus have 'We' made them subject to you that you may magnify Allah for His Guidance to you? And give glad tidings to the doers of good.

The types of animals which may be sacrificed are goats, sheep, cows and camels. It is forbidden to sacrifice sick, crippled or wounded animal. During Hajj, the sacrifices can be made in Mina or Makka, after stoning of the largest Jamarat. The sacrifice can be done by agent. The sacrifice should be performed on the tenth of Dhu'l-Hijjah but it is allowed to sacrifice up until the dusk of the 13TH.

This is His promise. Allah swt says in Surah Ankabut verse 69."As for those who strive hard in Us (Our Cause), We will surely guide them to Our Paths. And verily, Allah is with the good doers."

Here it explains that the heart towards God when doing sacrifice will bring reward and guidance from Allah. So making sacrifices brings revival to a believer. If somebody is willing to sacrifice their time, wealth, or resources, and their lives, or personal likes and dislikes, then all these are good deeds in the Islam.

In the Stoning at al-Jamaraat, the Muslims commemorate Ibraaheem (A) and remember how strong and firm he was against Shaytan (Satan) - our enemy since the time of Adam (A). The Muslims should remember how Satan does his utmost effort to distract us from doing what we're supposed to do to become closer to Allah and to enter Paradise. They say that "Allah has told us that Satan is our enemy and that we should be constantly in this life in a state of war with him." To show that attitude, people throw the stones. But the activity of throwing stones at Satan, worshipping stones find it's origin in pre Islamic pagan ritual in which stones were thrown to drive away evil spirits. This is only a physical act to resist the devil.

Jihad: The last one for the spiritual exercise is Jihad that is, exerting oneself to the utmost to disseminate the word of Allah to make it supreme. The aim is to live a life of dedication to the cause of Allah and, if necessary, to sacrifice one's life in the discharge of this mission. This is the highest spirituality, rooted in the real world, which the Islam wants to cultivate. Life-affirmation based on goodness and piety, and not life-denial, is what the Islam stands for.

A Muslim who follows all those above things fulfills the complete spiritual system and are also told in the Qur'an to read three other holy books: the Torah (the first five books of the Old Testament) the Zabur (Psalms of David) the Injeel (the Gospel of Jesus Christ)

Most of the religions teach that there is contradiction in between the physical yearning and spiritual yearning, but the Islam is different. They say both are equally important. For example the prophet Muhammad and his companions made wars, governed the lands, engaged in business and trade, and got married many wives. The Muslims assume that all these actions they did under the banner of spirituality. If we agree with the preceding assumption, why the Prophet Muhammad was relied on Jesus the son of Maryam for the rescue of his soul? If he came to that kind of conclusion how much more a normal Muslim should think about it?

The ultimate goal is to attain Allah's pleasure by being obedient to His words. In the Qur'an al- Imran 3:55, it says, 'Behold, Allah said, "O ISA (JESUS) I will take you and raise you to myself and clear you of those who disbelieve and I will make those who follow you to superior to those who disbelieve till the day of resurrection." Allah will be pleased if His creation listens to Him. The prophet Muhammad obeyed Allah and realized the truth and the key point. Even though he followed all the above 'spiritual exercise,' he knew that his soul is in the danger of entering into the hell; hence he relied on Jesus for the rescue of his soul and life.

Allah said, 'Those who follow Jesus will be superiors till the day of resurrection." As Allah said these words in the above statement let us proceed to know how to follow Jesus. What are the ways He taught? Why Jesus teachings pleased Allah to send Him to the earth the second time to judge all the people? How to get the spiritual strength in this world?

The spiritual life and the way of a follower of Jesus Christ are in accordance with the holy Bible.

The Way of Christian life -
the Spiritual exercise

Whoever is born in a Christian family is not a follower of Jesus Christ. The namesake Christians even though following traditions and carrying the name of the Christian religion, they do not know the truth; hence they are not enjoying the fullness and abundance of life in the Christianity.

Only the followers of Christ are Christians or His disciples. The term "born-again" refers to a "spiritual rebirth" of the "human spirit." We find this term in the New Testament. John 3:3: "Jesus replied, to Nicodemus, a ruler of the Jews, "Verily, verily I say unto you, no one can see the kingdom of God without being born again." Born again in Spirit means complete change in a person or become a 'Newman.' This action can not be taken place by person himself but it is a creative act of the HOLY SPIRIT but the condition of new birth is faith in Jesus Christ who was crucified, resurrected and sent His Holy Spirit to dwell in a believer.

According to the word of God when any one is born spiritually into a spiritual family he or she shall become son or daughter of God, be heirs of His kingdom and will be able to know the spiritual things. A born again Christian will be able to hear the voice of God. The term 'born again' is associated with the salvation. The believer is saved from the Eternal damnation. Those who are born-again have a personal relationship with Jesus Christ. When an individual repents for him or her sinful life, God graciously cleanses, and forgives the individual; in doing so they begin a new life (born–again) with God as they are now sealed with the promised Holy Spirit (Ephesians 1:13). Jesus Christ after His ascension sent the Holy Spirit as a comforter and a guide. '[16]The Spirit itself beareth witness with our spirit, that we are the children of God. [Romans 8:16] This privilege of children of God makes a person serene to stand still under any circumstance to see the salvation of God.

At the same time, the Bible makes it clear that faith is a true belief and real repentance before God. Faith can be explained from the word of God, Hebrews 11: 1, 11. Now faith is the substance of things hoped for, the evidence of things not seen. '[7]By faith Noah, being warned of God of things not seen as yet, moved with fear, prepared an ark to the saving of his house; by the which he condemned the world, and became heir of the righteousness which is by faith. [8]By faith Abraham, when he was called to go out into a place which he should after receive for an inheritance, obeyed; and he went out, not knowing whither he went. [9]By faith he sojourned in the land of promise, as in a strange country, dwelling in tabernacles with Isaac and Jacob, the heirs with him of the same promise: [10]For he looked for a city which hath foundations, whose builder and maker is God. [11]Through faith also Sara herself received strength to conceive seed, and was delivered of a child when she was past age, because she judged him faithful that had promised.'

Theoretical conviction of sin or it is coming from tradition of generations; it is not a real conviction. But the word of God says in James 2:17-20. '[17]Even so faith, if it hath not works, is dead, being alone.[18]Yea, a man may say, Thou hast faith, and I have works: show me thy faith without thy works, and I will show thee my faith by my works. [19]Thou believes that there is one God; thou doest well: the devils also believe, and tremble. [20]But wilt thou know, O vain man, that faith without works is dead.'

A true believer in Christ acts according to God's standards, since he is transformed into a new being with the Holy Spirit. Otherwise he proves that he is not really convinced of the truth of God's Word. 'He who says he abides in Him ought himself also to walk just as He walked.' (1 John 2:6). The Bible also presents faith as more than a mere acceptance of various regulations, a theoretical agreement with dogmas or a membership in a religious group. On the other hand, the Biblical faith could be called a firm, unshakeable trust in God rather than merely a humble recognition of God's sovereignty as it is in the Islam. The firm belief, which does not doubt, but becomes sure, before it sees, is considered exemplary in the Bible. Hebrews 11:1 defines faith as 'the substance of things hoped for, the evidence of things not seen.' The Faith leads a person into total dependence on God.

The Christian life is like a journey in a sea full of storms. All these storms in our life try to shake and weaken our faith with doubts and fears. Everyday believer's life is a challenge to strive through to attain victorious life. If we are steadfast in the faith we are victorious. God who has infinite wisdom knew it ahead. He knew our needs. He made provisions for us and gave us four anchors. By these four anchors we can be perfectly safe in our journey. We see them from the book of Acts 2:42. '42 And they continued steadfastly in the apostles' doctrine and fellowship, and in breaking of bread, and in prayers.' That is how the work began from the day of Pentecost after they received the Holy Spirit.

As a believer, I can tell my experience. Once a person is born of the Spirit, there will be hunger for the spiritual food (the word of God) just like when a child is born in the world. There will be hunger for nourishment. The believer grows spiritually day by day with the word of God. It brings change in her/his walk of life. It strengthens and opens the inner eye to understand the deepest things. The word makes us understand in which area of life we are weak and away from God. The living word helps us to be lively to respond to the Holy Spirit.

'⁶The words of the LORD are pure words: as silver tried in a furnace of earth, purified seven times.' [Psalms12:6] The word of God is sweeter than honey; it quickens us in our afflictions. The word gives us comfort and courage. In our daily life, God speaks with us appropriately in our need. The Word of God is light unto our path. We are able to see our faults in the light of His word. It rectifies us from our spiritual weakness and strengthens us, so that we shall attain perfection in our day to day life.

There are many precious promises in the Word of God, which really were fulfilled in my life. It made me to believe that it is the 'true word of God.' That is the reason the word of God became more than a treasure to me.

When I was a child this particular verse from Isaiah 49:16, '¹⁶Behold, I have graven thee upon the palms of my hands; thy walls are continually before me.' It was claimed by all our family because we observe every year a promise from the Holy Bible. As a family we all claimed that same verse throughout the year to be fulfilled on behalf of our family.

My father had a business in the other city. At that time he went to take care it. The next day around 13:00 pm, a fire broke in a house in our street where we lived. As it was a very hot summer day and wind was blowing so hard, it was quickly spreading and houses were burning. My mother, my sisters and I were home but my brothers were not home. The fire trucks and many people were trying their best to put out the fire. But it was in vain. The house right next to our house caught fire. We did not know what to do at that time. My mother and we knelt down and prayed and claimed the promise what our family believed for that particular year.

The fire was stopped right at our compound wall surrounded by our house. When we came out of the house the entire street was filled with the smoke. It was a terrible tragedy. All most all the houses in the street were burned. Only our house was left without any harm. Not even a single thing was touched by the fire. Many people thought that our house was burnt and visited us. But our trust worthy God kept His promise towards us. How faithful He is!

As we hear His voice and practice in our daily life, we acquire His divine qualities. In each and every letter of His word, there is strength and life; we see such a compassion, comfort, faithfulness and love. Our Lord's teachings are different from any other prophets. In Luke Gospel 6:27. [27]"But I say unto you which hear, Love your enemies, do good to them which hate you, [28] Bless them that curse you, and pray for them which despitefully use you" --- so on. There should not be any fighting for self defense. Zech 2:8. For thus saith the Lord of hosts:-"For he that toucheth you toucheth the apple of His eye".

I never forget this incident. Once again it is a very strong evidence of the truthfulness of God's promises from His word. When I was little, my parents came to know Lord Jesus Christ. They believed in the word of God. Our house was right on the high way in the town. We were the only people who were Christians. Many people witnessed when they were passing by at nights, noticed that our house was guarded by watch men. No one could dare to break our house. My father never hired any watchmen to guard our house. God sent His angels to protect us. What a privilege to His children! This kind of life experiences made me to trust His word more and more to enjoy in it.

The word of God or the Holy Bible is unchanged through out the years. Many believers through out the ages tested, tasted and witnessed. Because it is the true word of God it withstood all kinds of challenges, such as historic, literal, and scientific. [8]The grass withereth, the flower fadeth: but the word of our God shall stand for ever as it is written in Isaiah 40:8.

Many of the prophecies written in the word of God were fulfilled. Some prophecies are to be fulfilled. Surely, they will be fulfilled. It is written that, '[37]For no word from God will ever fail. (Luke1:37) All the promises in the word of God belong to those who trust in Him.

The last book of the Holy Bible is the 'Revelation.' The last verses at the end of the Holy Bible are written as follows: "[16]I Jesus have sent mine angel to testify unto you these things in the churches. I am the root and the offspring of David, and the bright and morning star. [18]For I testify unto every man that heareth the words of the prophecy of this book, If any man shall add unto these things, God shall add unto him the plagues that are written in this book: [19]And if any man shall take away from the words of the book of this prophecy, God shall take away his part out of the book of life, and out of the holy city, and from the things which are written in this book.' (Revelation 22:16, 18&19)

It is very clear that the word of God was given to the people to know the plan of God, the pattern of heaven, the future things and to be strengthened in the daily life. What a great privilege!

Prayer is not a ritual thing. It is a face to face communication of a person and God. But the prayer should be done with reverence and faith. It is clearly written in the word of God in Isaiah 59:2. The prayer can not be heard by God if there is sin in between God and the communicator. All the time the same prayer by memorizing and reciting can not achieve any purpose. It is not going to be effective. What I observed in my life is, when I was born again, most of my prayers are right away answered. I was considered as a little baby. My little faith was rewarded. Later on in my life what I tasted gave me strength and patience to wait upon God for His answers. That's how God improved my faith and patience and to come under His will. He made me to recognize that He is sole authoritative in my life.

The prayer can be offered at any time. For an example, if a person is in danger, when there is no help, simply by calling God as a father, God comes unto help. We consider Creator is our Father. In scriptures it says, "Even father and mother forsake, I never forsake you". Not only that, God said, even mother may forsake, I never, I carved you in my hands." The Prayers can be offer at any time.

Whenever the believer wants to worship God, and thank Him, to praise Him, to intercede, to express doubts, fears, and troubles, to express complaints, for forgiveness of sins, to get comfort or relief of stress or asking for a need. A believer prays for all the people (believers, non–believers, rulers, sick people and everybody, even for her or his enemies). There is no restriction of the place, dress, postures or language. The Prayers can be said in whole entire world in all languages in all situations.

But they should pray with all their heart and should believe that God is Omniscient and omnipresent and nothing is impossible to God. Even a beggar with filthy rags in a dirty place can utter a prayer and be closer to God in his spirit. A helpless sick person in bed also can communicate with God. If anybody is in hopeless and helpless condition, they need God, or need for God in the immediate present. That is why the name of our God is "I am that I am."

We see Jesus Christ words in Luke Gospel 18:1. He commended us to be in steadfast prayer. It means focus on God whatever we do in our life. It means persistent prayer. Lord Jesus Christ told His disciples, how to pray. This is called "Lord's prayer." It is with very simple words and compact with great wisdom, that any one can memorize. Dear reader! You could read it from the Gospels in the Holy Bible. In Lord's Prayer we learn outlines of the prayer. The powerful prayer can heal sickness and disease. We can see wonders and miracles through prayer. I saw many miracles with my own eyes.

God answered my prayers and my faith was increased through the years. From a tough problem to very least problem I lay it at His feet with simple faith and depend upon Him, Our faithful God answers and fulfill my requests. What else do I need rather than waiting upon Him? Nobody is such close to me in my life. I witness that our God is a prayer answering God. He proved in my life that He is a trust worthy God. God's assurance made me to satisfy in Him. I can sit hours together at His feet. There is no other place in this world that gives such a great relaxation and satisfaction. It is such a great privilege to meditate upon such a loving, great and awesome God.

If we are very close to Him God also reveals the up- coming things through our dreams or visions. At times the things will be seen even we are awake. Some times He gives us caution about the future. An unbeliever also can pray, for the merciful God answers him as well according to his situation, and lead him to God through the experience of the answered prayer. The collective prayers along with the fellow believers are so strong; God gave the promise that he will hear their prayer and answer them in His sanctuary (group of His people).

Our prayers will be answered if we fast and pray. It increases our faith in God and makes us completely immerse in God. We can hear the Holy Spirit speaking with us. We can solve any problem through fasting prayer, such as healing sick, casting out demons. The prayer and fasting when go together; we gain the power of the Holy Spirit. It will break the power of the evil.

In The New Testament, Jesus said we should make the fasting a secret. It should not be like the Pharisees who blew the horn and covered their heads with oil to show everyone how holy they were. No one should know that we are on fast unless one has health ailments that fasting may affect. Particularly short fasts, fasting ought to be between a person and God or a group of people and God.

A fasting program ought to include prayer, intercession, reading of God's word, (i.e. one way of listening to God) allowing God to speak from within. It can also include worshipping him with songs of praise collectively with fellow believers or personally. Listening to or watching sermons focusing on areas you are burdened with, is also edifying. A Christian prayer is always to heavenly Father and we submit in the name of Jesus Christ whom we knew in person. Only through Jesus Christ, we petition and file to Father Almighty.

How do we love and respect God in return? Our Great God did not come to us as an angel; instead He became one of us. He experienced human life. What a great love! Jesus taught to worship God in the Spirit and the truth as He is the Spirit. The believers thank Him for His great sacrifice, and His wondrous things in their daily life. They sing songs, worship and adore Him. It was written in Psalms 69:30-32, '³⁰I will praise the name of God with a song, and will magnify him with thanksgiving. ³¹This also shall please the LORD better than an ox or bullock that hath horns and hoofs. ³²The humble shall see this, and be glad: and your heart shall live that seek God. Praise ye the LORD. I will praise the LORD with my whole heart, in the assembly of the upright, and in the congregation. (Psalms 111:1) '²³Whoso offereth praise glorifieth me: and to him that ordereth his conversation aright will I shew the salvation of God.' (Psalms 50:23) It is so edifying when believers worship individually in the congregation of God.

Jesus answered Pharisees in Mathew Gospel 22:36-39. One of them asked Him, '³⁶Master, which is the great commandment in the law? ³⁷Jesus said unto him, Thou shalt love the Lord thy God with all thy heart, and with all thy soul, and with thy entire mind. ³⁸This is the first and great commandment. ³⁹And the second is like unto it, Thou shalt love thy neighbor as thyself.' Actually the love of a believer comes from all his heart because of the great sacrifice of the Savior and His trustworthiness. It is not coming with the fear of God.

Fellowship with the believers is one more thing to be strengthened in God. The early believers grew in the fellowship. It was not a good hand shake fellowship or meeting on a Sunday to be happy, or tea, coffee fellowship. They knew the power of the fellowship. They met together as often as they could to exchange and to share what they had received from the Lord. Praying for one another, sharing their experiences in God, bearing one another's burdens and help each other is very helpful to a Christian. It enhances our perspective of things. The believers really grow spiritually in the fellowship.

All the believers of Christ are considered as the body of Christ. Christ is the Head. According to God's word, the believers are God's house. God is building His temple to fill it with His glory. We experience His greatness and faithfulness in our daily life. When the people of God come together the believers will be strengthened by God's word and God will be glorified through them.

There are seven names in the Bible for 'the believers of Christ.' 1. Church (Jesus Christ pulled us out from the world with His strong hand) 2.God's family. (House hold of God) 3. The New man. 4. The Body of Christ. 5. God's workmanship. 6. Holy temple. 7. The Bride of Christ.

The singular name 'the church' explains the importance of being together to be filled with His fullness. '[18]May be able to comprehend with all saints what is the breadth, and length, and depth, and height; [19]And to know the love of Christ, which passeth knowledge, that ye might be filled with all the fullness of God.' (Ephesians 3:18–19) When believers are brought together, we taste His love in greater and full measure. His love and His purpose can never be comprehended by self. We required the help of all the saints as the believers are considered as one body of Christ. This is the mystery of our Lord. There are no barriers of caste, color or nationality. We are all one and we partake in only one Lord.

Baptism is the next fundamental and foundational principle of salvation. Repentance and faith are important to receive baptism. The baptism means immersion. In baptism a believer immersed into water by which he/she testifies that the Lord Jesus has completely washed his/her sins away. When some one is baptized, the whole person is put under the water for a moment. This symbolically represents death, burial, and resurrection. Some believers say that the baptism is not necessary. For nominal Christians baptism is a ritual, but for the believers it is a testimony.

There are 51 references in the Gospels and Epistles about the Baptism. There are three Scriptural reasons: 1. Baptism is commanded by Lord Jesus Christ (Mathew 28:19) and (Mark 16:16) He commanded the disciples to baptize in the name of the Father, the

Son, and the Holy Spirit. It signifies that a believer is born into the spiritual family and is intimately connected with the Father, having right to call God, "Father", connected with the Son the Savior and connected with the Holy Spirit who comes and lives in the believer. With this process, the Body of the believer becomes the temple of the Holy God. Then all together believers become the House hold of God. When a believer takes the Baptism in obedience he/she acknowledges the authority of the Lord Jesus Christ, and declares that He is the Lord of all.

2. Jesus Christ Himself was Baptized. Jesus Himself set us example by being baptized (Mathew 3:13-15) He is the Lord of all, yet He humbled Himself and was baptized. Through baptism we declare our union with the Lord Jesus Christ in His death, burial and resurrection. "Know ye not, that so many of us as were baptized into Jesus Christ were baptized into His death? Therefore we are buried with Him by baptism into death: that like as Christ was raised up from the dead by the glory of the Father, even so we also should walk in newness of life. For if we have been planted together in the likeness of His death, we shall be also in the likeness of His resurrection."(Romans 6:3-5) When we are saved we are baptized by the Holy Spirit into the body of Christ, which means we are joined to Him. We become members of His Body and His life begins to flow in us. In water baptism we declare the same spiritual union with the Jesus Christ. By faith we can enjoy fully our spiritual union with Christ. Every day we receive into us by faith the power of the death of the Lord Jesus die to our thoughts; the power of His burial to forget them; and the power of His resurrection to receive new life for victory over the sin and temptation. It is by oneness with Lord Jesus the believer get victory.

3. The Apostles preached and practiced Baptism. It is far better to follow the example of the Apostles, who were revealed the order, position, privileges and duties of the Church the Body of Christ rather than follow the traditional practices of men or own wisdom.

The next fundamental and foundational principle of salvation is laying on of hands (Hebrews6:2) In the holy Bible laying on of hands was used for different purposes such as showing relationships, oneness, equality and identification. We declare, our identification with Lord Jesus and all the saints, irrespective of nation, culture or education." There is neither Jew nor Greek. There is neither bond nor free, there is neither male nor female: for ye are all one in Christ Jesus." (Galatians 3:28) Every believer is equally precious in the sight of God as He made all the believers as His body. Thus after baptism, the elders of the Church lay their hands on the believer and pray in the congregation. This shows spiritual oneness with the church in the entire world.

The Pilgrimage is not obligatory in the Christian life. A disabled and very poor person is able to enjoy and have fellowship with God wherever he is. I knew a person who was a beggar on the road heard the Gospel and was born again. Later he composed a song about Jesus second coming. He composed it in such a way, whoever sings it will fully involve and experience the joy when Jesus comes. Whoever is listens his song will be thrilled.

A believer of Christ has to take part in the holy-communion. Lord Jesus same night in which He was betrayed took bread: And when He had given thanks, He broke it, and said, "take, eat: this is my body, which is broken for you: This do in remembrance of me." After the same manner also he took the cup, when He had supped, saying, "This cup is the New Testament in my blood: this do ye, as oft as ye drink it, in remembrance of me". (Luke Gospel 22: 19-20) It is better to have holy - communion as often as they could. Early Apostles did it everyday. Every one must examine before taking part in it, since the Lord is pure and holy. It opens the eyes of the believer to recognize Him as it was in Luke gospel 24:15-30. It is essential to take part in it to be pure like Him. It is a must to confess sins and ask Him forgiveness, and to cleanse in His precious blood, and be very cautious not to do same mistake, so that every one can take part in a worthy manner.

The bread indicated His body, because, the grain under go a process to become a bread. First crushed into flour, and should be made dough with salt and oil, and then it should go on the fire to become the bread. (Leviticus 2:13) Lord Jesus Christ body was bruised and crushed. Isaiah 53:5 -7, the prophecy about Jesus Christ was fulfilled. "He was oppressed and afflicted, yet he opened not His mouth. He was wounded for our transgressions; He was bruised for our iniquities." One of the offering to God in Torah (Leviticus 2:4, 5, 13) and if thou bring oblation of a meat offering baked in oven, it shall be unleavened cakes of fine flour mingled with oil. It is a thing that is most holy of the offerings of the Lord made by fire. It was foretold in the Torah. If we really think about it, it is very understandable why God had given the offering to be made as a symbol of 'fore coming Jesus Christ.'

Amazingly, the cup we drink is the indication of His holy blood in which we take part. The bread and cup are symbolic to His body and the blood. That is why in 1 Corinthians11:27-32, it is written, '27Wherefore whosoever shall eat this bread, and drink this cup of the Lord, unworthily, shall be guilty of the body and blood of the Lord. 28But let a man examine himself, and so let him eat of that bread, and drink of that cup. 29For he that eateth and drinketh unworthily, eateth and drinketh damnation to him, not discerning the Lord's body. 30For this causes many are weak and sickly among you, and many sleep. 31For if we would judge ourselves, we should not be judged. 32But when we are judged, we are chastened of the Lord, that we should not be condemned with the world.' It was warned very strictly in the word of God that a believer should take part in a worthy manner. The one who takes part without any discernment will be condemned. We have to fear and be pure to lay our hands since Jesus was holy.

The whole concept of becoming new born in the Spirit is to live separated life from the lust of the world. A believer of Christ should be separated from the world to lead a holy life because God is holy.

According to the God's word, 'be ye holy: for God is holy.' "Be ye Holy, for I AM Holy." (1 Peter 1:16)

It is written in the word of God that we are His dwelling place. In 1Corinthians 3:16, it says, '16Know ye not that ye are the temple of God, and that the Spirit of God dwelled in you? 17If any man defile the temple of God, him shall God destroy; for the temple of God is holy, which temple ye are.' The mystery of it is God wants us to be His habitation. Before we come to Him we were like a filthy rags and unclean to be His house. But now He purchased us with His own blood, cleansed us and made us His Habitation. He did it because God can not live in a filthy place.

That is why 'The will of God' for us is to live holy. '3For this is the will of God, even your sanctification, that ye should abstain from fornication: 4That every one of you should know how to possess his vessel in sanctification and honour; 5Not in the lust of concupiscence, even as the Gentiles which know not God: 6That no man go beyond and defraud his brother in any matter: because that the Lord is the avenger of all such, as we also have forewarned you and testified. 7For God hath not called us unto uncleanness, but unto holiness. 8He therefore that despiseth, despiseth not man, but God, who hath also given unto us his Holy Spirit.' (1Thessalonians 4:3-8)

The believer should abstain from all the worldly lusts. Here I am reminded of a believer. He was from a Hindu family having a Jewelry store and a wealthy man. He had no children with his wife. He had extramarital affairs and had a very beautiful daughter. He used to spend most of his time with the lady and his daughter. One day when he was sitting in his balcony he heard the Gospel from a street campaign of a group of Christians. They gave him a Gospel track. When he read it an amazing thing happened in his heart. He had curiosity to know more about the Gospel. He had the address at the back of the Gospel tract.

The next day he went there and came to know about Jesus. He accepted Jesus as his Savior and Lord. His life was changed from that day. He gave equal share to his wife and also to the lady who had child with him and ceased his relationship with her. He lived only with his wife. His wife accepted Jesus as her Savior. Later, the other lady and her daughter also were born again. He fulfilled all his responsibilities towards his daughter. He was an example to others. He and his wife did ministry all through their life.

In James- 4:4&1, it says, "⁴.Know ye not that the friendship of the world is enmity with God? Whosoever therefore will be a friend of the world is the enemy of God. ¹From whence come wars and fighting among you? Come they not thence, even of your lusts and war in your members?" A true Christian should experience and practically known all these things. If not, they are not close to God. We have to assume that they are drifted away from God.

It is written in the holy Bible that tenth of our income belong to God. Abraham was the first person to give tenth to the Lord. (Genesis 14:20) '²⁰And blessed be the most high God, which hath delivered thine enemies into thy hand. And he gave him tithes of all.' Proverbs3:9-10, '⁹Honor the LORD with thy substance, and with the first fruits of all thine increase: ¹⁰So shall thy barns be filled with plenty, and thy presses shall burst out with new wine.'

Not only tenth of their income, the believers extend their hand more as it is written in Proverbs 19:17, '¹⁷He that hath pity upon the poor lends unto the LORD; and that which he hath given will he pay him again.' In Proverbs 28: 27, 'He that gives unto the poor shall not lack: but he that hides his eyes shall have many a curse.' Psalms 41:1-3 says, "¹Blessed is he that considered the poor: the LORD will deliver him in time of trouble. ²The.LORD will preserve him, and keep him alive; and he shall be blessed upon the earth: and thou wilt not deliver him unto the will of his enemies. ³The LORD will strengthen him upon the bed of languishing: thou wilt make all his bed in his sickness."

To abide in His word, the believers are entitled to give first tenth of their income in God's house and alms to the poor. Our Father in heaven is so loving, caring and compassionate. We should be like Him. He called us 'high calling' to be like Him. Our God is Merciful and Compassionate God. He is not a dictator. He demonstrated by His self sacrifice and showed His compassionate nature.

In Mathew 6:1-4, Jesus explained how to give charity. 6. '¹Take heed that ye do not your alms before men, to be seen of them: otherwise ye have no reward of your Father which is in heaven. ²Therefore when thou doest thine alms, do not sound a trumpet before thee, as the hypocrites do in the synagogues and in the streets, that they may have glory of men. Verily I say unto you, they have their reward. ³But when thou doest alms, let not thy left hand know what thy right hand doeth: ⁴That thine alms may be in secret: and thy Father which seeth in secret himself shall reward thee openly.' That is how we get our reward.

A real believer gives their alms secretly. In some organizations people write on the paper how much they could give to the church. That kind of procedure of giving money to his house is not in accordance with the word of God. The believers give tenth from their income as gratitude towards God to the ministry and service of God, so that there is abundance in His prayer house. A believer gives to poor as a charity. A Christian (follower of Christ) should abide in faith, hope and charity. Greatest is the Charity. This is the reason why believers come forward to help whenever disasters happen in the world; we see the Christians are more charitable than any other people.

Lord Jesus Christ's final words were that we have to be His witnesses. As a Christian, we start witnessing about the wonderful things what we experienced in our life. In my life many of my visions were came true. God showed my future things ahead of the time.

Let me share with you the major things in my life. On March 29th 2010, Monday night in my sleep I saw my middle daughter put her hand on the chest, telling me that she was not able to breathe. The same thing happened as it is on April 4th 2010, the Sunday evening around 04:00 pm and she passed away to glory to be with the Lord. That was such a tragic incident. The terrific tragedy left inerasable physical pain in my heart but it made me to know unimaginable and unknowing secrets of the physical death and the eternity. God showed me a few visions about my daughter after she passed away. She is in a place of admiration. My heart was filled with surprise when I saw her in such a glory. Once again it confirmed me that there is an eternal assurance to those who believe in Jesus Christ and it confirmed me that the life on the earth is very temporary.

In 2011, on February 18th I worked night shift. I went to sleep at around 10 am on 19th morning. During my sleep, I heard and saw a huge thunder bolt struck the sky and the lightening hit the ground, the earth shook, and there was fire. The people of the earth were horrified. Multitudes of people were suffering in distress. This vision came true on March 11, 2011. A great earth quake in Japan with Tsunami and a nuclear plant caught fire. It was a chaos in Japan. I had very thrilling experiences in which God showed me the future things before they happen. What a wonderful privilege to be a friend of God.

Our loving God in the past regarded Abraham as His friend. We read in the Bible, Genesis 18;17-23, '17And the LORD said, shall I hide from Abraham that thing which I do; 23And the scripture was fulfilled which saith, Abraham believed God, and it was imputed unto him for righteousness: and he was called the Friend of God. Even now at present, the same privilege is to them that believe and trust Him.

If a God whom I believe is not a God of the whole universe, how did He show me the future things? It developed my belief in Him into a marvelous faith upon Him.

When we led by the Holy Spirit, we accomplish His will. Thereby God will be glorified, and He will be pleased. We will be victorious in overcoming temptations only if we obey God's voice. Then we will be fruitful. We bear fruits such as love, joy, peace, suffering, gentleness, goodness, faith, meekness, temperance. If we don't bear these fruits, we are not His children, or not lead by His Spirit. Because of the Holy Spirit we are able to bear these fruit. The person who does not have the Holy Spirit dwelling in him may not be having spiritual strength to bear the fruits of Him. In John Gospel 15:8, 'Herein is my Father glorified, that ye bear much fruit; so shall ye be my disciple.'

According to the word of God a real believer does not make any images, nor objects to kiss, prostrate or worship. No mediator in between God and man except only Jesus Christ. He is our representative to God. He reconciled us with God. Jesus Christ is a high priest. It is written very clearly in Hebrews 4:14-16. '[14]Seeing then that we have a great high priest, that is passed into the heavens, Jesus the Son of God; let us hold fast our profession. [15]For we have not a high priest which cannot be touched with the feeling of our infirmities; but was in all points tempted like as we are, yet without sin. [16]Let us therefore come boldly unto the throne of grace that we may obtain mercy, and find grace to help in time of need. And in Hebrews 7:24-25, '[24]But this man (Jesus Christ who was born as a man), because he continueth ever, hath an unchangeable priesthood. [25]Wherefore he is able also to save them to the uttermost that comes unto God by him, seeing he ever liveth to make intercession for them.'

The Christian life is an absolute trust in God. The Bible is filled with the promises, since we have so many fears in this world, stressing on many times "FEAR NOT." He knew that living in fear; distort the view and the relationship with God. God loves us and cares us. First He loved us and gave His life and taught us how to love Him. Our God is very near to those who pray with all their heart. There are so many proofs in my life. Let me share one of them.

Our second daughter passed away on April 6th, 2010. After a few months passed, one night I cried unto God. I said, "Father, I love you with all my heart. If you really wanted my daughter there, let your name be glorified through her death. I cannot understand thy ways. Let thy will be done in my life. But I loved her so much. Our second daughter loved us so much, and her devotion to you was so great. She was busy in your work, even on the same Sunday evening when she passed away. Lord, I just want to see my daughter again, I just want to kiss her, Please Father, could you send her to me?" That same night, on July 6th, 2010 my daughter came into my dream. Although, it seemed as if she was actually here with me, "not in my dream," but as if her presence was actually here with me. She was sitting next to me on my bed. I was surprised to see her at my bedside. In my previous dreams, initially I saw her far high into the skies. The joy I had for seeing my daughter again was uncontainable! I held her hand and kissed her. I kissed her until I was satisfied. She smiled and I was so shocked because her teeth were straight and the braces she wore on the earth were no longer there. I started talking to her, saying, "What happened to your braces? Nana, everyone will be surprised if I tell them you came back to life! We brought your death certificate, but now everyone will see such a great miracle on how you came back to earth." After I had said these words she disappeared from my sight.

I opened my eyes and realized God heard my prayers and sent my daughter just for a few minutes so that I could see, hold, and kiss her. This loving God who is the controller of the universe sanctioned my simple petition. I thanked God and my heart was full of gratitude towards Him. My heart towards Him was intensified with love, worship and faith.

Christ is sufficient for us. Even now in this life, spiritual wholeness and life abundance can be attained by the Holy Spirit. In real sense, even in this world, God's kingdom is around us. People can not see the kingdom of God with their physical eyes. It needs spiritual eyes to see the kingdom of God. Some people go to search the Garden of Eden. Can the eyes of man see the hidden things of God?

It is a joyful and peaceful life, since God's peace rules our hearts; we live with a greater sense of hope when faced with any kind of situation. Philippians 2:7: 'And the peace of God which passes all understanding shall keep our hearts and minds through Jesus Christ.' According to (Philippians 4:13) "I can do all things through Christ which strengthen me."

The kingdom of God is always in conflict with the demonic spiritual kingdom. No stoning on Satan works in this world to defeat him but we have "the word of God" which has the power and the power of His resurrection to defeat Satan. Jesus drove unclean spirits. Whoever has His Holy Spirit experience His resurrection power can do the same thing.

His disciples, Peter and Paul did so many miracles. '[11]And God wrought special miracles by the hands of Paul: [12]So that from his body were brought unto the sick handkerchiefs or aprons, and the diseases departed from them, and the evil spirits went out of them. [13]Then certain of the vagabond Jews, exorcists, took upon them to call over them which had evil spirits the name of the LORD Jesus, saying, we adjure you by Jesus whom Paul preacheth.' (Acts 19:11-13)

It is written in Ephesians by Paul in 6:10-18. "[10]Finally, my brethren, be strong in the Lord, and in the power of his might." It is explained; we need to '[11]Put on the whole amour of God that ye may be able to stand against the wiles of the devil. [12]For we wrestle not against flesh and blood, but against principalities, against powers, against the rulers of the darkness of this world, against spiritual wickedness in high places. [13]Wherefore take unto you the [1]whole armor of God that ye may be able to withstand in the evil day, and having done all, to stand.'

'[14]Stand therefore, having your loins girt about with [2]truth, and having on the breastplate of [3]righteousness; [15]And your feet shod with the preparation of the [4]gospel of peace; [16]Above all, taking the [5]shield of faith, wherewith ye shall be able to quench all the fiery darts of the wicked. [17]And take the [6]helmet of salvation, and [7]the sword of the Spirit, which is the word of God: [8]Praying always with all prayer and supplication in the Spirit, and watching thereunto with all perseverance and supplication for all saints;' And in 11Corinthians10:3-4, '³For though we walk in the flesh, we do not war after the flesh: ⁴ For the weapons of our warfare are not carnal but mighty through God to the pulling down of strong hold.' This shows complete dependence of God to defeat our enemies.

Lord Jesus Christ came to this world to give us His peace, joy and victory. When He spoke to His disciples in John Gospel 14, 15 and16, He assured of peace, joy and victory. Only through Jesus Christ, we are victorious over Satan but not by doing any physical acts like shouting or throwing of stones.

The Christians are like the pilgrims in this world. We take nothing of this world with us. We understand in our journey, how faithful our God is, and how much He loves us. The personal relationship with God will increase day by day. As we develop intimacy with God, we will transform into His likeness, means we attain His character. We submit ourselves more to our conscience. Our conscience is led by the Holy Spirit. We do not consider much the things of this world. We hear His soft voice to which we obey. Just like Jesus Christ, we develop a selfless and forgiving nature. We forgive even our enemies. We lead a responsible and disciplined life since we learn from Him that we have to give account to God for each and everything. We have such a great promises in the word.

The apostle Peter wrote in 2 Peter1:4-11, how to live diligently to make our highest heavenly call sure so that we can stand straight without falling. "⁴Whereby are given unto us exceeding great and precious promises: that by these ye might be partakers of the divine nature, having escaped the corruption that is in the world through lust. ⁵And beside this, giving all diligence, add to your faith virtue; and to virtue knowledge; ⁶And to knowledge temperance; and to temperance patience; and to patience godliness; ⁷And to godliness brotherly kindness; and to brotherly kindness charity. ⁸For if these things be in you, and abound, they make you that ye shall neither be barren nor unfruitful in the knowledge of our Lord Jesus Christ.'

'⁹But he that lacketh these things is blind, and cannot see afar off, and hath forgotten that he was purged from his old sins. ¹⁰Wherefore the rather, brethren, give diligence to make your calling and election sure: for if ye do these things, ye shall never fall: ¹¹For so an entrance shall be ministered unto you abundantly into the everlasting kingdom of our Lord and Savior Jesus Christ.'

Once a person is committed to Jesus Christ, He leads the believer in His ways. The relationship of the believer with Jesus Christ is compared as sheep and a shepherd. The believer walks with Him in the spiritual realm. He makes us to lie down in the green pastures: leads us beside still waters. Some times leads us into the deserts and provide Oasis, some times leads us into the valleys and send us the springs from the hills. Some times takes us to the mountain tops, sometimes take us through fire to make us pure as gold. Whatever is the situation, we understand His ways are higher than our ways. Since we love Him we commit unto His will. He leads us through all kinds of situations but His rod and His staff comforts us as it was written in Psalms 23:4. We daily grow into His likeness and into His character. This is the spiritual exercise to acquire love and devotion towards God to spend the eternity with Him.

The most awesome wonderful privilege is we can hear the voice of God. We hear His voice many times in our daily life. We hear it only if we have His Spirit living in us. To hear His voice, we need to be pure and be sanctified by His Spirit.

Any one whoever born in a Christian family can dare to say that he or she will enter into His kingdom? The answer is "no." Previously, we had been discussed that only those who are born again in spirit and walk in his ways will inherit the kingdom of God. "⁶²But Jesus said unto him, No man, having put his hand to the plow, and looking back, is fit for the kingdom of God.' (Luke 9:62) In the holy Bible Lot's wife was warned not to look back to the sinful Sodom and Gomorrah, but she did and became a pillar of salt. She was not rescued from the danger. This incident was written in the Bible for the caution of a believer in this world.

The believers have to be careful in all the things. "[12]Wherefore let him that thinketh he standeth take heed lest he fall." Paul wrote to the church at Rome, "[24]For the name of God is blasphemed among the Gentiles through you." (Romans 2:24) It is so sad that the people who say they are the Christians but some of them are not walking with God and never experienced His love and His promises. They did not taste how sweet His relationship is! Some of them are giving chance to Satan to accuse the Christians that they are drunkards, they expose themselves without dressing properly, and they give more importance to the vain things etc. Some Christians misunderstand the love and grace of God. They are not giving any priority to the plan of God and are not after the standards of God.

It reminds me the incident that occurred at the time of Noah in Genesis 8th chapter from the holy Bible. When Noah and all the living things on the earth were remained in the ark, God remembered them and restrained the rain from the heaven after forty days and forty nights of the rain. God made wind to pass over the earth, and the waters were continuously decreasing. After one hundred and fifty days the ark was rested upon the mountains of Ararat. Noah wanted to make sure whether the waters were dried up or not. '[7]And he sent forth a raven, which went forth to and fro, until the waters were dried up from off the earth. [8]Also he sent forth a dove from him, to see if the waters were abated from off the face of the ground; [9]But the dove found no rest for the sole of her foot, and she returned unto him into the ark, for the waters were on the face of the whole earth: then he put forth his hand, and took her, and pulled her in unto him into the ark. The raven did not come back to Noah because it found dead bodies to eat but dove came back to Noah. This is symbolic to two kinds of people in the world. One group of people is after the world and the other group of people is after the word of God and is separated from the world.

Since the believer had intimate relationship with Jesus Christ and trust in His promises they live with satisfaction in this world but they are not after the world.

The believer could say boldly, that, "I sought the LORD, and he heard me, and delivered me from all my fears. ⁵They looked unto him, and were lightened: and their faces were not ashamed. ⁶This poor man cried, and the LORD heard him, and saved him out of all his troubles. ⁷The angel of the LORD encampeth round about them that fear him, and delivereth them. ⁸O taste and see that the LORD is good: blessed is the man that trusteth in him. ⁹O fear the LORD, ye his saints: for there is no want to them that fear him. ¹⁰The young lions do lack, and suffer hunger: but they that seek the LORD shall not want any good thing.' (Psalms 34:4-10) The believers are as bold as lions to face second coming of Jesus Christ.

Finally the believers are looking forward for His second coming or should be ready whenever He calls to His presence to meet Him. They are bold enough to face Him because they are doing what he had told them. Those who don't obey His teachings are rebelling against Him. Whoever is not following Him should fear for His coming.

At the present, the signs of the end of the world and of His coming are at hand. The things that Jesus Christ told His disciples on the mount Olives are almost fulfilled. A few of them needs to be fulfilled. We read them in detail in Mathew Gospel 24, Mark Gospel 13 and Luke Gospel 21.We already had discussed about the end days in the second chapter of this book.

The Promised Return of Jesus (Bible): Based on the Hope

—◆—

There are almost 365 references in the New Testament about the second coming of Jesus Christ. God's love and His infinite wisdom is revealed in this to remind us every day to be vigilant, all 365 days in a year. The second coming of Jesus Christ is a very important subject in the whole Bible. It is an ultimate hope of a believer. Christians need to remind themselves and become continually aware of the second coming of Christ, because the hour and the time are not known to any one. But there is the lively hope in His promise. Jesus is the Truth. What He told was never failed. Jesus Christ promised His people that He will return to the earth to take them. Again this is the review of this subject as it should be reviewed everyday.

Matthew 24:3, states, 'as He sat on the Mount of Olives, the disciples came to him privately, saying, "Tell us, when will these things be, and what will be the sign of your coming and of the close of the age?"

Jesus answered His disciples clearly in the first part of the same chapter, (Mathew 24:4-14) as well as in the gospel of Mark chapter 13 and the gospel of Luke chapter 21. The following verses are spoken by Jesus to His disciples regarding His second coming: it is in two parts, one is the rapture of the church and the other is the second coming to all the people of the world.

The coming of Christ will be instantaneous and worldwide: '27For as the lightning comes from the east and shines as far as the west, so will be the coming of the Son of Man.' This will be the coming of Jesus to take the church with Him. He had given some hints that people can perceive His appearing on the clouds to receive saints. He explained this to his disciples with a parable about 10 virgins. We could read this parable in Mathew gospel 25:1-13. Jesus told this parable so that they could understand how vigilant they should be for the event of His coming. The believers, who ever are ready for His appearance will be received by Him on the clouds, the rest will be left behind in the world. The world will be continued as usual.

2. The coming of Christ will be audible: The believers who are ready and looking forward for His second coming will be heard the trumpet sound. '31And he shall send his angels with a great sound of a trumpet, and they shall gather together his elect from the four winds, from one end of heaven to the other.' (Mathew 24:31)

3. The two angels intervened about His second coming: We read this reference in Acts 1:9-11. The intervention of the angels took place at the time of his ascension to the heaven. '9And when he had spoken these things, while they beheld, he was taken up; and a cloud received him out of their sight. 10And while they looked steadfastly toward heaven as he went up, behold, two men stood by them in white apparel; 11which also said, ye men of Galilee, why stand ye gazing up into heaven? This same Jesus, who is taken up from you into

heaven, shall so come in like manner as ye have seen him go into heaven.'

4. Assurance of Jesus: We are strongly affirmed by His promise that one day He will return and take with him those who trust in him. On the day of His appearance, Christians who have died will be resurrected just as Jesus was resurrected from the death.

Jesus told His disciples in the Gospel of John 14:1-6: "Let not your hearts be troubled; you believe in God, believe also in Me. In My Father's house are many mansions; if it were not so, I would have told you. And if I go and prepare a place for you, I will come again and receive you to myself; that where I am, there you may be also. And where I go, you know, and the way you know." One of His disciples, 'Thomas said to Him, "Lord, we do not know where you are going, and how can we know the way?" Jesus said to him, "I am the way, the truth, and the life. No one comes to the Father except through me."

Dear Reader, what other proof do we need? Jesus clarified the way to salvation (through Him) and His promised return! This was face to face conversation between Jesus and His disciples, gives us a secure hope to a believer. No intermediation in between them. Because of His promise, believers have a living and secure hope!

After the Lord Jesus Christ's ascension, Paul had revelation about those who were dead in Christ. He wrote to the Thessalonians and Corinthian church about the hope of the dead in Christ. The resurrection of the righteous which are waiting on the promise of Jesus Christ and His return will occur on His second coming of the first phase, the rapture. (Taking off His church with Him) in addition to the above explanation)

Here below are the references from the Holy Bible about the rapture :(1Thessalonians 4:16) "16For the Lord himself shall descend from heaven with a shout, with the voice of the archangel, and with the trump of God: and the dead in Christ shall rise first. [17]Then we which are alive and remain shall be caught up together with them in the clouds, to meet the Lord in the air: and so shall we ever be with the Lord.' [1Thessalonians 4:17]

In 1Corinthians 15:52-57, it is written: '[52]In a moment, in the twinkling of an eye, at the last trump: for the trumpet shall sound, and the dead shall be raised incorruptible, and we shall be changed. [53]For this corruptible must put on incorruption, and this mortal must put on immortality. [54]So when this corruptible shall have put on incorruption, and this mortal shall have put on immortality, and then shall be brought to pass the saying that is written, Death is swallowed up in victory. [55]O death, where is thy sting? O grave, where is thy victory? [56]The sting of death is sin; and the strength of sin is the law. [57]But thanks be to God, which giveth us the victory through our Lord Jesus Christ.'

So far we have gone through the first phase of Jesus Christ's second coming, the rapture of the Church where Jesus comes back for the believers. (Dead and alive)

Now let's look at the references about the second phase of His coming. This is the appearance of Jesus Christ to the entire world to everybody. This happens at the end of the world. By this time all the believers will be out of this world. Jesus Christ explained to the disciples the signs of this period. He told them that in this event, the coming of Christ will be visible to all people: This is the second coming of Christ to the world. In the second phase of His coming, everybody will see Him even those who pierced and crucified Him.

In the word of God, the book of Revelation 1:7-8, John, the disciple of Jesus Christ wrote about the revelation of Jesus Christ. He wrote that everybody will see Jesus Christ with their eyes. "[7]Behold, He cometh with clouds; and every eye shall see him, and they also which pierced him: and all kindreds of the earth shall wail because of him. Even so, Amen.[8]I am Alpha and Omega, the beginning and the ending, saith the Lord, which is, and which was, and which is to come, the Almighty."

Jesus told His disciples (Mathew Gospel 24:29) --- The signs of the end days. "²⁹Immediately after the tribulation of those days the sun will be darkened, and the moon will not give its light, and the stars will fall from heaven, and the powers of the heavens will be shaken. ³⁰Then will appear in heaven the sign of the Son of Man, and then all the tribes of the earth will mourn, and they will see the Son of Man coming on the clouds of heaven with power and great glory." This takes place after the rapture of the church. This event takes place at the end time of the world. Lord Jesus Christ will return to the world with His saints to conquer the whole world and He makes war with Satan.

Lord Jesus Christ did everything in sequence. As a heavenly father He never skips any thing or hides anything from His children. Jesus personally gave us the gospel and showed us how to live a righteous life. Apart from it, He made a provision by sending His Holy Spirit into us to dwell when we are cleansed by His precious blood. He told signs of his coming in Luke 13:23 -30.

Since Jesus Christ is the king of the kingdom of God He told them who will be entering into His kingdom. '²³Then said one unto him, Lord, are there few that be saved? And he said unto them, ²⁴Strive to enter in at the straight gate: for many, I say unto you, will seek to enter in, and shall not be able. ²⁵When once the master of the house is risen up, and hath shut to the door, and ye begin to stand without, and to knock at the door, saying, Lord, Lord, open unto us; and he shall answer and say unto you, I know you not whence ye are: ²⁶Then shall ye begin to say, We have eaten and drunk in thy presence, and thou hast taught in our streets. ²⁷But he shall say, I tell you, I know you not whence ye are; depart from me, all ye workers of iniquity. ²⁸There shall be weeping and gnashing of teeth, when ye shall see Abraham, and Isaac, and Jacob, and all the prophets, in the kingdom of God, and you yourselves thrust out. ²⁹And they shall come from the east, and from the west, and from the north, and from the south, and shall sit down in the kingdom of God. [30]And, behold, there are last which shall be first, and there are first which shall be last.'

Most importantly, Jesus has specified that "He is the way, the truth, and the life" (John 14:6) and apart from Him there is no other way to receive the eternal life. Then before he left us, here he had given caution to His children to be against believing in false Christ's and/or false prophets.

Dear reader, despite this, let not your hearts be troubled! Scripture is very clear about Jesus' second coming and His glorious millennium ruling on the earth, and creation of the new heavens and the new earth! His kingdom will be forever, so do not be deceived by the false teachings after Jesus Christ!

Let us come to the final assumption of His second coming: All the believers (the Church) as His bride He will take them with Him. The remaining people will be left over on the earth. They will undergo through seven years of difficult period of great tribulation under Antichrist. And then Jesus Christ comes and makes war with Antichrist and false prophet and cast them into the lake of fire. An angel comes down from heaven, having the key of the bottomless pit and a great chain in his hand. And he laid hold on the dragon, that old serpent, which is the Devil, and Satan, and bound him for thousand years. (Revelation 20:1-2.)

Finally Jesus wins the battle and establishes His kingdom. He rules for thousand years literally on this earth.

After His ascension to heaven, the future kingdom which will be ruled by Him was shown to His disciple John. He wrote those coming events in the book of Revelation. In 19th chapter from 11th verse he wrote, '[11]And I saw heaven opened, and behold a white horse; and he that sat upon him was called Faithful and true, and in righteousness he doth judge and make war. [12]His eyes were as a flame of fire, and on his head were many crowns; and he had a name written, that no man knew, but he himself. ¹³And he was clothed with vesture dipped in blood: and his name is called 'The Word of God.'(This clearly shows He is Jesus Christ who came to this world as the word of God and offered his blood) ¹⁴And the armies which were in heaven followed him upon white horses, clothed in fine linen, white and clean. ¹⁵And out of his mouth goeth a sharp sword, that with it he should smite the nations: and he shall rule them with a rod of iron: and he treadeth the winepress of the fierceness and wrath of Almighty God. ¹⁶And he hath on his vesture and on his thigh a name written, KING OF KINGS, AND LORD OF LORDS.' Because of all this evidence there should be no doubt to believe in His future kingdom.

And when the thousand years are expired, Satan shall be loosed out of his prison, Again Satan tries to gather people to make war with saints: but fire will come down from God out of heaven, and devour them. Satan will be cast into the lake of fire and brimstone where Antichrist (the Beast) and the false prophet.

Then will be the white throne judgment. Everybody will be judged. Whose name is not written in the book of life will be cast into the lake of fire. And Death and Hell will be cast into the lake of fire. This is the second Death. (Revelation 20) And I saw a new heaven and new earth: for the first heaven and the first earth passed away; and there was no more sea. Please read (Revelation21 and 22) from the Bible to find out about new heaven and new earth.

The Second Return of Jesus in the Quran; Based on the Hope

———— ❦ ————

Muslim's believe Isa (Jesus) will return at a time close to the end of the world.

The Qur'anic verse eludes to us an indicator to Isa's (Jesus Christ's) future return, it states: [45] "And He Isa (Jesus) shall be a Sign for the coming of the Hour of Judgment: therefore have no doubt about the Hour, but follow ye me: this is a Straight Way." [Qur'an 43:61]

Sahih al Bukhari, 3:43:656: Narrated Abu Hurairah: Allah's Apostle said, "the Hour will not be established until the Son of Mary (Mary am) (i.e. Isa) descends amongst you as a just ruler; he will break the cross, kill the pigs, and abolish the Jizya tax. Money will be in abundance so that nobody will accept it.' (as charitable gifts). 'After the death of the Madhi, Isa will assume leadership. This is a time associated in Islamic narrative with universal peace and justice.

Islamic texts also allude to the appearance of Ya'juj and Ma'juj (known also as Gog and Magog), ancient tribes which will disperse and cause disturbance on earth. God in response to Isa' prayers will kill them by sending a type of worm in the napes of their necks. [46]'Isa' rule is said to be around 40 years, after which He will die. Muslims will then perform the Salat al – Janazah (funeral prayer) for Him and bury Him in the city of Medina in a grave left vacant beside Muhammad.[45]In this Qur'an narration Isa (Jesus) will come a second time to the world, He will live forty years, die, and will be buried in the city of Medina in a grave beside Muhammad.

Muhammad, Allah's Apostle, said His life and soul is in the hands of Jesus. Muhammad claimed Jesus' authority to rule, but denounced His character by making Him to subject to Al-Mahdi, the leader of all Muslims, and to help Al-Mahdi. In other words, Isa (Jesus) will be second in command.

According to the Qur'an, Jesus characteristics on His second coming will be:

1. He will be a devout Muslim.
2. He will kill Dajjal.
3. He will help Al-Mahdi to govern his caliphate and institute Sharia law throughout the world. He will break the cross- the symbol of Christianity.
4. He will turn the Christians away from the Christianity to become Muslims; Non-Muslims will be unprotected and will be put to death.
5. He will kill the swine, and abolish the jizya. He will kill and even decapitate those who refuse to submit to Islam.

The Muslims are waiting for the end days. They believe that Jesus will manage the entire world to become Islamic kingdom. The Muslims are expecting that Jesus will come and pay wages according to the good deeds. Money will be in abundance. His rule should be 40 years, He get marry, have children and he will die and will be buried next to Muhammad.

All the Muslims do not agree on every aspect of Muslim eschatology. There two different views in the Islam regarding Jesus rule. Sunnis and Shiites have a different view on the role of Al-Mahdi, who will arrive at the End times.

Some people say Jesus rules 40 years, some says Al-Mahdi rules 40 years. The Shiites believe that Al-Mahdi will establish order in the world and turn people to the Islam before the return of Jesus. According to the Shia sect, the Mahdi is the 12[th]Imam, Muhammad al-Muntazar, the Hidden Imam, who disappeared in 878 A.D. They believe he is alive and will reappear at the end of time to lead the Muslim armies. Jesus and the armies of Mahdi conquer the world and force everyone to become Muslims. The Dajjal, the Antichrist, and his force of 70,000 Jews will be destroyed.

The believers of the Islam do not have any further continuation about the world. In the Islam it was not written what happened to the present world? Or who will be ruling after Jesus Christ? There are no clear writings about the future things. There are so many questions and doubts arose from it.

Here below are many questions yet to be ananswered.

Will Jesus turn the Christians away from the Christianity to become the Muslims? Will He going to destroy His followers and make them to follow the Islam? Will He ignore all the four Gospels and His teachings? Why Jesus has to ignore the Torah, the Scripture and the Gospels? Four Gospels were written by the eye witnesses of Jesus Christ, when Allah gave revelation to consider Torah, Scripture and Gospels? His disciples and Apostles testified about Him in the Gospels. How could he reject and kill His own followers? Allah sent Jesus to fulfill the Torah Jesus did it accordingly? He several times pointed Torah which was witnessed Him.

Jesus taught Monotheism because He is 'the arm of God' according to the Scriptures. If we look into the Qur'an, the Prophet Muhammad had centered the Qur'an on the writings of the Torah, and Gospels. How could Allah and Jesus change their minds? If some one is disobeying Allah and Jesus words, then with what kind of hope, he or she can look forward for the second coming of Jesus Christ?

But there are some people who are looking forward for Jesus' return without following Him. How will He judge and give the rewards if the people don't follow His teachings why the people are killing innocent people without following the teachings of Jesus?? If the people are instilled with faith, why there is no faith in God? And no regard for Allah words? Why the people are miserable.

What is the definition of good works? What kind of good works we have to do to get good rewards and wages when Jesus comes? What are the good deeds that Jesus will be looking for in His ruling?

There are so many questions yet to be answered in the Islam.

In the Qur'an, there is no further explanation of the present world or the world after 40 years of Jesus and Madhi rule. It is very interesting that all the Muslims are waiting for the second return of Jesus to enjoy only 40 years of His rule.

There are two views in the Islam about the Resurrection and the Judgment.

1. 'Jesus shall be a Sign of the Hour of Judgment: therefore has no doubt about the Hour. It will be the hour of judgment. These are the words of the Prophet Muhammad. Everyone on the face of the earth will be resurrected because the second coming of Jesus will be the resurrection day. Even Muhammad will be resurrected to be judged by Jesus. Because of this reason, Muhammad said his soul and the life will be in the hands of Jesus."

When every one in the world is risen as it will be the final hour to judge the people and give rewards, how Jesus will be buried next to Muhammad tomb when Muhammad also will be resurrected and be judged by Jesus as he stated?

2. There is another concept that says in the Islam: Following the death and burial of Jesus, will be the resurrection of all the people. According to the Islam, this event will be preceded by the trumpet blast, which crushes the mountains. In the Islam all will be gathered and submit to Allah. And when

the trumpet shall sound one blast and the earth with the mountains shall be lifted up and crushed with one crash. Then, on that day will the Event befall. And the heaven will split asunder, for that day it will be frail. And the angels will be on the sides thereof, and eight will uphold the throne of thy Lord that day above them. On that day you will be exposed: not a secret of you will be hidden. [Surah 69:13-19] This explains the end of the world and the judgment. All the people have to go through the judgment and people will be separated and be punished.

From the above writing we conclude that there two resurrections, two judgments. And there are two different end days of the world. Even though there are varied ideas in the Islam, they do not want to search for the truth. Yet the Muslims are waiting forward for the second coming of Jesus to get their wages to have abundance of wealth and the Islamic kingdom all over the world.

The Forgiveness of the Sins in the Islam and the Christianity

In the Islam the forgiveness of the sins is very easy. The sins will be forgiven even though they are like the foam of the sea!

Narrated Abu Huraira: Allah's Apostle said,"Whoever says,'Subhan Allaahi Wa bihamdihi,{Allah is free from imperfection and His is the praise}. One hundred times a day, will be forgiven all his sins even if they were as much as the foam of the sea.(Bukhari, book #75, Hadith #414)

In the Islam, 'We Can Earn Over a BILLION Rewards in Just a Few Seconds!'Narrated 'Ubaadah that the Messenger of Allah said,"Whoever seeks forgiveness for the believing men and believing women, Allah will write for him a good deed for each believing man and believing woman."(Tabarrani) Just believing that Allah is only one God, Allah will right a good deed to them.

In the Islam there are forty very easy, quick & rewarding good deeds to do everyday! Earn a thousand good deeds in Minutes!

The Prophet Muhammad (Peace be upon him) said, "Is anyone of you incapable of earning one thousand Hasanah (rewards) a day?" Someone from the gathering asked," How can anyone of us earn a thousand Hasanah?" Prophet Muhammad (Peace be upon him) said: "Glorify Allah a hundred times by just saying,"Subhanallah" and a

Good deeds will be written for you, or a thousand sins will be wiped away."(Muslim 4:2073)

Allah is not a liar to write good deeds, even though we didn't do them. This indicates that forgiveness of sins can be attained only by praising God. How can Allah be pleased if we praise Him without doing any good deeds? If children do the same thing to parents, how do parents respond? Is Allah a liar to write what we did not do?

In the Gospels (Mathew 15:7-9) Jesus Christ (Word of God, Spirit from God) said, '⁷Ye hypocrites, well did Esaias prophesy of you, saying, ⁸This people draweth nigh unto me with their mouth, and honored me with their lips; but their heart is far from me. ⁹But in vain they do worship me, teaching for doctrines the commandments of men.'

In the Islam, "For these, there is hope that Allah will forgive: For Allah doth blot out (sins) and forgive again and again." [Surah 4:99] As per the Islam, a person commits a sin, and can have this sin forgiven merely by asking, but then can go out and commit the same sin over and over again, each time asking for forgiveness, and having it forgiven. In this aspect there is no repentance of the committed sin. By doing the same sin if we do good deed it will replace the committed sin. Because it was stated, 'replace the sin with some other good work.'

In the Islam, to do good work one should overcome 'the Self.' There is no help of the Holy Spirit. Thereby no firm decision of overcoming the sin. There is no support of God's Holy Spirit. There is a tendency of falling into the sin again and again with human spirit which is weak and frail. That is why, even our prophets such as Adam and Moses disobeyed God.

God in the Bible, not only forgives us from our sins but the difference is that when a person has trusted Christ, He cleans the believer so that the Spirit of God comes and dwells in him/her and will work in him/her to make him/her more like Christ who is by nature pure and holy.

According to the Bible, it is impossible to a human to live pure and holy. Even if we try our best, we can not live pure and holy.

Our thoughts themselves will defile us. But to the believer of Christ there will be immediate conviction then and there itself because of the indwelling Holy Spirit. For the human it is possible to overcome only through the Holy Spirit. It explains that God is Omnipresent. God is a Spirit being. He dwells in every believer, only if it is a holy place to live in. That is why we need cleansing of our heart. The holy Bible tells us that the one who abides in Him will keep himself pure with the help of the Holy Spirit. 'Whosoever abideth in him sinneth not: whosoever sinneth hath not seen him, neither known him.' (I John 3:6)

There is no provision in the Islam made for the removal of person's sins or moral filthiness; instead the perfect ness of a person depends upon himself. In the Qur'an it says, "If you avoid the major sins which you are forbidden, 'We' (Allah) will do away with your small sins and cause you to enter an honorable place of entering." [Surah4:31, Shakir translation] So the Islam explains that Allah allows people with small sins to enter into the heaven but not the major sins. The major sin in the Islam is Apostasy. The Apostasy from the Islam is not easily forgiven by Allah. In Islam if any one born in a Muslim family if change to other religion then that is also is an Apostasy. 'The death' is the only punishment for the Apostasy.

In the Islam no one enters into the heaven unless they go through the hell. That means every one must enter the hell without any escape because of the many sins which were not forgiven. This is a must because God is holy.

For the Muslims the only guarantee to get into the heaven is Jihad or holy war. Jihad literally means exerting force for God. One could be in Jihad by writing a book about the Islam, or by sharing faith to bring others to the Islam, or by physically fighting for the cause of the Islam. In the Islam they believe if a Muslim dies in Jihad, he definitely enters into the heaven. This belief makes them to exert force for God. In exerting force, the Muslims kill innocent people. We see this kind of incidents occurring in our daily life all over the world. Whoever kills an innocent person is a murderer. Instead of getting into the heaven, God judge them for the murdering the innocent people and whoever committed the murder goes straight to the hell fire. This truth is ignored by the people of Islam and still they exert force to kill the innocent people.

But God of the Torah, the Scriptures and the Gospel is entirely different in the aspect of sinful nature of man. Throughout the Old Testament and the New Testament it explains God is Holy God; He lives in the Holy city which is the Heaven. Nobody can enter into the heaven with sin. For that reason, He made provisions like obeying to commandments, sacrifices, and offerings to make people holy like Him so that they can live with Him in His Holy city the Heaven.

God of Abraham, Jacob, Isaac and Moses in the Torah (Leviticus 17:11-12) said to Moses, '¹¹for the life of the flesh is in the blood: and I have given it to you upon the altar to make an atonement for your souls: for it is the blood that maketh an atonement for the soul. ¹²Therefore I said unto the children of Israel, No soul of you shall eat blood; neither shall any stranger that sojourned among you eat blood. Muslims are very strict about not eating blood. Muslims eat only Halal meat in which they are obeying God. But they do not believe that only the blood can make the atonement for the souls.

In Exodus 12:1, 5-7, 12, 13, --- (Fore coming of the Lamb of God that will be sacrificed for redemption was fore shadowed in the Torah.)

It is written: 12. '¹And the LORD spake unto Moses and Aaron in the land of Egypt saying, ⁵Your lamb shall be without blemish, a male of the first year: ye shall take it out from the sheep, or from the goats: ⁶And ye shall keep it up until the fourteenth day of the same month: and the whole assembly of the congregation of Israel shall kill it in the evening. ⁷And they shall take of the blood, and strike it on the two side posts and on the upper door post of the houses, wherein they shall eat it. ¹²For I will pass through the land of Egypt this night, and will smite all the firstborn in the land of Egypt, both man and beast; and against all the gods of Egypt I will execute judgment: I am the LORD. [13]And the blood shall be to you for a token upon the houses. Where ye are: and when I see the blood, I will pass over you, and the plague shall not be upon you to destroy you, when I smite the land of Egypt.'

And God did exactly what he had told them. Those who had no blood on their posts as a token were destroyed by God. He smote all the land of Egypt and saved those who obeyed Him. Those who were not obeyed were damned, even the Israelites who were claimed to be the children of God. Most of the people perished because of not obeying God. God did not save them because of His spoken ordinance.

That is the reason God sent His Spirit in the human flesh (who was faultless) with the name of Jesus the Savior. He was offered as a sacrifice. Only His sinless blood can redeem human race from their sins and deliver them from the wrath of God.

That is why in 1Peter 1:18-19, it is written, '[18]Forasmuch as ye know that ye were not redeemed with corruptible things, as silver and gold, from your vain conversation received by tradition from your fathers; [19]But with the precious blood of Christ, as of a lamb without blemish and without spot.' From the word of God it is clarified that Lord Jesus Christ was the Lamb of God. Only through His precious blood, we shall be redeemed. Whoever believes in Him and repents of their sins will be redeemed by His blood and is eternally set apart for God. Secondly the Holy Spirit continually searches the person and makes the believer holy, day by day through the Scriptures. Complete sanctification awaits the appearing of the Lord Jesus Christ.(Ephesians 5 :27) '[27]That He might present it to Himself a glorious church, not having spot, or wrinkle, or any such thing; but that it should be holy and without blemish.

One day Jesus Christ will be coming to take His church and present it as a glorious church. If any one is not become part of His body (the Church) they will perish.

The Eternal Assurance in the Islam

The Prophet Muhammad said: "You have not been created for annihilation. You have been created for everlasting life. The only thing is that you are moved from one world to another."

In the beginning, the first man, Adam, was in the paradise but he went astray, Allah had driven him down to the earth. Did he get any eternal assurance to get back into the paradise? There is a very beautiful description of the paradise in the Qur'an. But is there any eternal assurance in the Islam? Let us find out from the Noble Qur'an.

As per the Qur'an, Allah did not give Adam any Eternal assurance to get back them into the Paradise. He expelled them from the Garden of Eden.

The Qur'an explains that people will be sleeping in the tomb until the resurrection day. According to the Islam, life continues in the grave after the body is buried. The Life in the grave is known as Barzakh. While a person died and is in the grave, two angels by names, Munkar and Nakir, question the newly died person. They ask the person three questions 1. Who is your God? 2. Who is your prophet? 3. What is your faith? The angels will make his grave comfortable, depending upon their answers. If that person answers correctly and says these three answers: 1. Allah. 2. Muhammad. 3. Islam, then his/her grave will be enlarged. If that person does not answer correctly, then the grave will be narrow and their ribs will be crushed. They hit them with hammer. This keeps on continuing while the person awaits judgment.

Allah never gave any eternal assurance. It is clear with Prophet Muhammad's final ultimatum that there is no assurance of eternity in the Islam. Because of this reason he sought the help of Jesus for the rescue of his soul and the life on the Judgment day. The good deeds should over weigh bad deeds to reach eternity but it is up to Allah. But in the Qur'an, there is no list of good deeds or bad deeds and there is no specification of good deeds or bad deeds. Hence there is no clarity of a way to reach paradise. In this world one can not estimate his or her good deeds or bad deeds. In the Islam there are no definite specifications for good and bad. No one is sure of which bad deed is equal to the good deed to cross it out. But the overall hope is that Allah is merciful so He definitely will grant the paradise.

Muslims believe that there will be a Day of Judgment.

The Prophet Muhammad said, "(Jesus) shall be a Sign (for the coming of) the Hour (of Judgment): therefore have no doubt about the (Hour), and his soul and life will be in the hands of Jesus when the hour comes." So there is no assurance from any other source except Jesus. What will be your reaction when the son of Mary (Jesus) descends and your Imam is among yourselves? (Sahih Muslim, bab nuzul isa, vol 2; Sahih Bukhari, Kitab bad' al-khalq wa nuzul isa vol 4) Here in this passage it is very interesting to note that the Prophet Muhammad questioned them, 'what will be your reaction when the son of Mary, Jesus descends and your Imam is among yourselves?' Even now, it is a question of great importance that every one should think of.

In the Islam, the Prophets are the chosen and distinguished persons in order to get in contact with Allah. They find out the truth and communicate it to the people. This kind of contact is called revelation. It is a special kind of contact between a prophet and Allah. According to the Islam, the Prophet with his inner eyes sees the mysteries of the universe, and with the ears of his heart listens to divine calls and conveys them to the people. In the Islam, the prophets have a high regard.

However, Allah never gave the Prophets any assurance of the eternity either. The Prophet Muhammad had no assurance of the eternity, so he relied on Jesus for the rescue of his soul. The prophet Muhammad said his soul is in the hands of Jesus, son of Mary. That may mean that all the Muslims need to rely on Jesus Christ for the rescue of their souls and life. But it is not clear from the Qur'an. The Prophet Muhammad had taken it very seriously. And he relied on Jesus for the rescue of his soul and the life. These are not my own words. It is very clear in the following quotation from the Sahih Muslim Book.

Sahih Muslim Book 041, number 6932: "By Him in whose hand is my life, the son of Mary, peace is upon him, will soon descend among you as a just judge. He will break crosses, kill the swine and abolish the poll–tax, and wealth will pour forth to such an extent that no one will accept it."

The Prophet Muhammad believed that Jesus is the one who comes to the world to judge; therefore, it is a wise thing to depend upon Jesus because Allah did not give any assurance. No one should blame the Prophet Muhammad for not writing about the eternal assurance, because all he knew was that Allah is merciful towards his believers, but he was not sure of his soul and his life. He turned to Jesus for the refuge of his soul and his life.

The Qur'an teaches the necessity of both faith and the good works for salvation: A believer of the Islam believes that Allah is merciful, but Allah does not make known the account of the persons standing. If a Muslim murders the innocent people and thought that he did it for the sake of Allah where does the believer go and ends up? Paradise or hell? Here is the explanation in the Qur'an: it encouraged the people to do it so but there is no explanation why the Merciful God allowed to kill the innocent people for His sake?

The Qur'an 47:4. Therefore, when ye meet the unbelievers (in fight), smite at their necks; At length, when ye have thoroughly subdued them, bind a bond firmly (on them: thereafter (is the time for) either generosity or ransom: Until the war lays down its burdens. Thus (are ye commanded): but if it had been Allah's Will, He could certainly have exacted retribution from them (Himself); but (He lets you fight) in order to test you, some with others. But those who are slain in the way of Allah, – He will never let their deeds be lost. Here, this verse of the Qur'an is teaching Muslim to fight for Allah.

God is not a selfish God who for His sake keeps aside the justice of His righteousness. God's words never change. His law is the law. A murderer is a murderer who will have punishment for the murder he committed.

How can a person reach the heaven which is a holy city in his/her filthiness, his hands with full of innocent blood without the cleansing? This issue of cleansing has no importance in the Islam. If everybody goes into the paradise with filthiness, the holy city the paradise will be corrupted. God is very merciful but because of the holiness of God and the holiness of great paradise, man hesitates or fears to go into that place. They will end up in the hell. That is the reason every one has to enter into the hell as per the Qur'an.

Even Adam and Eve when they disobeyed God in the Garden of Eden, they hid themselves. Merciful God did not reject them. He forgave them. But He sent them away from the Paradise. The same concept works with God regarding our disobedience and sinful nature. The way He treated Adam and Eve, He treats every one. He has no partiality. Only with one single sin, God separated Adam and Eve from Him and sent them down to the earth. It shows God's character that He is the most merciful but very holy. The people will fear because of their filthiness just like Adam and Eve. Now the same human race is trying their best to enter into the same Garden of Eden. If somebody commits many sins, what will be the consequence? There is a huge difference in between mercy and the holiness. So how do the same God who drove away Adam and Eve for one single sin, could admit the person who did many sins? Or more than one sin?

If a pig with all its mud and dirt comes into a very neat and beautiful place the beauty of the place will be spoiled. In the same way if a sinner goes into the heaven with the filthiness of sin it will be much worse than the act of a pig. Even a small stain, mark or a trace of filthiness can be clearly being seen in the holiness or bright light of God. That is the reason Adam and eve were driven out from the Garden of Eden for one single mistake.

Hence God sent Jesus as bright light to the world so that the people will be seen their filthiness and be cleansed before they go to the paradise. Please think for a moment how the filthy person feels when he was brought into a very bright and beautiful place? He desires to be cleansed and wear suitable garments to be fit in to accommodate. That is the reason why it is written in Hadiths and Qur'an that every Muslim will enter into the hell because of no cleansing. In contrast to this a believer of Lord Jesus Christ is cleansed with His precious blood and trying to live holy with the indwelling of the Holy Spirit and be prepared in this world by sanctification or (separation) to enter into the heaven.

Whereas the Qur'an is clear about the human suffering in the hell. In the Qur'an 19:67-72, (Pickthall) it says, "Do doth not man remember that We created him before, when he was naught? And by thy Lord, verily, "We shall assemble them and the devils, then 'We' shall bring them, crouching, around hell. Then we shall pluck out from every sect whichever of them of was most stubborn in rebellion to the Beneficent and surely We are best aware of those most worthy to be burned there in. there is not one of you but shall approach it. That is a fixed ordinance of thy lord. Then We (Allah) shall rescue those who kept from evil, and leave the evil- doers crouching there."

This above statement is a very clear explanation in the Qur'an that every Muslim will suffer in the hell. But, Tirmidhi hadith: 1475 tells us that bad Muslim or good Muslim when they are in the hell asks prophets such as Adam, Moses and Muhammad etc. But finally the Prophet Muhammad makes intercession to let them enter into the paradise.

However, here a doubt arises among the people, why did the Prophet Muhammad relies on Jesus Christ for his soul and life? He himself had no assurance of the eternity and was cautious about the Judgment day. Because, no Muslim can be perfect, even the prophet Muhammad, who has fulfilled all the spiritual pillars in the Islam. So, you may ask, what is the solution for the rescue of all the Muslims?

There are a lot of verses written about Allah's mercy and the beauty of the gardens and paradise. But before entering into these beautiful gardens, everybody has to enter into the hell. There is no surety of entering into the Garden of Paradise.

When someone converts to the Islam, Allah forgives all of their previous sins and deeds. By performing good deeds, we may erase some of the minor bad ones that we have done. The prophet Muhammad said, "Fear Allah wherever you are, and follow up a bad deed with a good one and it will wipe it, and behave well towards people." (Tirmidhi)

As to those who believe and work righteousness, verily 'We' shall not suffer to perish the reward of any who do a (single) righteous deed. (18:30) But still everybody has to go through hell. But after them there followed a posterity who missed prayers and followed after lusts soon, then, will they face Destruction,-Except those who repent and believe, and work righteousness: for these will enter the Garden and will not be wronged in the least,-Gardens of Eternity, those which (Allah) Most Gracious has promised to His servants in the Unseen: for His promise must (necessarily) come to pass." [Surah. 19:59-61]

According to these references from the Qur'an, people have salvation by having faith in Allah and by doing good works. However, it says, that Allah bestows on whom He pleases. Those who repent, believe, and do good deeds: God will change the evil deeds of such people into good ones.

Repentance for sin can be accomplished through acts such as, "fasting, giving charity, sacrificing an animal, and freeing a slave. In addition going on the hajj can serve as a form of repentance. [Qur'an Sura 25 ayat 70 [14 and 15]

According to Shaddad ibn Aws:

The Messenger of Allah, peace be upon him, said, "The lesser pilgrimage unto the lesser pilgrimage will expiate whatever sins were committed between them; and the accepted pilgrimage has no reward other than Paradise." — Sahih Bukhari, book 27, number 1.

With the masses of humanity and jinn assembled before the throne, the time comes for them to be divided, according to the judgment. The sins and actions of humanity recorded in the book of deeds will be placed before them.

Then as for him who is given his record in his right hand, he will say: "take, read my book!" [49]And the Book is placed and thou seest the guilty fearful of that which is therein, and they say: What Kind of a book is this that leaveth not a small thing or a great thing but hath counted it! And they find all that they did confronting them, and thy Lord wrongeth no one.' (Surah 18:49) 'Individuals whose good deeds outweigh their bad deeds will attain "Success". Those whose scales are light will loose their souls. The people will be gathered to the right and the left of the throne of God, which is upheld by eight angels.'(Surah 7:8-9)

Those on the right will enter the Gardens of Paradise; those on the left will get chains for hell. Both groups will then be forced to cross over the bridge of "Hell", called Sirat. However, regardless of one's outward deeds, God does not accept the forgiveness of those who are insincere in their repentance and only do so in order to avoid Jahannam.

It is not true repentance when people continue to do evil until death confronts them and then say, 'Now I repent.' — Qur'an, sura 4 Ayat 18

In the Islam the believer must always have faith on Allah, and believe that Allah is merciful in order to grant paradise. Other than that there are no other promises were given in the Islam. Muslims believe that there is no need for atonement, but they believe in sacrifice. According to the Islam, God determines the fate of all men. A Muslim has to wait until Allah decides. Every Muslim is looking forward for the Judgment day. The final inference according to the Qur'an 19:65-72, is every Muslim ends up in hell. Whoever kept their faith will come out from the hell, but evil doers end up there crouching. There is no eternal assurance in the Islam.

The Eternal Assurance
in the Christianity

In the beginning, God created an everlasting kingdom for man to enjoy and to live forever in Garden of Eden. But the first man Adam disobeyed and lost the opportunity to live forever with God. Is there any assurance in Christianity to get back into the everlasting kingdom? Let us look into the Holy Bible to find out.

The creation of God can be read in Genesis, the first book of the Holy Bible. It explains that, after God made the entire universe and saw everything perfect, then He made man in His own image. God created man in His own image with three components which are body, soul and spirit. He made man pure, beautiful and kept him in a beautiful garden. As a gift, God made him as a king over all His creation. At that time there was no sorrow, no sickness, no thorns, and no calamities, as it is written in Genesis.

Adam could command any of God's creation. God gave Adam dominion, authority and power over the whole creation. He could eat even the fruit of life which was within his reach. God gave only one restriction that Adam could not eat the fruit of the tree of knowledge good and evil.

Adam and Eve, both did not believe what God told them but believed in the words of the serpent. Adam and Eve did not obey His command. When they disobeyed God, they felt fear and shame. They hid themselves; and tried to cover their nakedness with fig leaves. It was in vain. The most merciful God did not get angry. Either His love or His purpose was not changed. God says, "For I am the Lord, I change not" (Malachi 3:6) Yet God drove them away from the Garden. Thus Adam and Eve lost the everlasting kingdom.

God made man in a special way and he regarded him as His friend. Even though man made a mistake, and went astray God forgave him and wanted him in right direction to get back into the eternal kingdom. God wanted Him to have everlasting life and everlasting kingdom.

Hence God made a way there and then itself in Genesis 3:15 and 21. '15And I will put enmity between thee and the woman, and between thy seed and her seed; it shall bruise thy head, and thou shalt bruise his heel. 21Unto Adam also and to his wife did the LORD God make coats of skins, and clothed them. But God put them out from the Garden of Eden.' Since they were driven out of the garden, they no more had the access for life of tree to eat the fruit and live forever. Later on Man's days on the earth were minimized by God to a certain limit. Most important result was man lost the everlasting life and the everlasting kingdom.

There is no one on the earth or in this universe ever talked about these heavenly words such as everlasting life and everlasting kingdom except Jesus Christ. The holy Bible is the only source for any one on this earth to find information about everlasting kingdom. Jesus Christ is the only one on the face of this earth who answered this particular question about eternity and also had given the assurance of the eternal kingdom. This explanation can be read from John Gospel, 3rd chapter.

"3.1There was a man of the Pharisees, named Nicodemus, a ruler of the Jews: 2The same came to Jesus by night, and said unto him, Rabbi, we know that thou art a teacher come from God: for no man can do these miracles that thou doest, except God be with him.' Nicodemus regarded Lord Jesus Christ as a heavenly teacher came from God. Anybody who comes to a teacher will come to learn something from them. And it is very interesting to notice that even before Nicodemus asked the question, Jesus knew his heart. He knew the hearts of the people. This divine character of Jesus Christ was reviewed in the previous chapters of this book. We see the same thing here in this passage. And it was written, Jesus answered before he even asked for it. We see it in this following verse. '³Jesus answered and said unto him, "Verily, verily, I say unto thee, except a man be born again; he cannot see the kingdom of God."

Nicodemus was living in the days that people were looking forward for the prophecies to be fulfilled. The prophets in the Old Testament had written about Messiah and the kingdom of God. Nicodemus might have read many prophecies in the scriptures about the kingdom of God, such as the prophecy about the kingdom of Jesus Christ written by the Prophet Daniel. Nicodemus who was a master of Israel might have read all these passages from the Scriptures but he could not understand the spiritual meaning of these events.

The truth is the kingdom of heaven came into midst of us with the birth of Jesus Christ in this world. Whoever is spiritually born again can see it, otherwise can not. Nicodemus was looking at it with his physical eyes. Even though, it was right in front of him, he could not see the kingdom of God because he was not born of the Spirit. He could not understand the fact that wherever is Jesus Christ there the kingdom of heaven is. Nicodemus came that night to Jesus Christ to ask Him about the Eternal kingdom.

Nowadays also, most of the people have the same question of how can we live forever. How can a man be in the Eternal kingdom? People strive to live long; if possible, they want to live a good life even unto the eternity. If someone lives longer than anybody else it goes into the world record. Man invented many medicines, physical fitness machines to strive on them to attain the goal of living long. The Ventilators were invented to prolong the days of survival. Yet, they could not prevent the death.

But here we have an explanation of the everlasting life which everybody likes to have. Jesus Christ explained it in the further verses of the same 3rd chapter. Lord Jesus stated in verse 12 &13, "12if I have told you earthly things and ye believe not, how shall ye believe, if I tell you of heavenly things? (Everlasting things) 13And no man hath ascended up to heaven, but He that came down from heaven, even the Son of man which is in heaven." A person who came from the heaven only can tell the heavenly things because he saw them.'

'4Nicodemus saith unto him, how can a man be born when he is old? Can he enter a second time into his mother's womb, and be born?' The ruler of the Jews, Nicodemus well educated teacher of the Jews could not understand the meaning of the word "born again" Many people can not understand the meaning of the word "born again." because they are not born of the Spirit.

'5Jesus answered, "verily, verily, I say unto thee, except a man be born of water and of the Spirit, he cannot enter into the kingdom of God." (Everlasting kingdom)' He repeated the same message five times in the same chapter, "Be born again" to see the kingdom of God. Jesus talked about the new life that should be received. The old life of that person should be changed and start a life that is divine and eternal to enter into the kingdom of God.

'6That which is born of the flesh is flesh; and that which is born of the Spirit is spirit. 7Marvel not that I said unto thee, ye must be born again.' Here in this verse Lord Jesus made it clear how important is to a person to be born again. A person has to born again in the spirit to acquire eligibility to enter into the Everlasting kingdom.

Then in the same chapter, 16th verse Lord Jesus had spoken about Everlasting Love which is God's love. Even though Adam lost the privilege to be with God forever in Garden of Eden, God's intention has not changed. Since his love for mankind is eternal, He still wanted man to be with Him. The purpose of creating man has not change at all.

That explains why God did an Eternal sacrifice by sending his only begotten son to this world and offered Him as a sacrifice. We read in John 3: 16. '¹⁶For God so loved the world that he gave his only begotten Son, that whosoever believeth in him should not perish, but have everlasting life. Jesus Christ left His throne and came to the world as a simple man and sacrificed His life.

God accomplished the Eternal sacrifice by offering His son on the cross. It is finished. No need of sacrifices anymore to satisfy God. Some people do sacrifices as a good deed to replace a bad deed. The further explanation is continued in John 3:19 Then Jesus spoke of the Eternal condemnation. '¹⁹And this is the condemnation, that light is come into the world, and men loved darkness rather than light, because their deeds were evil. Man did not want to come to the light because all his filthiness can be seen in light. He that believeth on him is not condemned: but he that believeth not is condemned already, because he hath not believed in the name of the only begotten Son of God.'

'⁴⁷Verily, verily, I say unto you, He that believeth on me hath Everlasting life. (John 6:47) '³⁶He that believeth on the Son hath Everlasting life: and he that believeth not the Son shall not see life; but the wrath of God abideth on him. (John 3:36)

It is written in 1Cor 2:9, '⁹But as it is written, Eye hath not seen, nor ear heard, neither have entered into the heart of man, the things which God hath prepared for them that love him.'

In the same chapter John 3:14, Jesus had spoken about the Everlasting victory: "Even so must the son of man be lifted up" here Lord Jesus Christ speaks of the cross on which he was lifted up and conquered death for eternity.

Next Jesus speaks of the Eternal judgment: '¹⁸He that believeth on him is not condemned: but he that believeth not is condemned already, because he hath not believed in the name of the only begotten Son of God. ²⁴Verily, verily, I say unto you, He that heareth my word, and believeth on him that sent me, hath Everlasting life, and shall not come into condemnation; but is passed from death unto life.' (John5:24) '⁴In him was life.' (John1:4) All these verses explain what we have to do to attain the Eternal life. Those who desire to be in the Everlasting kingdom of God should have the Everlasting life. This is the free gift of God that He offered to mankind to enjoy the Eternal kingdom. This is very crucial to those who don't believe in the name of Jesus Christ the son of God, because they have to face the Eternal judgment.

Thus God offered us the eternal life as the most precious and holy gift. But we can not receive it in our impure hearts. Our God is holy God. If we want to live with Him, we have to enter His holy city the heaven unto eternity. Lord Jesus Christ in His sermon on mount said "Blessed are the pure in heart: for they shall see God." (Mathew 5:8). But no one can say that he or she is pure. '²³For all have sinned, and come short of the glory of God (Romans3:23) ¹⁹For out of the heart proceed evil thoughts, murders, adulteries, fornications, thefts, false witness, blasphemies.'(Mathew 15:19)

That is the reason, God did the eternal sacrifice. The holy blood of a faultless, pure and holy person, Lord Jesus Christ was shed for the redemption of many. Only His blood can cleanse a sinner and make him clean to enter into the holy city, the Eternal kingdom so that we can enjoy and live with our holy God unto the eternity. It is very interesting to note that Jesus Christ was buried in a new sepulcher in a garden where He was resurrected by defeating the death. Adam lost the eternal kingdom in the garden and Jesus Christ restored the eternal life to enjoy only in the garden.

The above explanation by Lord Jesus Christ to Nicodemus, revealed seven eternal or everlasting or heavenly things that people are not able to understand. 1. Everlasting kingdom. 2. Ever lasting love. 3. Eternal sacrifice. 4. Everlasting life. 5. Everlasting victory. 6. Eternal judgment. 7. Eternal condemnation.

Born in a Christian family or having a lot of knowledge or doctorate in theology can not take a person into the eternity. Lord

Jesus Christ stressed the key point that a person should be born again. One should receive new life, life that is divine and eternal to enter into the kingdom of God. Only those who have everlasting life can enjoy everlasting kingdom. '³⁶He that believeth on the Son hath everlasting life.' (John 3:36) Because of God's eternal sacrifice and eternal victory we received everlasting life. Since we believed in Him we escaped eternal judgment and eternal damnation.

Not only explaining all these seven heavenly things, there is one more assurance by Lord Jesus Christ, He said in John 14:1-3, 14. "¹Let not your heart be troubled: ye believe in God, believe also in me. ²In my Father's house are many mansions: if it were not so, I would have told you. I go to prepare a place for you. ³And if I go and prepare a place for you, I will come again, and receive you unto myself; that where I am, there ye may be also."

What a blessed assurance by Lord Jesus Christ to those who obey Him and born again! They will walk with God and live forever with Him and enjoy the Eternal kingdom. Yes, there is Eternal assurance in the Christianity to inherit the everlasting life in the Eternal kingdom or Everlasting Kingdom.

The Heaven and the Hell
belief in the Islam

⎯⎯⎯⎯⎯⎯⎯⎯

According to the Islam there is Heaven and there is Hell.

In the Islam one can reach the heaven by self effort or positive achievements. The principle is 'Submit to God and follow the Qur'an.' The Judgment involves weighing up of good and bad deeds of the person. Even then, entry into the heaven depends upon mercy of Allah. But there was no promise of Allah or surety of Allah even to the prophets to grant the paradise. The good deeds should out weigh bad deeds then there is a scope to get mercy of Allah. The Muslims continue their faith hoping that Allah may grant them the paradise if they fear God. No Muslim is sure about his destination.

There is a very good description of the paradise in the Qur'an. The Gardens of Eden which the All-Merciful has promised to His servants in the Unseen as per His promise is always kept." Qur'an. [Surah Maryam, 61]

Allah has promised the men and women of the believers Gardens with rivers flowing under them, remaining in them timelessly, forever, and fine dwellings in the Gardens of Eden. And Allah's good pleasure is even greater. That is the great victory. [Surat at-Tawba, 72] "They will not hear therein ill speech or commission of sin. But only the saying of: Peace! Peace!" [Qur'an 56:25–26] "Belief and Righteous Deeds are two of the best routes to Jannah (Paradise).

The door of righteous deeds is wide and the ways of obtaining rewards are vast, as Allah says, 'And those who believe and do good deed, them are the inhabitants of Paradise, in it they shall abide." [Qur'an 2:82]

According to the Islam there are many paradises. And there are seven heavens. All sensual love can be satisfied in the Paradise. In the Qur'an 55: 46–54, "46.But for Him who feareth the standing before his Lord there are two gardens. 47. Which is it, of the favors of your lord that ye deny? 48. Of spreading branches. 49. Which is it, of the favors of your Lord that ye deny? 50. Wherein are two fountains flowing 51.Which is it, of the favors of your Lord that ye deny? 54. Reclining upon couches lined with silk brocade, the fruit of both gardens near to hand. 55. Which is it, of the favors of your Lord that ye deny? 56. Therein are those of modest gaze, whom neither man nor Jinni will have touched before them."

Taqwa is the fear of the Most Merciful, and acting in accordance with the Qur'an and the Sunnah of the Messenger of Allah, sallallahu alayhe wa sallam. That is: hoping for the reward of Allah and avoiding disobedience of His Guidance and fearing His Punishment. For Allah says, "Surely those of Taqwa shall be in the midst of Gardens and fountains."[Qur'an15:45]

If you enter the Paradise, you will live a very happy life without sickness, pain, sadness, or death; God will be pleased with you; and you will live there forever. "But those who believe and do good deeds, we will admit them to Gardens (Paradise) in which rivers flow, lasting in them forever...." [Qur'an 4:57]

Here are some paraphrases which tell us that Allah will bring a believer out from the darkness to the Light: The believer means those who believe in Allah, angels and His messengers. But they are still in the darkness.

"He it is who sends blessings on you, as do His angels, that He may bring you out from the depths of the Darkness into the Light: and He is full of Mercy to the Believers." [Quran 33:43]In the case of those who say, "Our Lord is Allah," and, further, stand straight and steadfast, the angels descend on them (from time to time): "Fear ye not!" (They suggest), 'Nor grieve! But receive the Glad Tidings of the Garden (of Bliss), that which ye were promised! [Qur'an 41:30]

"It is not righteousness that ye turn your faces towards East or West; but it is righteousness to believe in Allah and the Last Day, and the Angels, and the Book, and the Messengers; to spend of your substance, out of love for Him, for your kin, for orphans, for the needy, for the wayfarer, for those who ask, and for the ransom of slaves; to be steadfast in prayer, and give zakat; to fulfill the contracts which ye have made; and to be firm and patient, in pain (or suffering) and adversity, and throughout all periods of panic." [Qur'an 2:177] "You be foremost (in seeking) forgiveness from your Lord, and a Garden(of Bliss), the width whereof is as the width of heaven and earth, prepared for those who believe in Allah and His messengers: that is the Grace of Allah, which He bestows on whom He pleases: and Allah is the Lord of Grace abounding." [Qur'an 57:21]

Those are limits set by Allah. "Those who obey Allah and His Messenger will be admitted to the Gardens with rivers flowing beneath, to abide therein (for ever) and that will be the supreme achievement. But those who disobey Allah and His Messenger and transgress His limits will be admitted to a Fire, to abide therein: And they shall have a humiliating punishment." Qur'an (4:13-14)

"But those who believe and work righteousness, no burden do 'We' place on any soul, but that which it can bear, they will be Companions of the Garden, therein to dwell (forever)." [Qur'an 7:42]

The Qur'an description of the heaven includes plentiful food and drink: "A similitude of the Garden which those who keep their duty (to Allah) are promised: Therein are rivers of water unpolluted, and rivers of milk whereof the flavor changeth, and rivers of wine delicious to the drinkers, and rivers of clear run honey: therein for them every kind of fruit, with pardon from their lord (Are those who enjoy all this) like those who are immortal in the fire and are given boiling water to drink so that it teareth their bowels?" [Qur'an 47:15] (Pickthall)

Those who find the favor of Lord would get all comfort. They will get so many favors. But there is no clarification of any good deed or bad deed. Allah's decision will be final. Those who get favor of Lord will get into the Paradise but the punishment of those who wage war against Allah and His Messengers.

According to the Noble Qur'an, Taqwa should be the ultimate result of all forms of worship. Fear of God, which in Arabic means Taqwa, is the soul of fasting. In the Islam, being just is considered to be a necessary condition or being pious and God-fearing, the basic characteristics of a Muslim. The Noble Qur'an says: "...Deal justly; those is nearer to pity, and observe your duty to Allah. Surely Allah is well aware of what you do. Love your God more than your soul." (Qur'an 5:8).

The Islam teaches that Hell is a real place prepared by God for those who do not believe in Him, rebel against His laws, and reject His messengers. The Hell is an actual place, not a mere state of mind or a spiritual entity. The horrors, pain, anguish, and punishment are all real, but different in nature than their earthly counterparts. The Hell is the ultimate humiliation and loss, and nothing is worse than it. In the Islam there are minor sins and major sins. The primary sin in Islam is Apostasy. It can not be easily forgiven by Allah. In the Islam there is no cleansing of the sins.

Every Muslim has to follow the law very strictly. As we know, that the Divine law can not be changed. We assume that God is the most Merciful and He always forgives. But yet there is no surety. While the Islam teaches that it will be simply forgiven by saying, 'Muhammad is Allah's messenger,' why God sent Adam and Eve out of the Paradise even though God had forgiven them? When the sins of the people are forgiven by saying 'Muhammad is a messenger,' why Muhammad himself is relying on Jesus to rescue his soul? Then how can we believe the statement that if we say Muhammad is the messenger then all the sins will be forgiven?

In the Islam there is no clarification of any good deed or bad deed. Every one has to wait until the final judgment to know how many good deeds or bad deeds he or she did. Allah's decision will be final. Those who get favor of Lord will get into the Paradise. But the punishment of those who wage war against Allah and His Messenger, and strive with might and main for mischief through the land is: execution, or crucifixion, or the cutting off of hands and feet from opposite sides, or exile from the land: that is their disgrace in this world, and a heavy punishment is theirs in the Hereafter; Whoever doesn't believe that Allah is only God, their punishment will be hell. Those who don't believe Allah as God, they are in their sin.

It says in the Qur'an, 'seize ye him, and bind ye him, And burn ye him in the Blazing Fire. Further, make him march in a chain, whereof the length is seventy cubits! This was he that would not believe in Allah Most High. And would not encourage the feeding of the indigent! So no friend hath he here this Day. Nor hath he any food except the corruption from the washing of wounds, which none do eat but those in sin.'[Qur'an 69:30–37]

"Our Lord, Surely, whom you admit to the Fire, indeed you have disgraced him, and never will the wrongdoers find any helpers." [Qur'an 5:33; 3:192]

Yet there are other passages in the Qur'an that strongly states that there are no intercessors or helpers besides Allah since He is sufficient: But again, the Hadiths clearly teach that the righteous do seek the aid of the prophets and will receive it, at least on the Day of the Judgment.

Narrated 'Abdullah bin 'Umar' about the Day of Resurrection:

The Prophet said, "A man keeps on asking others for something till he comes on the Day of Resurrection without any piece of flesh on his face." The Prophet added, "On the Day of Resurrection, the Sun will come near (to the people) to such an extent that the sweat will reach up to the middle of the ears, so, when all the people are in that state, they will ask Adam FOR HELP, and then Moses, and then Muhammad (p.b.u.h)." The sub–narrator added, "Muhammad will intercede with Allah to judge amongst the people. He will proceed on till he will hold the ring of the door (of Paradise) and then Allah will exalt him to Maqam Mahmud (the privilege of intercession, etc.). And all the people of the gathering will send their praises to Allah. [Sahih Al- Bukhari, volume 2, book 24, number 553]

There is another explanation in the Islam about the Resurrection Day.

Every living creature will die, even the angels, causing all to submit to the oneness of God, tawhid [Surah 55:26-27, 28:88] Then all will be resurrected, including the angel who blows the trumpet to the resurrection. This event will be preceded by the trumpet blast, which crushes the mountains. All will be gathered and submit to Allah. And when the trumpet shall sound one blast and the earth with the mountains shall be lifted up and crushed with one crash, then, on that day will the Event befall. And the heaven will split asunder, for that day it will be frail. And the angels will be on the sides thereof, and eight will uphold the throne of thy Lord that day above them. On that day you will be exposed: not a secret of you will be hidden. Then as for him who is given his record in his right hand, he will say: take, read my book! [Surah 69:13-19]

All people will be gathered before the throne of God to be judged for their deeds. On this day, two groups will be separated. The believers will have joy and the disbelievers will face doom. The above passages show that there are two different ways of explanation in the Islam about the Resurrection day as well as the Judgment Day.

In the Qur'an, 19:67-72, (Pickthall) it says, "Do doth not man remember that We created him before, when he was naught? And by thy Lord, verily We (Allah) shall assemble them and the devils, then We shall bring them, crouching, around hell. Then we shall pluck out from every sect whichever of them of was most stubborn in rebellion to the Beneficent and surely We (Allah) are best aware of those most worthy to be burned there in. there is not one of you but shall approach it. That is a fixed ordinance of thy lord. Then We (Allah) shall rescue those who kept from evil, and leave the evil-doers crouching there."

This above verse is a very clear explanation in the Qur'an that every Muslim has to enter into the hell. It shows that there is no way for mankind to avoid disobedience? Adam disobeyed and Moses also disobeyed. Even the Prophets disobeyed, so it is difficult for the human being to live with obedience to God. That is the reason, it is a fixed ordinance that every one must enter into the hell according to the Qur'an.

The Heaven and the Hell belief
in the Christianity

The Christians believe there is heaven and hell. The Christians who follow Jesus have a great promise and assurance of their eternal home. Jesus Christ said in John14:1- "¹Let not your heart be troubled: ye believe in God, believe also in me. ²In my Father's house are many mansions: if it were not so, I would have told you. I go to prepare a place for you. ³And if I go and prepare a place for you, I will come again, and receive you unto myself; that where I am, there ye may be also. ⁴And whither I go ye know, and the way ye know." The place that Jesus went to prepare is in heaven which is an abode of God Almighty. The holiness is the main and unique in the Heaven. There are many Christian believers that are sure about their destination. There is concrete evidence in the holy Bible about heaven.

This place heaven was shown to John, one of the disciples of Jesus after His ascension to heaven. He personally wrote whole book about it. Not only heaven, the detail truth of the past, present, future was revealed to the disciple John in Patmos, where he was exiled by a Roman emperor, Domitian. According to the history, the Apostle John was banished in Patmos Island by the emperor Domitian for preaching the Gospel at Ehesus. The Gospel declares that Jesus is Lord and God, but Domitian required to be called Dominus et Deus "Lord and God." Domitian had John thrown into a cauldron of boiling oil before the Porta Latina at Rome but John suffered no injury! The only way that Domitian could get rid of him was to exile him.

During those days early Christians were going through severe persecution. It was probably about sixty years after the crucifixion of Jesus Christ. John was so desperate because of the persecution of the church. At that situation he was carried to heaven when he was in the spirit. Angel came and showed him many interesting events which he never even dreamed of. The book of Revelation is the eye witness of Saint John. There in Patmos, John wrote all what he had seen in "Revelation, the last book of the Holy Bible.

John wrote, '[10]I was in the Spirit on the Lord's day, and heard behind me a great voice, as of a trumpet,' when he turned to see, Christ appeared in His glory to show John that He did not leave His mission. He assures John that He is in control of all the things. Jesus Christ reaffirms His nature and identity. Here we noticed that John was in such a distress because of the persecution of the early mission of Jesus Christ. When John was in such dismay, he heard voice of Jesus calling by his name from behind. In other words Jesus knew the perspective of John about his situation. Yet Jesus was not appeared in front of Him, where he was seeing the son of man with whom he spent a period of time. Jesus wanted John to look in the other direction where the son of man could be seen in His glory so that he could understand his thinking and his ways are different than his Master Jesus.

In Revelation 1st chapter, 12–20 verses: John wrote, "[12]And I turned to see the voice that spake with me. And being turned, I saw seven golden candlesticks; [13]And in the midst of the seven candlesticks one like unto the Son of man, clothed with a garment down to the foot, and girt about the paps with a golden girdle. [14]His head and his hairs were white like wool, as white as snow; and his eyes were as a flame of fire; [15]And his feet like unto fine brass, as if they burned in a furnace; and his voice as the sound of many waters.

[16]And he had in his right hand seven stars: and out of his mouth went a sharp two-edged sword: and his countenance was as the sun shineth in his strength. [17]And when I saw him, I fell at his feet as dead.

And he laid his right hand upon me, saying unto me, "Fear not; I am the first and the last: [18] I am he that liveth, and was dead; and, behold, I am alive for evermore, Amen; and have the keys of hell and of death. [19] Write the things which thou hast seen, and the things which are, and the things which shall be hereafter; [20]The mystery of the seven stars which thou sawest in my right hand, and the seven golden candlesticks. The seven stars are the angels of the seven churches: and the seven candlesticks which thou sawest are the seven churches."

The above verse explains that at present Jesus Christ is working in the midst of His church.

I beseech every reader to focus on the above verses, especially the 18th verse. God showed John that Lord Jesus Christ was dead but alive and He had the keys of the hell and the death. He is alive and He is living in them whoever believed in him. Once again the truth of His death on the cross and the resurrection was confirmed to John. In these above verses the seven candle sticks are the seven churches.

According to the Bible the church is body of Christ. As we read in the above paragraph, Jesus is in the midst of the seven candle sticks which are the seven churches in different locations and in different era.

Seven churches represent seven periods in the church history along with their respective characteristics.

1. The first apostolic church was Ephesus 33–70AD. (Paul 35–64AD) It had lost its first love.
2. The church of Smyrna 70–313. (During this church period John exiled in Patmos. Bitter sweetness (church persecuted)
3. The church of Pergamos 313–1157. (Divorce, church as state religion, spiritually married to Rome)
4. The church of Thyatira 1157–1367(constant labor)

5. The church of Sardis 1367–1517(of the flesh)
6. The church of Philadelphia 1517–1874(brotherly love)
7. The church of Laodicea 1874 – present (people opinion)

God promised every church era, a selective distinguished gift to those who are victorious throughout their lives. Despite of their constant struggle and persecution, whoever has perseverance they will receive such gifts when they go to heaven.

The church of Jesus Christ since beginning until now is still going under persecution. Every time the Satan imprisoned His people, it resulted in greater blessings to the church. Christ loved the church, and gave Himself for it; " [26]That he might sanctify and cleanse it with the washing of water by the word, [27]That he might present it to himself a glorious church, not having spot, or wrinkle, or any such thing; but that it should be holy and without blemish." From this explanation, one can understand how dear the church is to Lord Jesus Christ. He holds the seven stars in His right hand as it was shown to John in Patmos. Now the church is waiting for Jesus Christ to come on the clouds as He was promised to take it to the heaven.

According to the Bible, when a believer dies, he or she goes to the Heaven until the resurrection occurs. As we had read in the previous chapters, only Jesus Christ had such authority to grant the place in heaven. In Luke Gospel 23:43, 'He told the thief when [42]he said unto Jesus, Lord; remember me when thou comest into thy kingdom. [43]And Jesus said unto him, Verily I say unto thee, today shalt thou be with me in paradise.' Because of this direct evidence, we knew when believers die they straight a way goes to the paradise.

We have other evidence that there is heaven. Paul went to the third heaven and he heard unspeakable words. Paul wrote in 2 Corinthians 12:1–4. 12."It is not expedient for me doubtless to glory. I will come to visions and revelations of the Lord. '[2]I knew a man in Christ above fourteen years ago, (whether in the body, I cannot tell; or whether out of the body, I cannot tell: God knoweth;) such an one caught up to the third heaven. ³And I knew such a man, (whether in the body, or out of the body, I cannot tell: God knoweth;) ⁴How that he was caught up into paradise, and heard unspeakable words, which it is not lawful for a man to utter."

But at the end days, Jesus returns to the earth. It will be His second return. He will take His people with Him. The believers who are alive as well as dead will hear the sound of trumpet, all their mortal bodies will put on immortal bodies in a moment and go with Lord Jesus. But all other people and the world remain same as it is. We had been discussed about the Second coming of Jesus in the earlier chapters of this book.

After the church has taken up, there will be a great tribulation period for seven years on the earth. At the end of that period, Jesus Christ will come along with all the saints with His glory literally to the world to make war with Anti Christ. This return of Jesus Christ to the earth will be seen by everybody even those who pierced Him as it is written in the holy Bible.

"⁷Behold, He cometh with clouds; and every eye shall see him, and they also which pierced him: and all kindred of the earth shall wail because of him, Even so, Amen. ⁸I am Alpha and Omega, the beginning and the ending, saith the Lord, which is, and which was, and which is to come, the Almighty." Revelation 1:7-8

Then there will be a thousand years rule and reign of Christ on the earth. It is mentioned in the Bible as the Millennium. Jesus will rule with the iron rod. The Saints the believers who are victorious from the temptations of the world will rule and reign with Him. "Jesus rule on the earth and His kingdom" is written in Revelation 19ᵗʰ chapter. "⁶Blessed and holy is he that hath part in the first resurrection: on such the second death hath no power, but they shall be priests of God and of Christ, and shall reign with him a thousand years.'

"⁷And when the thousand years are expired, Satan shall be loosed out of his prison. ⁸And shall go out to deceive the nations which are in the four quarters of the earth, Gog, and Magog, to gather them together to battle: the number of whom is as the sand of the sea. [9]And they went up on the breadth of the earth, and compassed the camp of the saints about and the beloved city: and fire came down from God out of heaven, and devoured them. [10]And the devil that deceived them was cast into the lake of fire and brimstone, where the beast and the false prophet are, and shall be tormented day and night for ever and ever."

Then the 'White throne judgment' will take place. "[11]And I saw a great white throne, and him that sat on it, from whose face the earth and the heaven fled away; and there was found no place for them. [12]And I saw the dead, small and great, stand before God; and the books were opened: and another book was opened, which is the book of life: and the dead were judged out of those things which were written in the books, according to their works. [13]And the sea gave up the dead which were in it; and death and hell delivered up the dead which were in them: and they were judged every man according to their works. [14]And death and hell were cast into the lake of fire. This is the second death. [15]And whosoever was not found written in the book of life was cast into the lake of fire."

Finally, there will be eternity with new heaven and new earth.

When we come to the last chapters of the same book 21-22, John wrote a clear description of the heaven. He described what he had seen. When we picture the description of John it is a very splendid and spectacular place. Whoever missed to enter this place will definitely regret. Here below I quote some verses from the description of John to show the glimpse of the heaven.

'[11]Having the glory of God: and her light was like unto a stone most precious, even like a jasper stone, clear as crystal; [14]And the wall of the city had twelve foundations, and in them the names of the twelve apostles of the Lamb. [15]And he that talked with me had a golden reed to measure the city, and the gates thereof, and the wall thereof. [16]And the city lieth foursquare, and the length is as large as the breadth: and he measured the city with the reed, twelve thousand furlongs. The length and the breadth and the height of it are equal. ¹⁷And he measured the wall thereof, an hundred and forty and four cubits, according to the measure of a man, that is, of the angel.' (Revelation 21:11-17)

'¹⁸And the building of the wall of it was of jasper: and the city was pure gold, like unto clear glass. ¹⁹And the foundations of the wall of the city were garnished with all manner of precious stones. The first foundation was jasper; the second, sapphire; the third, a chalcedony; the fourth, an emerald; ²⁰The fifth, sardonyx; the sixth, sardius; the seventh, chrysolyte; the eighth, beryl; the ninth, a topaz; the tenth, a chrysoprasus; the eleventh, a jacinth; the twelfth, an amethyst. ²¹And the twelve gates were twelve pearls: every several gate was of one pearl: and the street of the city was pure gold, as it were transparent glass. ²³And the city had no need of the sun, neither of the moons, to shine in it: for the glory of God did lighten it and the Lamb is the light thereof.' (Revelation 21:18-23)

'³And I heard a great voice out of heaven saying, Behold, the tabernacle of God is with men, and he will dwell with them, and they shall be his people, and God himself shall be with them, and be their God. ⁴And God shall wipe away all tears from their eyes; and there shall be no more death, neither sorrow, nor crying, neither shall there be any more pain: for the former things are passed away. (Revelation 22:3-4)

John clarified the truth in Revelation7:9-14: "'⁹After this I beheld, and, lo, a great multitude, which no man could number, of all nations, and kindred, and people, and tongues, stood before the throne, and before the Lamb, clothed with white robes, and palms in their hands; ¹⁰ And cried with a loud voice, saying, Salvation to our God which sitteth upon the throne, and unto the Lamb.¹¹And all the angels stood round about the throne, and about the elders and the four beasts, and fell before the throne on their faces, and worshipped God,¹²Saying, Amen: Blessing, and glory, and wisdom, and thanksgiving, and honor, and power, and might, be unto our God forever and ever. Amen.[13]And one of the elders answered, saying unto me, what are these which are arrayed in white robes? And whence came they? [14]And I said unto him, Sir, thou know. And he said to me, these are they which came out of great tribulation, and have washed their robes, and made them white in the blood of the Lamb." They entered into the eternal life because they were washed in the precious, atoning blood of Christ.

John heard a voice, "[5]And he that sat upon the throne said, "Write: for these words are true and faithful. [6]And he said unto me, It is done. I am Alpha and Omega, the beginning and the end. I will give unto him that is athirst of the fountain of the water of life freely. [7]He that overcometh shall inherit all things; and I will be his God, and he shall be my son."

"[8]But the fearful, and unbelieving, and the abominable, and murderers, and whoremongers, and sorcerers, and idolaters, and all liars, shall have their part in the lake which burneth with fire and brimstone: which is the second death." (Revelation 21:5–8)

The Christians believe that there is Hell along with the Heaven. The Hell was mentioned in the Bible more times than it mentioned the heaven, because God does not want anybody to enter into the Hell. There is no rest in the Hell. In the Hades (Hell) there is complete darkness and an ever burning fire. There is no light in the Hades because God is not there. Explanation of it can be read in Luke Gospel 16th Chapter from the Bible.

Those who are thrown into this fiery pit will never die. I heard a real testimony of my oldest brother. He was not a born again Christian. Our family and other fellow believers were always praying for his salvation. He was a Christian but was not born again. He never repented for his sins. He was a smoker and, alcoholic even though attending family prayers. One day he had a heart attack, threw up blood when he was in a restaurant. He was in coma for 4 days. Doctors gave up their hope, yet he remained in the coma for four days.

But on the fourth day he woke up from his coma. He shared his testimony as follows: When he was in the coma, he was going in a pitch dark path. He saw afar fire, horses, and out of their mouth issued fire and smoke. He was so terrified, immediately he cried "God please forgive me, I want to live for you". As soon as he uttered those words, he came back to life. We all were very thankful to God for saving my brother from his death bed and also from his ultimate destruction. The prayers of the fellow believers never had been wasted! Now he is still alive as a testimony that there is Hades (bottomless pit). God did not neglect to explain about the Hell. It is very well explained in the word of God the Bible.

Those who are not washed their clothes in the blood of Lord Jesus Christ will enter into the Hell. It is written in Revelation 21:8. The fearful, and unbelieving, and the abominable, and murderers, and whoremongers, and sorcerers, and idolaters, and all liars, shall have their part in the lake which burneth with fire and brimstone: which is the second death. (Spiritual death which is eternal separation from God)

Whoever wanted to escape the hell fire or second death should come to Jesus Christ who defeated death with His resurrection power.

Dear Reader, any body would regret missing the heaven as his or her Eternal destiny. They could not escape from the Hell once they enter into it. If any one enters into the hell because of wrong beliefs and teachings, they could not forgive themselves and there will be no end to it. If anybody misses the Heaven they will end up in the hell, an ever burning fire, and those who are thrown into it never die.

The Hell and the Heaven were created because God is a Just God; the creation of the Hell is a proof of God's righteousness. God did not create the Hell for humanity. He created it for Satan and His angels who are demons; (Matt 25:41) but because of the sin and the lack of repentance, humanity ends up in the Hell and there are more that perish than those who reach His glory. The

Satan and the demons are trying to deceive the people to take with them to the Hell. Therefore, Jesus gave His life for the humanity so it would not perish and end up in a place the hell. One can call or pray God 7 times or several times a day with respect and reverence, but still without the holiness, one cannot enter into the Holy city which is the Heaven. Without repentance and forgiveness of the sins and cleansing with the precious blood of Jesus, one cannot be holy enough to enter into it!

Jesus Christ as a savior and ruler, He saves and protects but never likes to smite unbelievers; He showed how to love our enemies and help them to be saved from eternal damnation. He is knocking at the door! Revelations 3:20 states, "20Behold, I stand at the door, and knock: if any man hears my voice, and opens the door, I will come in to him, and will sup with him, and he with me." It is a great promise! Those who open the door of their heart to Jesus will inherit these wonderful promises. There Jesus gave a great warning to take heed and not to yield to false teachings, because they take them to eternal damnation.

Here is an important question to be asked. After all this future things were shown to His disciple John, did God change His entire plan and showed other plan to enter into paradise to Muhammad? Every person has to think deeply into this great question!! Jesus said he is the only way to enter into His heavenly kingdom. There is on other way. He also warned that false Christ and false teachings will come after Him. He gave us caution to be aware of them.

It is essential to come to the cross and BELIEVE in Christ for the salvation, because Jesus said there is no other way to the heaven! It didn't say that name sake or nominal Christians can reach the heaven. It says, "Only those who trust Jesus Christ as their personal savior enter into the heaven." It is questionable to those who don't accept Him as a savior and ruler to enter into the heaven.

The following verses end the book of Revelation. These are Jesus Christ personal warnings to every one.

"¹¹He that is unjust, let him be unjust still: and he which is filthy, let him be filthy still: and he that is righteous, let him be righteous still: and he that is holy, let him be holy still. ¹²And, behold, I come quickly; and my reward is with me, to give every man according as his work shall be. ¹³I am Alpha and Omega, the beginning and the end, the first and the last. ¹⁴Blessed are they that do his commandments that they may have right to the tree of life, and may enter in through the gates into the city. ¹⁵For without are dogs, and sorcerers, and whoremongers, and murderers, and idolaters, and whosoever loveth and maketh a lie. ¹⁹And if any man shall take away from the words of the book of this prophecy, God shall take away his part out of the book of life, and out of the holy city, and from the things which are written in this book."

The Facts to realize in the Islam and the Christianity

The Islam: Faith in Allah. A believer should live for Allah and die for Him.

1. The believers chose Allah to be their God.
2. Allah is distant.
3. A believer is slave to Him. He is not dwelling in the hearts of people.
4. No guarantee of salvation.
5. Fight those who fight with you.
6. Death to infidels.
7. Pray Allah to destroy your enemies.
8. Keep your duty to Allah.
9. No assurance of Going to paradise. Allah decides by weighing good and bad deeds.
10. Reaching paradise depend upon keeping all five pillars of Islam.
11. Kill infidels to get higher level in paradise.
12. Looking forward to enjoy sensual pleasures in paradise.
13. Peace will be reached through violence because when the entire world becomes Islamic then peace will be established.
14. There is no guarantee of escaping the Eternal damnation.

The sequence of the end of the world occurs according to the Islam as follows:

15. Looking for the second coming of Jesus for the rewards.
16. Jesus get marry, have children and died after 40 years rule.
17. Everybody will die at the end of the world.
18. At the end comes Resurrection and books will be opened.
19. The Judgment at the throne of God.
20. Good people and bad people will be separated.
21. Those on the right will enter the Gardens of Paradise; those on the left will get chains for the hell.
22. Both groups (good people and bad people) will then be forced to cross over the bridge of "Hell", called Sirat.

However, regardless of one's outward deeds, God does not accept the forgiveness of those who are insincere in their repentance and only do so in order to avoid Jahanna.

Main teaching in the Qur'an is belief in Allah. He is only one God. Other than that is evil. Whoever doesn't believe is an unbeliever and committing major sin by not accepting Allah as a God. It was written that Allah is the most Merciful and Compassionate but He punishes unbelievers without any mercy.

Here below are some Qur'an teachings: These references are taken from the Noble Qur'an. It teaches the believers to be very careful of non believers and it also teaches there is severe punishment to unbelievers. In Islam religion means surrendering to Allah. There are some fixed ordinances by Allah about non believers. Non believers have no invitation to enter into believers.

*Punishment for apostates: Allah will never pardon them, nor will He guide them unto a way. {Qur'an 16: 106/ 3: 86–88 and 90/ 4: 137}

*Torment to Non-believers: Lo! Those who disbelieve Our revelations, we shall expose them to the fire. As often as their skins are consumed We shall exchange them for fresh skins that they may taste the torment. Lo! Allah is ever Mighty, Wise [Qur'an 4:56]

*Only Islam Acceptable: And whoso seeketh as religion other than the Surrender (to Allah) it will not be accepted from him, and he will be a loser in the Hereafter [Qur'an 3:85]

*No friends from outsiders: O ye who believe! Take not for intimates other than your folk, would spare no pains to ruin you; they love to hamper you. Hatred is revealed by their mouths, but that by their breasts hide is greater. We have made plain for you the revelations if ye will understand.[Qur'an 3 : 118]

*No friends with Jews, Christians: O ye who believe! Take not the Jews and Christians for friends. They are friends one to another. He among you who taketh them for friends is (one) of them. Lo! Allah guideth not wrong doing folk. [Qur'an 5:51]

*No friends with non believers: Let not the believers take disbelievers for their friends in preference to believers Whoso doth that hath no connection with Allah unless (it be) that ye but guard yourselves against them, taking (as it were) security. Allah biddeth you beware (only) of himself. Unto Allah is the Journeying.[Qur'an 3:28]

*No friends with parents/siblings if not believers: O ye who believe! Choose not your fathers or your brethren for friends if they take pleasure in disbelief rather than faith. Whoso of you taketh them for friends, such are wrongdoers. [Qur'an9:23]

*Fight non-believers; O ye who believe! Fight those of the disbelievers who are near to you, and let them find harshness in you, and know that Allah is with those who keep their duty (unto Him) [Qur'an 9:123]

*Kill non-believers: They long that ye should disbelieve even as they disbelieve, that ye may be upon a level (with them) So choose not friends from them till they forsake their homes in the way of Allah; if they turn back (enmity), then take them and kill them wherever ye find them, and choose no friend nor helper from among them. [Qur'an 4:89]

*Killing Idolaters: Then, when the sacred months have passed, slay the idolaters wherever ye find them, and take them captives and besiege them, and prepare for them each ambush. But if they repent and establish worship and pay the poor due, then leave their way free. Lo! Allah is Forgiving, Merciful.

*Idolaters are unclean just because they are idolater: O ye who believe! The idolaters only are unclean. So let them not come near the Inviolable place of Worship after this their year. {Qur'an 9:28}

*Forcing Christians and Jews to pay tax : Fight against such of those who have been given the Scripture as believe not in Allah nor the Last day and forbid not that which Allah hath forbidden by His messenger, follow not the religion of truth, until they pay the tribute readily, being brought low{ Qur'an 9:29}

*Cast terror in the hearts, smite the neck and cut fingertips of unbelievers: When thy Lord inspired the angels (saying) I am with you. So make those who believe stand firm. I will throw fear into the hearts of those who disbelieve. Then smite the necks and smite of them each finger { Qur'an 8;12}

*Severe Punishment for non–believers: But as for those who disbelieve, garments of fire will be cut out for them; boiling fluid will be pour down on their heads. 20. Whereby that which is in their bellies, and their skins too, will be melted; 21 and for them are hooked rods of iron.22. Whenever, in their anguish, they would go forth from thence they are driven back therein and (it is said unto them); taste the doom of burning. { Qur'an 22:19-22}

*The Torment of Hell:{ Qur'an 44: 43-58}

*Non believers go to hell : { Qur'an 4: 140 & 7: 36}

*Threat of punishment for not going to war : {Qur'an : 9:38-39& 48:16}

*Intentionally preventing unbelievers from Understanding: And when thou recitest the Qur'an, We place between thee and those who believe not in the Hereafter a hidden barrier; And We place upon their hearts veils lest they should understand it, and in their ears a deafness; and when thou makest mention of thy Lord alone in the Qur'an, they turn their backs in aversion. [Qur'an : 17: 45-46]

*It is God who causes people to err and He punishes them for that: And he whom Allah guideth, he is led aright: while as for him whom he sendeth astray, for them thou wilt find no protecting friends beside Him, and We shall assemble them on the day of Resurrection on their faces, blind, dumb and deaf, their habitation will be hell: whenever it abadeth. We increase the flame from them. { Qur'an 17:97}

*Intentionally misguiding those whom he pleases to: And We never sent a messenger save with the language of his folk, that he might make (the Message) clear for them. Then Allah sendeth whom He will astray, and guideth whom He will. He is the Mighty, the Wise{ Quran 14:4}

*God causes human to err: he who Allah leadeth, he indeed is led aright, while he whom Allah sendeth astray– they indeed are losers [Qur'an 7:178]

The Christianity:

1. The believer is saved by the grace of God.
2. God sacrificed and died to save a sinner to rescue him from the Eternal damnation to live with him forever.
3. Guarantee of the salvation unto the eternity through Jesus Christ because Jesus means savior and Christ means anointed. God Himself came to the world to show how deep His love is. And gave His direct assurance and provided a straight path to reach Him.
4. The cleansing of the sin is only with the precious blood of Jesus Christ. He is forgiving God.
5. God as a Holy Spirit comes and lives in a believer and enable the believer to live better life separated from the sinful world.

6. God is our comforter and friend to whom anybody can talk and pour out their heart and to be filled with the Holy Spirit.

7. Watch and Pray and Love your neighbor even your enemies.

8. Read the word of God to be strengthened and pray fervently for all the people. Always being joyful and speaking to yourselves in psalms and hymns and spiritual songs, singing and making melody in your heart to the Lord.

9. Through faith in God you will be healed and miracles or super natural things will happen.

10. Giving thanks always for all things unto God and the Father in the name of our Lord Jesus Christ.

11. Love thy neighbor like yourself. If it be possible, as much as lieth in you, live peaceably with all men. Dearly beloved, avenge not yourselves, but rather give place unto wrath: for it is written, Vengeance is mine; I will repay, saith the Lord. Therefore if thine enemy hunger, feed him; if he thirst, give him drink: for in so doing thou shalt heap coals of fire on his head. Be not overcome of evil, but overcome evil with good. If any unbeliever comes to kill a real believer, he has to forgive and show love of God.

12. There is an assurance of paradise once if get saved and live faithfully in right with God. It is a privilege of resting of soul until resurrection.

13. Escaped from the Eternal damnation.

14. Looking for the second coming of Jesus Christ for the rapture.

The sequences will be as follows:

15. He appears on the clouds to receive the church and takes with him. The Church is compared with Bride. John in Patmos wrote in the last book of the Bible, Revelation, "And after these things I heard a great voice of much people in heaven, saying, Alleluia; Salvation, and glory, and honor, and power,

unto the Lord our God: '8And to her was granted that she should be arrayed in fine linen, clean and white: for the fine linen is the righteousness of saints.'

16. 20And the beast was taken, and with him the false prophet that wrought miracles before him, with which he deceived them that had received the mark of the beast, and them that worshipped his image. These both were cast alive into a lake of fire burning with brimstone.'

17. '20And I saw an angel come down from heaven, having the key of the bottomless pit and a great chain in his hand. 2And he laid hold on the dragon, that old serpent, which is the Devil, and Satan, and bound him a thousand years, 3And cast him into the bottomless pit, and shut him up, and set a seal upon him.'

18. Then Millennium. '6Blessed and holy is he that hath part in the first resurrection: on such the second death hath no power, but they shall be priests of God and of Christ, and shall reign with him a thousand years. 7And when the thousand years are expired, Satan shall be loosed out of his prison, and again goes to deceive people.'

19. '9And they went up on the breadth of the earth, and compassed the camp of the saints about and the beloved city: and fire came down from God out of heaven, and devoured them. 10And the devil that deceived them was cast into the lake of fire and brimstone, where the beast and the false prophet are, and shall be tormented day and night for ever and ever.'

20. Then there will be white throne judgment. And I saw the dead, small and great, stand before God; and the books were opened: and another book was opened, which is the book of life: and the dead were judged out of those things which were written in the books, according to their works. '13And the sea gave up the dead which were in it; and death and hell delivered up the dead which were in them: and they were judged every man according to their works.'

21. '¹⁴And death and hell were cast into the lake of fire. This is the second death. ¹⁵And whosoever was not found written in the book of life was cast into the lake of fire.'

22. '¹And I saw a new heaven and a new earth: for the first heaven and the first earth were passed away; and there was no more sea.²And I John saw the holy city, new Jerusalem, coming down from God out of heaven, prepared as a bride adorned for her husband. ³And I heard a great voice out of heaven saying, Behold, the tabernacle of God is with men, and he will dwell with them, and they shall be his people, and God Himself shall be with them, and be their God. ⁴And God shall wipe away all tears from their eyes; and there shall be no more death, neither sorrow, nor crying, neither shall there be any more pain: for the former things are passed away.'

The main teaching in Christianity is just to believe in Lord Jesus Christ that He came and died for the people to give salvation and the repentance is needed for the forgiveness of the sins. He had authority to forgive the sins and gives a believer a new life. He is forgiving God. His Holy Spirit comes and lives in us, only when we are cleansed and gives us spiritual energy to follow His teachings. It says in the Bible, that He is knocking at the door with an unconditional love and unfailing patience. Revelations 3:20 states, "²⁰Behold, I stand at the door, and knock: if any man hears my voice, and opens the door, I will come in to him, and will sup with him, and he with me."

God is so gracious and merciful. He gave His life for every one. The only must is we should become holy to enter into HIS CITY. A sinner can not stand in such a holy place by self effort. Everyone should believe that His blood only has the power to cleanse a sinner.

Here are His main teachings to attain His character. These are as follows:

These are taken from The Holy Bible: Mathew Gospel 5th chapter. 5.[1]And seeing the multitudes, Lord Jesus Christ went up into a mountain: and when he was set, His disciples came unto him:

[2]And he opened his mouth, and taught them, saying,

[3]Blessed are the poor in spirit: for theirs is the kingdom of heaven.

[4]Blessed are they that mourn: for they shall be comforted.

[5]Blessed are the meek: for they shall inherit the earth.

[6]Blessed are they which do hunger and thirst after righteousness: for they shall be filled.

[7]Blessed are the merciful: for they shall obtain mercy.

[8]Blessed are the pure in heart: for they shall see God.

[9]Blessed are the peacemakers: for they shall be called the children of God.

[10]Blessed are they which are persecuted for righteousness' sake: for theirs is the kingdom of heaven.

[11]Blessed are ye, when men shall revile you, and persecute you, and shall say all manner of evil against you falsely, for my sake.

[12]Rejoice, and be exceeding glad: for great is your reward in heaven: for so persecuted they the prophets which were before you.

[37]But let your communication be, yea, yea; nay, nay: for whatsoever is more than these cometh of evil.

[38]Ye have heard that it hath been said, an eye for an eye, and a tooth for a tooth:

[39]But I say unto you, that ye resist not evil: but whosoever shall smite thee on thy right cheek, turn to him the other also.

[40]And if any man will sue thee at the law, and take away thy coat, let him have thy cloak also.

[41]And whosoever shall compel thee to go a mile, go with him twain.

[42]Give to him that asketh thee, and from him that would borrow of thee turn not thou away.

[43]Ye have heard that it hath been said, Thou shalt love thy neighbour, and hate thine enemy.

[44]But I say unto you, Love your enemies, bless them that curse you, do good to them that hate you, and pray for them which despitefully use you, and persecute you;

[45]That ye may be the children of your Father which is in heaven: for he maketh his sun to rise on the evil and on the good, and sendeth rain on the just and on the unjust.

[46]For if ye love them which love you, what reward have ye? Do not even the publicans the same?

[47]And if ye salute your brethren only, what do ye more than others? Do not even the publicans so?

[48]Be ye therefore perfect, even as your Father which is in heaven is perfect.

The discussion of the Truth

Please let us walk further deep into some of the thoughts which are very questionable about the truth. Let us go on one by one to understand the truth.

It was revealed in the Gospels and in the Qur'an that, "Jesus is truth." His promises are true and His teachings are from God. But there came up some contradictions among the people, making Jesus Christ and Allah words false. These contradictions showing the people that they both were deviated from their previous sayings. Let us see in detail how these contradictions suppress the 'Truth' to mislead the people into wrong direction.

Here is one truth that we have to realize. The Muslims and the Christians believe that Jesus (Messiah) will come to the world the second time.

In the previous chapters of this book, as per the Islam we came across about the hour will not be established until Jesus comes. It is stated in Sahih Al Bukhari, 3:43:656: Narrated Abu Hurairah: 'Allah's Apostle said, "the Hour will not be established until the Son of Mary (Mary am) (i.e. Isa) descends amongst you as a just ruler; he will break the cross, kill the pigs, and abolish the Jizya tax. Money will be in abundance so that nobody will accept it (as charitable gifts). "After the death of the Madhi, Isa will assume leadership.

This is a time associated in the Islamic narrative with the universal peace and justice. The Islamic texts also allude to the appearance of

Ya'juj and Ma'juj (known also as Gog and Magog), ancient tribes which will disperse and cause disturbance on the earth. God in response to Isa' prayers will kill them by sending a type of worm in the napes of their necks. [46] Isa' rule is said to be around 40 years, after which He will die. The Muslims will then perform the Salat al – Janazah (funeral prayer) for Him and bury Him in the city of Medina in a grave left vacant beside Muhammad." [45]

Now, the Muslims and the Christians, all are waiting for Jesus' second return so that all the above narration to be fulfilled and all the believers to be saved. Even the Prophet Muhammad will be there and he claimed that Jesus will save him. Muslims are waiting for 40 years glorious period whereas the Christians are waiting for them to take home with Him and later a glorious period of 1000 years which they call Millennium which will be ruled by Jesus Christ and the believers will be reigned with Him. At His first advent, Jesus was born with the human flesh. He died and was raised with the glorious body. It is a fact that He was raised with His glorious body otherwise He can not live in the heaven with ordinary human body.

Presently, Jesus is in the heaven and at His second return; He will be descending on the shoulders of two angels without being born as a human (mortal). It means He will be coming with His glorious body with which He was raised to Allah. In fact He will be coming as the spirit of God. Here are some questions to be considered and probe into if the Muslims believe the same Jesus who was announced by the angel Gabriel to Mary at His birth and came once to the world through Mary. If that same Jesus Christ will be coming back the second time to the world, then the questions are as follows:

How could Jesus as a Spirit being coming on the shoulders of the two angels get marry, get children, live forty years and die? What would be the benefit for the people who are waiting for Jesus' return as a ruler if He will live only forty years and be buried in a grave beside Muhammad? If Jesus will be buried next to Muhammad, how Muhammad relied on Jesus for the rescue of his soul?

Now let us focus on Jesus' direct words and His direct guidance whether He will be coming to save the souls and take them with Him as per the Christianity or to get marry, have children, live 40 years and be buried in Medina next to Muhammad as per the Islam?

Jesus is the Truth according to the Qur'an and the Bible so we have to believe His words not some one else's words or assumptions.

According to His words, Jesus will be coming the second time, not to die and be buried (since he already defeated the death) but to come as a just judge, to rule and to reign for thousand years.

Jesus came to the world the first time with the purpose of redeeming all the people from the law and the second time God will be sending Jesus to judge the people.

According to the Islam, "the hour will not be established until the son of Mary (i.e. Jesus) Jesus descends amongst you as a ruler." (Sahih Al Bukhari 3:43–656)

The people who read and follow the Bible are very confident of this event because of His promise that He will come and take them with Him.

In the Holy Bible, the last book 'Revelation' was written by John at Patmos Island. As we came across it many times in this book, he wrote what he had seen. He stated and confirmed whom he had seen. He saw the same "Son of Man" Jesus who was born to Mary but in His glory. Once John lived with Jesus but now as a normal human being John could not stand when He saw Jesus in His glory. He wrote unimaginable description of the Glory of Jesus Christ. Angel showed John the prophecy of Jesus and he also showed John the present situation of Jesus.

John the disciple testified about Jesus Christ in the first chapter of Revelation. "⁹I John heard behind me a great voice, as of a trumpet, ‘¹¹Saying, I am Alpha and Omega, the first and the last: and, what thou seest, write in a book, and send it unto the seven churches which are in Asia; ¹²And I turned to see the voice that spake with me. And being turned, I saw seven golden candlesticks; ¹³And in the midst of the seven candlesticks one like unto the Son of man, clothed with a garment down to the foot, and girt about the paps with a golden girdle. [14]His head and his hairs were white like wool, as white as snow; and his eyes were as a flame of fire; [15]And his feet like unto fine brass, as if they burned in a furnace; and his voice as the sound of many waters. [16]And he had in his right hand seven stars: and out of his mouth went a sharp two edged sword: and his countenance was as the sun shineth in his strength.'

John wrote that, '[17]And when I saw him, I fell at his feet as dead. And he laid his right hand upon me, saying unto me, "Fear not; I am the first and the last: [18]I am he that liveth, and was dead; and, behold, I am alive for evermore, Amen; and have the keys of hell and of death. [19]Write the things which thou hast seen, and the things which are, and the things which shall be hereafter;"

These words of Jesus in the above verses 17–19, which says, that "He is first and last and he is alive for evermore and He has the keys of hell and death." These are contrary to the teachings in the Islam that Jesus lives only 40 years and be buried at the side of the Prophet Muhammad in Medina. "[8]Jesus Christ is the same yesterday, and to day, and for ever.' (Hebrews 13:5) He confirmed with John "[8]I am Alpha and Omega, the beginning and the ending, saith the Lord, which is, and which was, and which is to come, the Almighty. [18]I am he that liveth, and was dead; and, behold, I am alive for evermore, Amen; and have the keys of hell and of death." (Revelation1:8 &18) Jesus affirmed these words to John. How could any one deny this truth and accept the information of another person rather than Jesus Christ.

Here the problem arose because people do not want to take Jesus direct words but wanted to know about Jesus' information from the third person who came after seven hundred years. Some people do not want to believe the eyewitness but ready to believe the information from a person who never even saw Jesus Christ.

John was His eyewitness who wrote: '[20]The mystery of the seven stars which thou sawest in my right hand, and the seven golden candlesticks. The seven stars are the angels of the seven churches: and the seven candlesticks which thou sawest are the seven churches.' Presently, Jesus Christ is in midst of seven churches working among them to make them like gold.

The church (The body of Christ or the believers) who go through many afflictions and persecution are compared as the gold. The Spiritual meaning of gold is the Divine nature. Jesus is working with all His house hold to build His divine house with the people who are going through trials and tests like fire to become as real gold that means God is taking them through the situations in their life to acquire divine qualities. Jesus is making the people in the church to attain His characteristics so that they can withstand His glory in the coming Eternal kingdom.

In the Islam, they believe, Jesus lives only 40 years on this earth, get marry, have children and be buried in Mecca, next to Muhammad's tomb as an ordinary man. Those whoever wrote this kind of information about Jesus, might have forgotten or not analyzed about His life on the earth when He came the first time to the world.

Jesus on this earth never tried to conquer the world nor got married. He proved that He is not of this world. As it was written in John 3:31, '31He that cometh from above is above all: he that is of the earth is earthly, and speaketh of the earth: he that cometh from heaven is above all.' Jesus Christ never fought to conquer the kingdoms of the earth. His kingdom is the everlasting kingdom. He never wanted to enjoy with wives or never tried to get earthly riches. If He wanted to enjoy earthly life He might have conquered everything in this world only with one word as He is the word of God. He proved there is power in His words. As we all came to know in the history, He healed all kinds of diseases and He even raised the dead. He fed thousands of the people with five bread loaves and two fish. He did many miracles and wonders even from He was an infant on the earth.

Jesus Christ many times explained difference between the earthly and the heavenly things. He said in John Gospel 8:44. "⁴⁴Ye are of your father the devil, and the lusts of your father ye will do. He was a murderer from the beginning, and abode not in the truth, because there is no truth in him. When he speaketh a lie, he speaketh of his own: for he is a liar, and the father of it. Allah was well pleased with the teachings of Jesus Christ. That is the reason, God is sending Jesus Christ second time to judge all the people. He will judge according to His own teachings. How could any one abandon their own teachings and judge by other's teachings?

In the Islam, the believers are wishing to be in Jihad to enter directly into the heaven so that they can enjoy sensual pleasures in the heaven. The sensual pleasures are the lusts of this world. And they are the desires of the earthly body which limits only with this world. This kind of act is against to God if we understand the above verse which was quoted in John 8:44. The suicide bombing is against the teachings of Jesus Christ. He had invited everybody with love and warmth. God loved each and every one and made them in His image. No need of killings to enter into the kingdom of God. If we kill unbelievers, how they will come to know the love of God? Whoever murders is a murderer. God's law is law. His word is the word. It never changes.

In the above paragraph, As per the teachings of Jesus Christ, the Satan is the murderer from the beginning. Whoever murders any human is the child of the Satan, the destroyer. The life comes from God.

God does not need any human help to kill the people for Him. He can kill any one or He can destroy any one if He wishes. He is sovereign God. All the creation is in His powerful hands. God is so great. Psalmist, King David described the majesty and power of God. '²Who coverest Thy self with light as with a garment; Who stretchest out the heavens like a curtain; ³Who layeth the beams of his chambers in the waters; Who maketh the clouds his chariot;

Who walketh upon the wings of the wind; ⁴Who maketh winds his messengers; Flames of fire his ministers;' (Psalms 104:2-4) '6 Whatsoever the LORD pleased, that did he in heaven, and in earth, in the seas, and all deep places. ⁷He causeth the vapours to ascend from the ends of the earth; He maketh lightning for the rain; He bringeth the wind out of his treasuries.'(Psalms 135:6-7)

God with His one word can give life or He can destroy the worlds.

Jesus came to the world not to kill but to give life. "²⁵Jesus said unto her, "I am the resurrection, and the life: he that believeth in me, though he was dead, yet shall he live."(John 11:25-27) Here in this verse He promised that whoever believes in Him would live. Why He will die after the 40 years of His rule and will be buried?

The Noble Qur'an and the Holy Bible says He comes on the clouds with His glory to be seen by the whole world. Why He stays on this earth, get marry, have children, die and be buried in Mecca? Whoever had written this kind of statement misunderstood the difference between earthly and heavenly. When He was in this world He proved that He had authority to bring the dead to life. Jesus is not of this world to have the lust of the flesh to get marry and have children like an ordinary man. He is the Spirit of God. As it is written, for the desires of the flesh are against the Spirit, and the desires of the Spirit are against the flesh. It proves that He is the Eternal Spirit. Jesus Christ challenged about His life style.

The Muslims take the Scriptures into consideration as the Prophet Muhammad mentioned in the Qur'an but are not opening their inner eye to see the prophecies written about Jesus' first coming and the second coming. Jesus Christ had power to give life. As we all knew only God has the ability to give life. Jesus proved the same ability when He came to the world but some people are neither following His teachings, nor trying to go in straight path by following Him.

The essential thing that people have to notice in the Islam is that Allah sent Jesus to the world first time as a bright light and with wisdom to teach the Torah, the Scriptures and the Gospel. In the Qur'an it had been written that Allah said that He makes people superior whoever follows Jesus until the day of the resurrection. The following statement explains the meaning of this verse from the Qur'an.

Qur'an al- Imran 3:55: Behold, Allah said, "O ISA (JESUS) I will take you and raise you to myself and clear you of those who disbelieve and I will make those who follow you to superior to those who disbelieve till the day of resurrection."

The above verse explains, that Allah gave authority to Jesus that whoever follow Jesus will be superiors up until the Resurrection day. Please notice here in the preceded statement "until the day of Resurrection. Nothing should be changed in the mean time of this statement and the Resurrection day. On the Resurrection day, every one whoever born on this earth even the Prophet Muhammad also should resurrect and there will be judgment to the whole world.

It reveals the truth that Jesus is not from this earth that is why Allah raised Him up from dead to Himself. The Spirit from God came to the world in the human form through Mary. He belongs to the place where Allah abodes. They compare Adam and Jesus by ignoring all these facts. They could not understand the key point why God did not raise Adam to Himself. But Allah said to Jesus, "I will raise you to Myself." And He raised Jesus to Himself.

Even, in the later writings of the Islam, it is explained that Jesus will be coming on the clouds in the end days on the shoulders of angels as it was written in (Qur'an, Az-Zukhuruf, 43:61) "Allah will send Maseeh ibne Maryam (Messiah son of Mary). Thus he will descend near the White Eastern Minaret of Damascus, clad in two yellow sheets, leaning on the shoulders of two angel (Sahih Muslim, Vol. 8, P. 192-193) The son of Mary will kill the Anti-Christ (Dajjal) at the door of Ludda.(Tirmidhi and Ahmad) By

Him in Whose Hand is my life, Ibn Maryam (Jesus Christ) would certainly pronounce Talbiyah for Hajj or for Umrah or for both (simultaneously as a Qarin) in the valley of Rawha." Sahih Muslim book 7, number 2877.

Even though Jesus never fought or participated in the wars when he was in the world, Yet Allah is sending Him to defeat Dajjal. (AntiChrist) It is important to note that every one is looking forward for Jesus to come to defeat Dajjal. (Anti Christ) Otherwise there will be no rescue to the world from Dajjal. (Anti Christ)

Every one must think about this great issue why God is sending Jesus who never even did any wars in the world? Muhammad did many wars to occupy other lands to establish the Islam? Why God did not plan to send the angel Gabriel or the prophet Muhammad to fight with Dajjal or to destroy him? Why God is sending Jesus to destroy Dajjal? Here is the answer. Jesus was pleased God by His teachings and the purpose God sent Him to the world. God gave Him the power and the authority.

Why God can not come to the world to judge? Why He is sending Jesus to judge the people and to give rewards?

Here is the secret. Since no one is able to approach or go near to the super power God, there is no choice rather than sending His Spirit (His Son as Jesus who came to fulfill the Torah. Only Jesus Christ has the authority to be near to Him because He is a Spirit of Him. The angels are the spirit beings which minister to God but they are not the Spirit of God. They are also the creation of God. Even the angel Gabriel is not the Spirit of God. All the angels are only the spirit beings. But Jesus is the Spirit of God in the image of Son. God lowers Himself as the Son. He came as Son in the name of Jesus means the Savior.

The Bible revealed the truth. It was prophesied even before God appeared as the Son on the earth. God knew that no human could stand at Him. That is the reason God made a provision to reach Him by sending "His arm as Jesus Christ" to give salvation and forgives who are inclining their ears and minds towards His great salvation. Secondly as a just God He decided to judge the people whom he made in His image whether they obey Him or not? That is why God is sending Jesus as a judge to the entire world. There is a very clear explanation in the following reference from the Bible to reveal the plan of God to the human race.

These following words were prophesied by Isaiah the Prophet in the ancient times, around 700BC. Isaiah 53:1-6, '¹Who hath believed our report? And to whom is the arm of the LORD revealed?'(Isaiah 53:1) '"⁴Hearken unto me, my people; and give ear unto me, O my nation: for a law shall proceed from me, and I will make my judgment to rest for a light of the people. ⁵My righteousness is near; my salvation is gone forth, and mine arms shall judge the people; the isles shall wait upon me, and on mine arm shall they trust. ⁶Lift up your eyes to the heavens, and look upon the earth beneath: for the heavens shall vanish away like smoke, and the earth shall wax old like a garment, and they that dwell therein shall die in like manner: but my salvation shall be for ever, and my righteousness shall not be abolished." A very clear cut explanation in this prophecy that Jesus as the arm of the Lord, salvation and His righteousness. He will judge all the people of the world according to His own teachings with what God had sent Him to the world the first time.

Jesus Christ at His second advent, will be coming straight from the heaven on the clouds as it was written in the Noble Qur'an and the Holy Bible. He is holy and He is from above. He is not a mortal to get marry and have children. We also have to think about the Prophet Muhammad why he said, "(Jesus) shall be a Sign (for the coming of) the Hour (of Judgment): therefore have no doubt about the (Hour), and his soul and life will be in the hands of Jesus when the hour comes. He said that it will be the hour of judgment."

There is a marked demarcation in the meaning of earthy and heavenly in both of their life style. In this passage we clearly came to know that the Prophet Muhammad declared," Jesus shall be sign of the hour of judgment; therefore his soul and his life will be in the hands of Jesus."

The judgment will be the final hour. All the tombs will be empty. How Jesus gets marry, have children, rule forty years then die and be buried at the side of Muhammad? According to the above verses, Muhammad will be there when Jesus comes as it was described as the Resurrection day. He also will be resurrected for the final judgment hour and he also said that his soul and life will be in the hands of Jesus when the hour comes means the judgment of every person will be in the hands of Jesus.

Jesus Christ's words are of great assurance that He will come and take His believers home where He abodes as it is written in John 14:1-3, 14, "Let not your heart be troubled: ye believe in God, believe also in me. ²In my Father's house are many mansions: if it were not so, I would have told you. I go to prepare a place for you. ³And if I go and prepare a place for you, I will come again, and receive you unto myself; that where I am, there ye may be also." Please notice the promise of Jesus. He did not say that He stays back in the world to get marry, have children, live forty years and die. He is not coming as a mortal.

In Revelation 22: 6-7 &12-13, Jesus said to His disciple John, "⁶These sayings are faithful and true: Behold, I come quickly: blessed is he that keepeth the sayings of the prophecy of this book.¹²And, behold, I come quickly; and my reward is with me, to give every man according as his work shall be. ¹³I am Alpha and Omega, the beginning and the end, the first and the last." In Luke Gospel 9:26. "²⁶For whosoever shall be ashamed of me and of my words, of him shall the Son of man be ashamed, when he shall come in his own glory, and in his Father's, and of the holy angels." (Luke 9:26)

We should be holy so that we won't be ashamed when Jesus comes. Because Jesus came first time and gave His life and offered his blood in the heaven as a high priest, we have the precious blood of Jesus Christ for washing, cleansing and purging. We have a chance of getting cleansed. We must be partakers of God's holiness that we may be able to live in the holy city, the heaven. He was challenged Himself and proved Himself as pure and holy. Only His holy blood can wash sinners. As we researched and went through many chapters of this book, He was very much different from all the human beings.

He was not of this world. His deity was confirmed by saying and proving His power to give life and there will be no judgment to those who believe in His words. "²¹For as the Father raiseth the dead and giveth them life, even so the Son also giveth life to whom he will. ²²For neither doth the Father Judge any man, but he hath given all judgment unto the Son; ²³that all may honor the Son, even as they honor the Father. He that honoreth not the Son honoreth not the Father that sent him. ²⁴Verily, verily, I say unto you, He that heareth my word, and believeth him that sent me, hath eternal life, and cometh not into judgment, but hath passed out of death into life. ²⁵Verily, verily, I say unto you, the hour cometh, and now is, when the dead shall hear the voice of the Son of God; and they that hear shall live." (John 5:21–25)

Only the righteous will hear his voice and be raised from the dead. Those who don't here His voice they will die in their sins and face the second death.

As per the Holy Bible (Revelation 22:12) and the Noble Qur'an (Al-Nisa 4:173) Jesus will be coming to judge the world and give rewards or wages according to everybody's works.

There is another misconception of the truth. In the Islam as we read about the end days, Jesus at His second return breaks the Cross, abolish Jizya tax and kill Christians where as the cross was the fulfillment of the eternal plan according to the Christianity.

"The Cross" was the fulfillment of the Scriptures? He was crucified on the cross and became a sacrifice for all the people's sins. He provided salvation to the human race. When Satan tried to bruise His feet on the cross, He crushed Satan with His feet. The first covenant made by God in Genesis 3:15, was fulfilled on the cross.

There on the Cross Jesus became very obedient unto death because He wanted to finish the purpose of His first coming to the earth. He fulfilled one of the covenants of God.

Why would Jesus Christ abolish Jizya tax and kill the Christians who are His followers?

Jesus Christ promised that whoever follows Him will inherit His kingdom. Many believed His words and died as martyrs for His name sake. Many were persecuted through the ages for continuing Jesus' mission. Moreover, Jesus promised in John 1:12, '¹²But as many as received him, to them gave He power to become the sons of God, even to them that believe on his name: Can any father abandon his own children?' Jesus said, "³⁷And him that cometh to me I will in no wise cast out." (John 6:37)

Jesus promised the eternal life to the believers. "⁴⁰And this is the will of Him that sent me, that every one which seeth the Son, and believeth on him, may have everlasting life: and I will raise him up at the last day." (John 6:40)

Anything contrary to His promises is insanity!

Even in the Qur'an, Allah sent Jesus as His word and His Spirit, and ordained the people that everybody has to listen to Him. Allah sent Him for a purpose. Allah was pleased with Him because He accomplished what Allah's intention was. He taught people how to worship God. He said, whoever worships God should worship Him in spirit and in truth with all their heart. He also taught them several things which we could read in the Gospels. He told them He is the way the truth and the life. No one can reach God except through Jesus. Allah knew what Jesus taught. He was pleased by His teachings. He raised Him to Himself. God wants Jesus to judge and rule all the people. That is the reason God is sending Him second time to the earth.

Why Allah reverse the Torah, the Scripture, and the Gospel? With which He sent Jesus to the world? How will Jesus ignore His own teachings with which Allah sent Him to the world? And Allah said, in Al Nisa [4:172-173] 172 "The MESSIAH ---- whoever hates worshipping HIM and is conceited --- so very soon He will gather them all towards Him." 173."Then to those who believed and did good deeds, He will pay their wages in full and by His munificence, give them more, and those who hated (worshipping Him) and were proud, He will inflict a painful punishment; and they will not find for themselves other than ALLAH, any supporter or any aide.

How can we neglect this above revelation about Jesus in the Qur'an, when Allah mentioned His name 'Messiah' and addressed all the mankind to reveal about Jesus and also instructed to follow Him? The revelation of Jesus is very important because it is from Allah. The main misconception of the truth is that the people misunderstood the revelation about Jesus in the Islam. They turned away from Allah's words. They underestimate Jesus' power and majesty with which God sent Him to the world. Even though Allah specifically told them that Jesus is the bright light.

In Al Nisa 4:174, we read, 174. "O mankind! Indeed the clear proof from your Lord has come to you, and we have sent down to you a bright light." (Please refer --- The Holy Prophet is clear proof from ALLAH.) and in Al- Maidah 5:46.[46] "And We sent, following in their footsteps, ISA, the son of Mary, confirming that which came before him in the Torah; and We gave him the Gospel, in which was guidance and light and confirming that which preceded it of the Torah as guidance and instruction for the righteous." Here Allah is witnessing that Jesus Christ is the 'Bright light' not an ordinary light. Allah sent Him as a bright light so that people can see their filthiness, uncleanness (dirt) and know their sins to repent. Allah mentioned the word "bright light" only to refer Jesus. In the Noble Qur'an, Allah is addressing to the whole world. Please notice the word "O mankind!" It is not only to the Israel nation. He mentioned Jesus as bright light to the whole mankind.

He Himself is the straight path and is a bright light as it was specified in the above statements from the Qur'an. These are not my words. The above statements are from Allah.

Why Allah reverse these above statements which are from the Qur'an about Jesus? God never alter His words. When Jesus was on the earth, multitude of people followed Him. They marveled at His teachings and His miracle works. Since Allah was pleased with Jesus He is sending Him again the second time to be a judge to the whole world and to rule.

Even in the holy Bible, it is written in Romans13:11-14. '[11]And that, knowing the time, that now it is high time to awake out of sleep: for now is our salvation nearer than when we believed. [12]The night is far spent, the day is at hand: let us therefore cast off the works of darkness, and let us put on the armour of light. [13]Let us walk honestly, as in the day; not in rioting and drunkenness, not in chambering and wantonness, not in strife and envying.[14]But put ye on the Lord Jesus Christ, and make not provision for the flesh, to fulfill the lusts thereof.' This is for the Christians to wake up out of their sleep.

Let us come to the point whether the Muslims do have any assurance, promise, or strong hope if they don't follow Jesus? When Jesus comes where they will stand? Do they win the favor of Jesus?

The Islam started with the correct revelation of Jesus, His birth, His miracles and it claimed Allah raised Him to Himself. And they are waiting for His coming to kill Dajjal (Anti Christ) and predicted that He rules. But gradually, they turned away from following Jesus. Some of them refused to follow the command of Allah and forgot that Allah told them that He sent Jesus, the Messiah as a bright light. Whoever does not want to come to the bright light can not see their way because they are in the darkness hence their way is obscure. Since God is a great intense Light, none could reach Him with their own effort. The Islam teaches that Allah weighs and decides their abode. How could any one stand in front of the super power God? He is the intense light. It is impossible to stand before Him.

Whoever did not come to the bright light are imperfect and have no strength to stand in front of the great and holy God who is too bright to reach. "[15]Which in his times he shall shew, who is the blessed and only Potentate, the King of kings, and Lord of lords; [16]Who only hath immortality, dwelling in the light which no man can approach unto; whom no man hath seen, nor can see: to whom be honor and power everlasting. Amen." (I Timothy 6:15-16)

Whoever is not holy can not approach Holy God in His holy city. Maybe because of this reason it was written in the Qur'an that everybody has to go through hell fire before they enter the paradise. God sent Jesus as a bright light to the world so that people can see their filthiness and go to him for cleansing. He was sacrificed His life. He became as a Lamb of God gave his precious blood for the cleansing of the human race. In the Qur'an, 10:94, it was written, "And if thou wert in doubt as to what 'We' have revealed unto thee, then ask those who have been reading the book before thee." If Torah and Gospel had been changed, how could be such command given by Allah? God's message is always unchanged.

There is no Gospel after Jesus Christ. He fulfilled the eternal plan. This heavenly plan to redeem the human was fulfilled by His sacrifice. He finished it in the cross. It is not time to win the kingdoms in the world but it is important to reach the Eternal kingdom. This is the teaching of Jesus Christ. In the Qur'an Allah said that Jesus will punish those who do not follow Him. The Muslims and the Christians are looking forward for Jesus' return and His ruling, but whoever is not following Him can not stand at Him. Whoever do not believe in Jesus Christ as their savior but waiting for Him to save them from Dajjal is absurd! In fact, it is a crisis because they do not know whether Jesus will give them good wages or punish them. Allah stated that Jesus will inflict a painful punishment; and they will not find for themselves other than Allah, any supporter or any aide.

Conquering the whole world, losing their souls from the eternity is a profound loss. The people who misrepresent the Holy Spirit and follow the false teachings, those are in the spiritual darkness. Some people missed the way to the eternity because they disregarded Jesus words. He said, "I am the way the truth and the life, no man cometh to the Father but by me." Whoever do not follow the straight path or not obeying Jesus are jeopardizing the truth and stumbled at the way, hence can not reach the Eternal kingdom, because they did not understand Allah's words or the purpose of sending Jesus to the world. They ignored Allah and did not come to the Bright light which is Jesus Christ. They can not see their filth because they don't come to the bright light. Alas! They are faint in their hope because they were misguided and are going away from the right path. Hence they will be perplexed and utterly fall at the second return of Jesus Christ.

God created man for such a great purpose to be His sons not to be His slaves. Because of this reason God made man in His own image. In this verse Allah told Muhammad to read the previous Scriptures, and the Gospel, if he is in doubt of what Allah is telling him. If any body says that the Scriptures and the Gospel were corrupt, he or she is not in accordance with Allah's words. If they were corrupted, Allah might not say these words to Muhammad. God knew the end before the beginning. We always have to remember there is no change in God's word.

It is wise to search the truth and follow it; instead of getting angry and violent. Extremists of the Islam use force and violence and die in order to get into the paradise. They are under the false teaching and think that they are doing good deeds. It says: In Proverbs19: 19-20: '[19]A man of great wrath shall suffer punishment: for if thou deliver him, yet thou must do it again. [20]Hear counsel, and receive instruction, that thou mayest be wise in thy latter end.' It is better to open eyes and see which one is a straight path to reach the eternity.

It clearly states in the Word of God, 'there is no mediator between God and the man except Jesus Christ.' (1Timothy: 2:5) The Islam also believes that Allah is sending Jesus to judge the people. Allah gave Him the authority to judge all the people. Whatever He judges Allah would accept it because He was pleased with Jesus teachings. If not He might not decided to send Jesus Christ the second time to the world.

Muslims believe that God sent Muhammad as a comforter. However, we must realize it is impossible for one person to comfort everyone in the whole wide world. A one universal human comforter is unrealistic because man's life is limited on this earth. Man with the physical body can not interact within another individual. That is why Jesus Christ after He left this earth, He sent the Holy Spirit to live in us.

God wants to reach and comfort everyone in different parts of the whole world with His love and words though His Spirit. God designed us to be eternal. He made man in His image. Since the human sinned against God, was defiled and was cast out from there. But because of His grace He did not abandon the human race. He sent the Eternal Spirit to communicate man through His spirit. Therefore the Comforter that God has given us should be in the form of the Spirit.

God as a comforter is not pertained to a particular place or people. He belongs to every one. Only God's Spirit can dwell everywhere and is the guidance to every one.

The concept of the Spirit of God interact the spirit of mankind, gives us clarification that the Prophet Muhammad's short duration of life was not sufficient to be a life time comforter to the whole world. He himself did not know the future things. He could not heal his sickness. He died with sickness. He was desperate when his enemies came upon him. He was stressed out with his family problems. Many times, he was needed a comforter. That is the reason he himself was relied on Jesus the son of Mary.

In the Qur'an, the angel Gabriel was considered as the Holy Spirit. This is another misunderstanding of the Truth.

There are so many incidents in the Bible that shows angels are the servants of God. Jesus was not born when the angel Gabriel blew into Mary as it was written in the Qur'an Mary19; (part16):17, "Then We sent unto her Our spirit and it assumed for her the likeness of a perfect man." In 18th verse, Mary said: "Lo! I seek refuge in the Beneficent One from thee, if thou art God fearing." These verses in the Qur'an, are creating a meaning that the angel himself bestows on her a faultless son.

It was written in the Qur'an that Mary had chosen seclusion from others; Gabriel appeared to her in the likeness of a perfect man. When she saw, she sought refuge of God the Beneficent. She also asked the angel, "If thou art God fearing. In this narration from the Qur'an shows plural words such as 'We' and 'Our' pertain to God and the angel Gabriel appeared to her in the likeness of a perfect man. God and angel Gabriel came together to Mary. They exalted the angel Gabriel as a God.

The most important key point we have to understand is the angel Gabriel is only a messenger to convey good news to the saints of God. In the Holy Bible it is very clearly mentioned that the angel Gabriel is only a messenger. "[35]And the angel answered and said unto her, The Holy Ghost shall come upon thee, and the power of the Highest shall overshadow thee: therefore also that holy thing which shall be born of thee shall be called the Son of God." (Luke 1:35) Here in this verse, it was very well explained that 'Holy Ghost or the Spirit of God come upon thee' means God's anointment came upon her.

The Highest or unseen Spirit will overshadow Mary, means that God's Spirit did the impossible thing without her knowledge. The angel Gabriel was just a messenger came to convey her good news of God. It clarifies that Jesus was not born when the angel Gabriel came as a perfect man to blow into her. In the other words Jesus is God's Spirit. The same Spirit came in to this world to fulfill the fore plan of

God for the human race. There are many types of angels mentioned in the Bible. The angel Gabriel is one of them.

Jesus promised His disciples that He will send His Holy Spirit after His ascension and He sent. We have discussed about 'the Holy Spirit and His significance' in the other chapter of this book. It is very important to have the Holy Spirit to guide us and to lead us. In this concept also the people abandoned the Truth in the words of Jesus. Therefore they don't have the privilege of having the Comforter in their lives.

It is one of the fundamentals in the Islam that God exists without a place and has no resemblance to His creations. For instance, God is not a body and there is nothing like Him. In the Qur'an it says what it mean "nothing is like Him in any way." Allah is not limited to dimensions. [Qur'an 42:11] Because of this verse in Qur'an 42:11, it is wrong to worship any object or black stone at Kabah? It is a disobedience to Allah. There is none to compare with God.

The Islamic theology identifies Allah as described in the Qur'an is same as the God of Israel who covenanted with Abraham. As per the Qur'an, we have to take the Torah, the Scripture, and the Gospel. Please refer Qur'an 10:94. And God spoke all these words in the Torah. (First five books of Old Testament) It was written by Moses. Muslims quote that the true God "El" of the Bible is the same as Allah of the Qur'an.

If the Muslims take God of the Bible, who had the hosts of heavens, all angels are His servants and He rides upon heavens of heavens. He said, in Exodus 20:2-5. (Second book of the Torah) "²I am the LORD thy God, which have brought thee out of the land of Egypt, out of the house of bondage. ³Thou shalt have no other Gods before me. This command is very well observed in the Islam (Monotheism). ⁴Thou shalt not make unto thee any graven image, or any likeness of any thing that is in the heaven above, or that is in the earth beneath, or that is in the water under the earth. (Some Muslims are dishonoring Allah by disobeying this law).⁵Thou shalt not bow down thyself to them, nor serve them: for I the LORD thy God am a jealous God, visiting the iniquity of the fathers upon the children unto the third and fourth generation of them that hate me." (Some Muslims are disobeying this law)

It is very clear in the above written verses; we can not make, kiss or bow to any object. We provoke God to wrath. It is rebelling against God." That is why we should not follow any one, except God's word. The Word of God was written by inspiration of His Spirit. Isaiah the Prophet in the Old Testament had written about the habitation of God. Isaiah 66: 1-2. '¹Thus saith the LORD, The heaven is my throne, and the earth is my footstool: where is the house that ye build unto me? And where is the place of my rest? ²For all those things hath mine hand made, and all those things have been, saith the LORD: but to this man will I look, even to him that is poor and of a contrite spirit, and trembleth at my word.' '⁵¹Ye stiffnecked and uncircumcised in heart and ears, ye do always resist the Holy Ghost: as your fathers did, so do ye.' (Acts7:51)

And again from Deuteronomy (fifth book of the Torah) the word of God said, "⁷Remember, and forget not, how thou provoked the LORD thy God to wrath in the wilderness: from the day that thou didst depart out of the land of Egypt, until ye came unto this place, ye have been rebellious against the LORD." [Deuteronomy 9:7] By making other objects as God, they provoked God.

God made this clear, by giving this message to Jeremiah. Jeremiah was the Prophet who lived around 556 BC. We could read this message of God from the book Jeremiah 31:31-33, from the holy Bible. '³¹Behold, the days come, saith the LORD, that I will make a new covenant with the house of Israel, and with the house of Judah: ³²Not according to the covenant that I made with their fathers in the day that I took them by the hand to bring them out of the land of Egypt; which my covenant they brake, although I was an husband unto them, saith the LORD: ³³But this shall be the covenant that I will make with the house of Israel; After those days, saith the LORD,

I will put my law in their inward parts, and write it in their hearts; and will be their God, and they shall be my people.' This is the new covenant. This was foretold to the Prophet Jeremiah that the Holy Spirit will come and dwells in us. Fulfillment of this covenant took place after Jesus came into the world.

As per the Surah Al Maidah 5:46-47, Sahih International, Allah sent Jesus as a guidance and instruction for the righteous. When Jesus came to the world, He taught how to worship God because those days they used to go to mountain to worship or go to Jerusalem to worship. Jesus said in John Gospel 4:24. '24God is a Spirit: and they that worship him must worship him in spirit and in truth.' Whoever is not listening to Jesus is disobeying Allah.

In 1John 3:4 it says, "Whosoever committed sin transgressed also the law: for sin is the transgression of the law.' The Muslims should be cautious about this. The Muslims are saying God is one but they kept a black stone wrapped in a cloth at Kabah. They perform Hajj, going there and kissing, doing traditions, just like idolatry. God is not permitted to one place (Mecca). The Muslims are disobeying the Qur'an 41:37, where it says, "You prostrate before Allah and do not prostrate before the sun or the moon". It explains that we have to prostrate before God the creator who has no dimensions. He is not limited in a small black stone. The black stone is His creation.

In the Old Testament, 1 Kings19: 14-18, '14And Elijah the Prophet said, I have been very jealous for the LORD God of hosts: because the children of Israel have forsaken thy covenant, thrown down thine altars, and slain thy Prophets with the sword; and I, even I only, am left; and they seek my life, to take it away. 15And the LORD said unto him, go, return on thy way to the wilderness of Damascus: and when thou comest, anoint Hazael to be king over Syria: 16And Jehu the son of Nimshi shalt thou anoint to be king over Israel: and Elisha the son of Shaphat of Abelmeholah shalt thou anoint to be prophet in thy room. 17And it shall come to pass, that him that escapeth the sword of Hazael shall Jehu slay: and him that escapeth from the sword of Jehu shall Elisha slay. **¹⁸Yet I have left me seven thousand in Israel, all the knees which have not bowed unto Baal, and every mouth which hath not kissed him.'**

In this above passage, God is counting on them whoever is not kissing and kneeling at the idol Baal. Whoever does such abomination God's wrath will kindle against them.

'⁹For the eyes of the LORD run to and fro throughout the whole earth, to shew himself strong in the behalf of them whose heart is perfect toward him. Herein thou hast done foolishly: therefore from henceforth thou shalt have wars.' (2 Chronicles 16:9). How true are God's words? The founder of the Islam since he started, he participated in twenty seven battles, personally fighting in nine of them. God gave him reprobate mind to preach hate and war against enemies. He started the Islam a message of tolerance toward other religions but later, earlier Surahs of tolerance were abrogated by the new revelation exhorting Muslims to Jihad against the unbelievers.

The Islam strongly prohibits all form of idolatry but they do not realize that they are doing the idolatry. In the Qur'an, it was explained that God is above all comprehension, "No vision can grasp Him, but His grasp is over all vision. He is most courteous well acquainted with all things. (Qur'an 6:103) The most interesting thing to note is a stone was kept in the mosque, and changed the shrine into mosque had led people into idolatry. It is an abomination to God.

Whoever committed sin by transgressing Mosaic Law is against God's commandments. Whoever led people to face Kabah when they pray, limited Allah to a particular place. Whoever made it as an obligatory to go to Mecca is answerable to God because some people are not able to go there. Some people when they go there, kiss and bow at the black stone? Hindus claim in Vedas the stone and temple was their shrine in ancient times. They say Hinduism is far more ancient than the Islam. They are claiming that black stone belong to Hindus. It is idolatry to kiss and bow at the black stone.

The Muslim theologians believe in the sinless ness of the Prophets or the absolute sovereignty of God, but have never been formulated into a statement of faith and sinless ness binding on all the believers. But in our history even the great Prophets made mistakes starting from Adam. Here we have to notice that the Islam and the Christianity accept the fact that Jesus is the only man who was sinless even right in His birth until He was raised to heaven.

In addition to that there is no one sinless in the sight of God. For until the law the sin was in the world: but the sin is not imputed when there is no law. If we say that we have no sin, we deceive ourselves, and the truth is not in us.

Since the law came into existence the mankind is aware of which is good and which is bad. If man is good, he should always do good deeds. Why should he do bad deeds? Why this many differences exist in the world? The Sin touches in every aspect of the human life. If Adam did not sin, they might have been in Eden (Paradise) for ever. If Adam did not eat the good and evil fruit, we might not know about the sin or differentiate the good and the evil. Because they sinned against His word, God drove away Adam and Eve from the Garden of Eden. It indicates that Adam did sin.

Let us take examples from our Prophets. Adam sinned against God. Adam's son murdered his brother Abel. Moses could not enter into Canaan because of His disobedience. King David tried his best to be favorable to God but He committed adultery and cried unto God. "Behold, I was shape in iniquity; and in sin did my mother conceive me." [Psalms 51:5.] Muhammad confessed, "O Allah, I seek refuge with you from the sins and from being in debt."

In Isaiah Chapter 64:6, 'we are all unclean and all of our righteousness is as filthy rags. In Jeremiah 17:9, our heart is deceitful above all the things and is desperately wicked. Isaiah the Prophet when he saw the glory of God in his vision, he cried out. 'Then said I, Woe is me! for I am undone; because I am a man of unclean lips, and I dwell in the midst of a people of unclean lips: for mine eyes have seen the King, the LORD of hosts.' Isaiah the Prophet could not even see God clearly. He saw only the glory of God and he could not stand.

We commit many unholy mistakes and think sinful thoughts, thus we are unholy. We cannot perfect ourselves by our own power. If we depend on our selves, 'The Self' gets defeat many times a day even in very simple things. Because of these reason, we have to accept the fact that the Prophets who feared God also committed mistakes.

The Qur'an is very strict about the fear of God and the hope for rewards from Allah. The main principle in the Islam is 'Avoid disobedience of His guidance and fearing His punishment.' Taqwa is the fear of the Most Merciful, and acting in accordance with the Qur'an and the Sunnah of the Messenger of Allah, sallallahu alayhe wa sallam. That is: hoping for the reward of Allah and avoiding disobedience of His Guidance and fearing His Punishment. We have to notice and look into the life style of great Prophets, then we will understand the truth that mankind is susceptible to sin.

For example: Even though God made Adam with His own hands still Adam disobeyed. Moses the prophet who had fear of God, led 600,000(men 20-60 years of age) = wives and children and old people. But Moses could not reach Canaan because of his disobedience. God told him to speak with rock but he did not speak with the rock; instead he hit the rock. (The book of Numbers 20) No matter how much the mankind tries their best with the fear of God, they make mistakes. 'The Self' is not enough to achieve the full righteousness.

God's law was handed over to Moses on the Mount Sinai to ancient Israelites on one of the Pentecostal day. When Moses came down from the mount, the Israelites by making idol sinned against God. Moses anger waxed hot and he cast the tables out of his hands, and breaks them beneath the Mount. And there fell of the people that day about three thousand men. (Exodus 32: 19-28) When they received the law, the people died. There is always punishment in the law.

If we come to the New Testament, the law was replaced by the grace of Lord Jesus Christ. Let us look in to Acts 2:2-4 and 41. 2. 'And when the day of Pentecost was fully come, they were all with one accord in one place. ²And suddenly there came a sound from heaven as of a rushing mighty wind, and it filled all the house where they were sitting. ³And there appeared unto them cloven tongues like as of fire, and it sat upon each of them. ⁴And they were all filled with the Holy Ghost.' ⁴¹Then they that gladly received his word were baptized: and the same day there were added unto them about three thousand souls.'

In the Old Testament on the Pentecostal day, by receiving the law three thousand people died. In the New Testament on the same day the law was replaced by the grace of our Lord and three thousand people were saved. The plan of God is awesome.

Actually, God gave the Law so that people might understand God's definition of Sin. We read in Romans 3:20, "Therefore by the deeds of the law there shall no flesh be justified in his sight: for by the law is the knowledge of Sin." Secondly, the law was given to the people to understand the God's holiness. The law was there and according to the law it is clear which is right which is wrong, but when the people tried their best not to commit sin, they failed and had to admit that not a single person had the strength or human energy to obey and fulfill what God said and thus the whole world became guilty, and every mouth was stopped before God as it is written in Romans 3:19.

Thirdly, the Law was given to help us to understand how dangerous, horrible and destructive the sin is. One thought or one desire is enough to bring destruction to a life, a home and even to a society or the world. How much darkness by one single dark step?

Who is righteous in front of God? There is none that could fulfill all the law to stand in front of God. He sent the Prophets but they were also weak and went astray. They made mistakes. They were disobedient to God. God's moral law proceeds from the righteousness of God and can never be abolished. Hence the Mosaic Law has been superseded by another law that is the standards of grace revealed in the New Testament. The believer is under the law of Christ. (1Cor 9:21) & (Romans 8:2-4)

There is no salvation under the Law. It can not make any one righteous and bring him /her near to God. "Wherefore the Law was our school master to bring us to Christ, that we might be justified by faith." Galatians 3:24. "For Christ is the end of the law for righteousness to every one that believeth." Romans 10:4. We have come under His grace only by believing which is very simple.

Only by His grace Jesus intercedes for our weaknesses. That is the reason John saw Jesus Christ in his vision as a high priest. Jesus is the only mediator in between man and God. Otherwise there is no access to man to approach the great intense light, and super power God in all His awesome glory.

Hence God made provision by sending His Spirit who is able to fulfill all the law. Jesus Christ justified the punishment of the law by His death. This is possible only to God's Spirit. No one else is perfect to accomplish it. He left His throne in the heaven and came to redeem us and gave his life. This act we call as Grace. He loved us since He made us in His likeness.

But some people do not want to accept the truth. The Islam taught some key points about Jesus, but it could not explain it fully. They assumed that God left the mankind at half way without making any plans to save the people. There is no process of cleansing, purging and saving. There is no Holy Spirit guidance to go in a right direction. The consequence of this is very fatal to a believer. In the Islam it is a fixed ordinance to every one either believer or unbeliever; every one has to go through the hell fire.

The Muslims assume that for the righteous people the hell fire is not going to harm. But there was no real experience of any one who went to hell and told it in the Islam. This is only an assumption. But the key point in the Qur'an stated very clearly that, "We are best aware of those most worthy to be burned there in. There is not one of you but shall approach it. That is a fixed ordinance of thy Lord. By knowing this truth, if some one follows the same path it is very unwise or imprudent.

There is a narration which gives a hope that Prophet Muhammad will intercede with Allah to judge amongst the people but at the same time, he himself will be seeking the help of Jesus. Here below is the passage for the evidence:

Narrated by 'Abdullah bin 'Umar (one of the companions of the Prophet Muhammad): The Prophet said, "A man keeps on asking others for something till he comes on the Day of Resurrection without any piece of flesh on his face." The Prophet added, "On the Day of Resurrection, the Sun will come near (to the people) to such an extent that the sweat will reach up to the middle of the ears, so, when all the people are in that state, they will ask Adam FOR HELP, and then Moses, and then Muhammad." (p.b.u.h).'

The sub-narrator added, "Muhammad will intercede with Allah to judge amongst the people. He will proceed on till he will hold the ring of the door (of Paradise) and then Allah will exalt him to Maqam Mahmud (the privilege of intercession, etc.). And all the people of the gathering will send their praises to Allah." (Sahih Al-Bukhari, volume 2, book 24, number 553)

The certainty of this above verse is doubtful because the Prophet Muhammad said, that he will be seeking help and refuge from Son of Mary, as it was written in Sahih Muslim, book 041, number 6932, "By Him in whose hand is my life, the son of Mary, peace is upon him, will soon descend among you as a just judge."

Until then dead shall be in their tombs. The Muslims believe that Jesus will be coming to establish peace on the earth and he will be coming as a judge. The final solution should be as that of Muhammad who believed that his life is in the hands of son of

Mary, Jesus who gives rewards according to everybody's work on the judgment day. Then how could we believe that Muhammad will make an intercession when he himself seeks the help of Jesus for his life and soul? Every Muslim should think this matter very seriously. The prophet Muhammad made a wise decision for himself. He was cleared of himself.

Whoever relies on Jesus will be saved. His love and His power attract the people towards Him. He became a stumbling block to the Jews because He was an access to any one whoever comes to Him. He was not only permitted to Jews. He showed His love and compassion to all kinds of the people. He treated rich and poor in the same manner. He healed all kinds of the people. He gave access to every one to enter into the heavenly kingdom. He loved the sinners. He never rejected any one. Being a Jew he went to Samaritans, Gentiles and touched outcast lepers, and healed them. He even delivered an adulterer from the stoning. Since He had power to forgive sins, He forgave her.

Dear earnest reader! Does it please Jesus when he comes as a judge, if we smite unbelievers? If we do so how could we escape His judgment and the hell? If Jesus rejects, how could Allah accept? Those who are disobedient to Jesus are also disobedient to Allah. If Allah is not merciful and compassionate, all souls will be destroyed. The Islam teaches Allah is Most Merciful and most compassionate but teaches to kill those who are away from Allah.

The people are misunderstanding Allah and showing Allah as a very Cruel and Ruthless by writing contradictory statements against His attributes. In the Qur'an it states that He never forgives apostasy and there is very severe punishment to unbelievers. It is very stunning if we look into the Qur'an that shows Allah's character as follows:

'And slay them wherever ye catch them.' {Qur'an 2:191}

'And fight them on until there is no more Tumult or oppression.' {Qur'an 2:193}

'Fighting is prescribed for you, and ye dislike it. But it is possible that ye dislike a thing which is good for you.'{Qur'an 2:216}

'Let not the believers Take for friends or helpers Unbelievers rather than believers: if any do that, in nothing will there be help from Allah.' {Qur'an 3:28}

'Then fight in Allah's cause - Thou art held responsible only for thyself - and rouse the believers. It may be that Allah will restrain the fury of the Unbelievers; for Allah is the strongest in might and in punishment.'{Qur'an 4:84}

'And never will Allah grant to the unbelievers a way (to triumphs) over the believers.' {Qur'an 4:141}

'The punishment of those who wage war against Allah and His Messenger, and strive with might and main for mischief through the land is: execution, or crucifixion, or the cutting off of hands and feet from opposite sides, or exile from the land: that is their disgrace in this world, and a heavy punishment is theirs in the Hereafter;'{ Qur'an 5:33}

'I will instill terror into the hearts of the unbelievers: smite ye above their necks and smite all their finger-tips off them.' {Qur'an 8:12}

'O ye who believe! When ye meet the Unbelievers in hostile array, never turn your backs to them. If any do turn his back to them on such a day - unless it be in a stratagem of war, or to retreat to a troop (of his own)- he draws on himself the wrath of Allah, and his abode is Hell,- an evil refuge (indeed)!'{Qur'an 8:15-16}

'It is not ye who slew them; it was Allah: when thou threwest (a handful of dust), it was not thy act, but Allah's: in order that He might test the Believers by a gracious trial from Himself.' {Qur'an 8:17}

'Against them make ready your strength to the utmost of your power, including steeds of war, to strike terror into (the hearts of) the enemies, of Allah and your enemies, and others besides, whom ye may not know, but whom Allah doth know. Whatever ye shall spend in the cause of Allah shall be repaid unto you, and ye shall not be treated unjustly.' {Qur'an 8:60}

'O Prophet! rouse the Believers to the fight. If there are twenty amongst you, patient and persevering, they will vanquish two hundred: if a hundred, they will vanquish a thousand of the Unbelievers.'{Qur'an 8:65}

'But when the forbidden months are past, then fight and slay the Pagans wherever ye find them, and seize them, beleaguer them, and lie in wait for them in every stratagem.' {Qur'an 9:5}

'Fight them, and Allah will punish them by your hands, cover them with shame, help you (to victory) over them, heal the breasts of Believers.' {Qur'an 9:14}

Since Allah is the most merciful and the most compassionate, these above references from the Qur'an are not reflecting God's character. All the above verses are contrary to His mercy and compassion. Those verses are drawing away people from Allah.

In the Qur'an it was ordained by Allah that we have to consider the Torah, the Scripture and the Gospel in which it shows His mercy and compassion.

Let us read the Scripture: In the Scriptures, the book of Isaiah 1:15, it says, "And when ye spread forth your hands, I will hide mine eyes from you: yea, when ye make many prayers, I will not hear: your hands are full of blood." God revealed this truth to the Prophet Isaiah in the Old Testament.

Let us see the character of Jesus who came from God. He was so compassionate even to His enemies who tried to kill Him. We see how He demonstrated His kindness. Here is a passage from the Gospels, when Jesus hour came to be taken away from His disciples, [48]But Jesus said unto him, Judas, betrayest thou the Son of man with a kiss? [49]When they which were about him saw what would follow, they said unto him, Lord, "shall we smite with the sword?" [50]And one of them smote the servant of the high priest, and cut off his right ear. [51]And Jesus answered and said, "Suffer ye thus far. And he touched his ear, and healed him." Jesus healed His enemy. Here we see God's attributes such as Mercy and Compassion. Because of these qualities Allah was pleased by Jesus and gave the authority to Jesus. He raised Jesus to Himself. We should be like Him to meet Him in person without any shame and can enter into the heaven where He was raised.

That is the reason Allah said, "Whoever follow Jesus is superior until the resurrection day."

Some people argue that even Jesus have God. They say, He prayed when He was in the form of the man on the earth. Certainly He did. He came to be an example to all the mankind in all the things. He showed them how to follow Him. He told them about His sufferings and dying and will be raised on the third day. But no one believed His words. Even a voice came from the heaven to clarify that He is the son of God but some people did not believe it.

Jesus told them indirectly so many times that He was there before the foundations of the earth, yet some people did not believe His words he said, "[5]And now, O Father, glorify thou me with thine own self with the glory which I had with thee before the world was."(John17:5) "[39]Search the scriptures; for in them ye think ye have eternal life: and they are they which testify of me." He said that He has an authority to give life and take life. He gave life to the dead. Even by seeing His deeds, they could not believe Him. He had authority to grant or do if any one asks Him. He said, "¹³And whatsoever ye shall ask in my name, that will I do, that the Father may be glorified in the Son." Yet some people do not want to believe.

He did many miracles. His life itself is an evidence for His divinity yet some people do not want to believe. Some people rebuke Him for no reason. If He did not come from God, how did God raised Him to Himself from the dead? Even God raised Him some people does not want to accept the truth that Jesus came from God.

Whoever has no belief on Him should think that if Jesus Christ claimed directly that He is God, do any one trust Him? Certainly not! They might have stoned him. Many times Jews tried to stone Him and tried to kill Him for His teachings but Allah was pleased by Him.

When Jesus was passing the other side into the country of the Gergesenes, two men possessed with demonic spirits cried out, saying, 'what have we to do with thee, Jesus, thou Son of God? Art thou come hither to torment us before the time? (Mathew 8:29) Here in this verse demons knew that Jesus is the son of God but mankind does not want to accept this truth.

His first priority to come to the world is to sacrifice Himself to redeem all the people. He came to fulfill the law. "²³For the wages of sin is death" Whoever wrote 'the Will' should die, then only 'the Will' be effective. God is the one who ordained that law. He commanded Adam and told him that He will die if he eats the forbidden fruit. Unless some one who is worthy should pay the penalty of sin which the death. Otherwise there is no justification for His word since the wages of sin is death. God is a just God. He is not a God to alter His words. He came and justified the law. (His commands)

That is why God Himself came as a human and died. He made Himself as a human to die for the sins of the human race. Since

He had authority over the life, He resurrected and ascended to the heaven and offered His pure and innocent blood. He made a way to the humans to enter into the heaven. He finished the purpose of His coming to save the sinners.

If He came as a God with all His glory no one dare to crucify Him. Then the task of the redemption will be left incomplete. That is the reason He was shown in His glory to John in Patmos Island after His ascension. There He cleared all his doubts about this subject. He told John, He is Alpha, Omega, beginning and ending. When He came as a human to be with mankind, He was still there in the heaven with all His glory since He is Omniscient.

Any one whether a Christian, a Muslim, a Jew, a Hindu or white, black, yellow, pink or brown skin or from any part of the world, whoever may be if they are not cleansed by the blood of Jesus Christ is not eligible to enter into the holy city.

In Surah 6:34, 6; 115; 10:64 and 50:28, 29 clearly say to the Muslims, there is none to alter the decisions of Allah: According to 6:115, "Perfect is the word of thy Lord in truth and justice. There is naught that can change His words. He is the Hearer, the knower. There is no changing in the words of Allah – that is the Supreme Triumph.

He saith: Contend not in My presence, when I had already proffered unto you the warning. [29]The sentence that cometh from Me can not be changed, and I am in no wise a tyrant unto the slaves." Allah stated such unaltered statements, and in the "Family of Imran." It was written, that He revealed in the name of Allah, the Beneficent, and the Merciful. "[1]Alif. Lam. Mim. [2]Allah! There is no God save Him, the Alive, the Eternal. [3]He hath revealed unto thee (Muhammad) the Scripture with truth, confirming that which was revealed before it, even as He revealed Torah and the Gospel. [4]Aforetime for guidance to mankind" so the Torah, the Scripture and the Gospels are correct, because Allah did verify this fact as per the Qur'an.

If anybody alters Allah's words, they make the Qur'an false; because it contradicts Allah's words. To make these accusations against Jesus Christ and to twist and change His teachings on the earth is an abomination to the Most Holy God! They will be incurred to severe punishment. Those who don't follow Jesus are not in accordance with Allah. They are against Allah. Jesus fulfilled God's fore plan to redeem all the people. He was an example of deity (sinless or faultless, merciful and compassionate)

Dear friend! Take heed and remember Jesus' own words in Mathew Gospel 24:24: "²⁴For there shall arise false Christs, and false prophets, and shall shew great signs and wonders; insomuch that, if it were possible, they shall deceive the very elect." "¹⁴Because strait is the gate, and narrow is the way, which leadeth unto life, and few there be that find it. ¹⁵Beware of false prophets, which come to you in sheep's clothing, but inwardly they are ravening wolves." (Mathew 7:14–15) Jesus Christ with his own mouth He cautioned us to beware of the false prophets! Even though Jesus warned that He is the way, the truth and the life, no man come to the father except through Him. Whoever does not listen to these teachings of Jesus Christ and following another way which make them ashamed when they stand in front of Jesus on His second return!

The revelation of Jesus is very important because it is from Allah. Why Allah reverse these statements which are from the Qur'an about Jesus? God never alter His words. When Jesus was on the earth, multitude of people followed Him. They marveled at His teachings and His miracle works. Since Allah was pleased with Jesus He is sending Him again the second time to be a judge to the world and to rule. If Jesus taught what was not from Allah, Allah might not send Him back to judge all the people.

Let us search and believe in the truth. There is correct evidence in the Torah, the Scriptures and the Gospels. (4 Gospels which are the biographies) The fact that the four Gospels present a Person rather than a complete biography indicates the spirit in which they should be approached. They gave us complete revelation even though they did not give us complete story. The Old Testament is the inspired introduction to the New Testament. In the New Testament, The Christ of the Gospels is the perfect manifestation of God's grace. The Gospels reflect His divine image. Here is the plan of God we understand. God's intention was somehow a sinner must be redeemed, saved and justified as righteous to earn son ship of God and eventually attain His glorious image. That is the reason God created man in His own image.

Here I would like to share a story which was told by a God servant Bro. G. John. Once upon a time there was a murderer. He was running away to a solitary place to hide. He was in dirty clothes without bath and was starving for food. He was very tired and dozed in his way.

He had a dream in his sleep. 'There was a terrible storm on his way. He was running for a shelter. He came across a building; he went near to that building. It was written 'a holy place' on the door. He was not dared to knock the door. He passed on and found a house. It was written on the door 'any one who is truthful' will get entrance. He had no access to enter as he can not confess them that he was running away to escape from the punishment of the murder he committed. He ran away from that door post. He found a place with a gate where it was written, 'No entrance except you are righteous.' He was so much discouraged and fled away from it. He had no hope because of his present situation. He was completely wet with storm and his body was bruised and hurt. He reached a place where it was written "Grace" on the door. He had no strength to go forward. He knocked at the door. A person came and opened the door and took him inside and gave him shelter.' He opened his eyes and it was only a dream.

Yet he found out that only through the Grace he will be saved. Otherwise there is no other way for him to be saved. In this we learned there is no entrance to a sinner. Only through the grace of God, a sinner could find shelter in His presence.

Since God is very holy, He is unreachable. Because of this reason, He sent Jesus Christ as the Lamb of God. Only His blood has the power to cleanse a sinner to be eligible to enter into His holy presence.

God showed His abundant grace towards the human race. 'God's Riches At Christ's Expense' (GRACE) God invited all the people to be saved by His grace and inherit His eternal kingdom.

Believe in the one who has defeated the death in the grave than in the one who is seeking refuge for the punishment in the grave! If you do so you will surely see Lord Jesus Christ will be coming on the clouds. We will see Him face to face and be joyful with exceeding happiness because we followed Him and did what He had told us to do. He never forsakes us because we believed in His promises and trusted Him with all our heart.

Even the Prophet Muhammad sought refuge, by saying: "By Him in Whose Hands my soul is, son of Mary (Jesus) will shortly descend amongst you people (Muslims) as a just ruler." Allah's apostle the Prophet himself claimed that His soul is in the hands of the son of Maryam (Jesus). Sahih Muslim, book 1, number 287 & Sahih Muslim, book 041, number 6932, it is clear that Jesus will govern the people, according to His own teachings. If a king is ruling we have to follow only his rules. Only a traitor will betray his/her king and get severe punishment.

Everybody's soul (life) is in the (king's) hands. Everybody should think about this fact, whom to follow. The Prophet Muhammad had chosen to rely completely on Jesus Christ son of Mary for the refuge but the Muslims are relying for their refuge on Muhammad.

Please stop for a moment and think diligently whom you have to seek refuge? Best choice makes up the vast difference.

My personal assumption through my life- experience

The Qur'an writings are based on the Bible for the topics of the human creation, heaven, hell, Jesus Christ, His life on the earth and His second coming to the world. We had been discussed many topics which are from the both religions.

The Muslim scripture clearly ascribes titles and functions to Christ which point to His Divine pre human existence, e.g. Christ is God's Word which He gave to Mary and a Spirit that proceeded from Him. The second coming of Jesus Christ is the final hour and resurrection day because Muhammad also will be there since he stated that his soul will be in the hands of Jesus.

Then in the later writings, whole concept was changed. There is no importance for Jesus' teachings. They do not realize that Muhammad himself rely on Jesus and sought refuge for his soul. Instead of believing in Jesus, they believe in Muhammad teachings. It made the Muslims to neglect Jesus and His teachings, and making allegations that Christian doctrines are wrong and was corrupted.

The later writings of the Qur'an were deviated from the earlier writings. These later writings of the Qur'an drew away the people from the salvation. Thus they are far away from the grace. It made them to do their own efforts to enter into the heaven. Since the own efforts of man are not sufficient to the holy heaven, every Muslim has to enter first into the hell according to the Qur'an. There is no surety to enter into the heaven. They are looking forward for Jesus second coming even though they are not abiding in His words and not following Him. They left the complete plan of God why He made man in His image or in His likeness. They made man as a slave to God.

Because of that reason they could not discern that the Bible is the main resource of all their roots of the Islam. They could not realize that the Bible is one book and is a progressive unfolding truth of the plan of God and His great act of providing salvation to all the people from the second death of the human race. God's entire plan for the human race to escape the eternal damnation which was incurred from the first man Adam is embedded in it and was revealed in the Bible. No other book is needed for the plan of God for the human race. The revealed truth of God's plan from the Bible is fully manifested and was accomplished when Jesus appeared on the earth the first time. Next the second coming will be for the judgment of the world.

The explanation is as follows: God's desire for the human is to be with Him and enjoy the fullness of joy. That is the reason God gave Adam all the necessities in abundance and dominion over all His creation. Adam even had the access to the tree of life. But Adam failed to eat it and ate what God did not want him to eat. He lost the great privilege of having the eternal life and fellowship with God. But God did not leave the human race. Since He made man in His image and likeness and gave His breath of life. His plan was unchanged and He knew how to restore it. God is the only one who could justify His own words. He specified His future plan in the first book Genesis of the Bible in the beginning itself. (Genesis 3:15)

God said in Jeremiah 31:3, "³Yea, I have loved thee with an everlasting love: therefore with loving kindness have I drawn thee." God showed His heavenly plan in the Old Testament for all the nations and kingdoms of the earth to the people like Moses,

Nebuchadnezzar (heathen), Daniel, Ezekiel and John etc. All the plan of God was fulfilled according to the foretold prophecies. Because of His unconditional and unchanged love, Our God is God who can be experienced; a God whom we can understand; whom we can hear; and whose presence is every where; we could feel it wherever we are and we be lead by Him. He is a God who wants to reveal Himself in every true sense. He is our strength and He is our salvation.

God is not an imaginary. He is a person. "I am that I am" is His name. He is a Spirit being. During the Old Testament days, God's voice can be heard only by the prophets and high priests. But later, when the time was fulfilled, His Holy Spirit in the form of human as Lord Jesus Christ came to the world as a Savior, shed His precious blood to cleanse us so that His Holy Spirit can come and dwell in us to guide us until we go to the eternity. We will be perfected day by day with His voice and His word and he revealed that we are His body. By being a part of His body, His life flows into the believer. It explains a very close relationship in between Jesus and the believer.

How can we hear God's voice during these end times in such a tumultuous world? Since He is the Spirit, our spirit should be sensitive to the voice of His Holy Spirit. To be sensitive we should be born again in to the holy family of God. Then the believer is eternally joined with our Mighty and Great God. We can call Him at any time. We enter into His presence day and night and enjoy life with Him in greater measure. If any one has doubt about Him, he or she should cry out with all his/her heart to find out who the real God is, definitely He will reveal Himself. God said, "[3]Incline your ear, and come unto me: hear, and your soul shall live; and I will make an everlasting covenant with you." We have great assurance and promises in Him. (Isaiah 55:3)

It says in the holy Bible 'Lean not unto your own understanding. Incline your ears unto His voice.' We can hear His voice only if we have peace in our heart. This inward peace will come only if the prince of peace comes into our heart. Who is this Prince of peace?

This is very clearly written in the book of Isaiah 9:6. '6For unto us a child is born, unto us a son is given: and the government shall be upon his shoulder: and his name shall be called **Wonderful, Counsellor, The mighty God, The everlasting Father, and the Prince of Peace.**' This prophecy in the Old Testament is very clear in telling us Jesus is the son, the mighty God, the everlasting Father and the Prince of Peace. The people, who doubt Jesus as God, must open their eyes from their spiritual derision and read this prophecy foretold by Isaiah the prophet.

I am the least of all the believers yet I testify that I hear His voice everyday many times because He is the unchanging God. His promises are real and He is trust worthy God. His love is unfathomable.

If you need that same privilege come unto the Lordship of Prince of peace. Though you may know about the Bible, you may not know the meaning of the atonement and the new birth, or of justification or redemption, or restitution: but if Lord Jesus Christ becomes your peace, then by that peace you will hear His voice. Then you will find God's will in your everyday life. By this inward peace we will be protected from all the unbelief and doubts. He did not leave us helpless. He gave His word to us to know about Him and be strengthened. Get that word fully in you and get into a fellowship of real children of God who follows His word. There in His word He had shown His love and encouragement in our spiritual journey.

The Holy Bible is the word of God. It is a unique book in which it is written directly to the reader or to the listener. It is full of the words like "Verily, verily I say unto you," "The word of the Lord came expressly," "The word which came unto," "The word of the Lord came second time," "Thus saith the Lord the maker thereof, the Lord that formed it to establish it; the Lord is His name," "The Lord of hosts hath sworn, saying" " I am the Lord thy God," " I will go before thee, and make the crooked places straight; I will break in pieces the gates of brass, and cut in sunder the bars of iron; I will give thee the treasures of darkness, and hidden riches of secret places, that thou mayest know that I, the Lord," "I am the Lord, and there is none else, there is no God beside me. I form the light, and create darkness," "Fear not I am with thee," For I am the Lord thy God, the Holy one, thy Savior," I, even I, am the Lord; and beside me there is no savior," etc.

This book the holy Bible contained the Old Testament and the New Testament. It was compiled by many authors but throughout we hear only one voice and one message of only one God who is unchanged forever. God stretched forth His hands towards us and calling us to turn towards Him. This message is to all the mankind, whether born in Christian family or non Christian family. Everybody is invited by Our Supreme God, only one God. The invitation is steadfast.

In the Old Testament in the book of Isaiah, it was written, "[18]Come now, and let us reason together, saith the Lord: though your sins be as scarlet, they shall be as white as snow; though they be red like crimson, they shall be as wool. [19]If ye be willing and obedient, ye shall eat the good of the land."

And in the New Testament, Mathew Gospel 11:28–30, Jesus said, "[28]come unto me, all ye that labor and are heavy laden, and I will give you rest. [29]Take my yoke upon you, and learn of me; for I am meek and lowly in heart: and ye shall find rest unto your souls. [30]For my yoke is easy, and my burden is light." These are the words that were spoken by Jesus. He assured us with His personal words. As soon as we accept that we are sinners and repent of our sins He cleanses and purges us by His precious blood then His Holy Spirit comes and lives in us as a comforter and guide. We will find rest. Please remember a savior never leaves whom he rescues. He comforts and guides until the rescuer gets secured and rest. Jesus Christ accomplished the task of salvation. He is our savior. Jesus Christ is our ultimate rescuer, comforter and guide to take us to an everlasting destination.

The depth of the holy Bible in all sixty six books is beyond human finite mind. It is one continuous story which reveals a progressive unfolding Truth. Even though written by many authors in different time period, every book has one voice and same message. It explains sovereignty of only one God. He is singular but exists in three phases to accomplish the complete work of the human creation in fullest measure.

The central theme of the Holy Bible is the manifestation of Jesus Christ. God revealed Himself as a human in Jesus Christ to rescue all the mankind and to redeem them from their sins and to raise them to Him. God's great love was shown in this great act. The roots of all these subsequent revelation about Jesus Christ are planted in the Old Testament. The promised Messiah was appeared in the human history in the New Testament. Before He left the world, Jesus promised, "I will come again and receive you to Myself." (John14:3) He will definitely take those whoever believe and walk in His ways. His name is Truth. That is the reason every believer with steadfast faith is looking forward for His second coming.

The Bible is full of God's promises that you could claim and see fulfilled throughout the life of a believer. Even a small fragment in the Bible speaks with people. The Bible comforts you and keeps you in all life's situations; it is the spiritual food that every one needs to acquire strength to live a holy life in this world. Personally, God has fulfilled several promises in my life and I do not want you to miss these golden opportunities from the True God.

I want you to have the same life-changing experience several others and I had! So, Come, Taste and See, and you will know. With passionate urge I invite you to become children of God and inherit the kingdom of GOD and escape the hell and punishment from GOD.

God made human in His image to have fellowship with Him and to reign with Him. He made all plans to take us with Him to be with Him. Remember our God is Most Holy, Most Merciful, and Most

Compassionate and truthful God. He is inviting every one to have a sweet fellowship with Him now and unto the eternity! He never rejects any one even if he or she is an unbeliever.

By the time you finish reading this book, you might have heard God's voice. Did you hear it? If you hear it, please don't ignore His sweet voice. Please yield unto His voice and submit unto Him. Definitely He will take you to the eternity. God bless you and keep you in His arms!

The Conclusion

I urge you to discern which way to follow to inherit the heaven, the Islam or the Christianity? I tried my best to put in the truth of two religions as much as I could. It is not a matter of choosing a religion but the main intention is to choose straight path to reach eternity. Dear reader, my decision should not be an obligation to your choice. I left the facts right in front of you. God gave everyone freedom to choose the best way. But don't be reluctant to the voice of God!